SCYTHIAN ART

SCYTHIAN ART

CRAFTS OF THE EARLY EURASIAN NOMADS

by Georges Charrière —

with an introduction by

M.L. Artamonov
(former director of the Hermitage Museum, Leningrad)

ALPINE FINE ARTS COLLECTION LTD.
Publishers of Fine Art Books
New York, New York

Published by: The Alpine Fine Arts Collection, Ltd.
527 Madison Avenue
New York, New York 10022

ISBN: 0-933516-05-3

Color illustration printed in France
Text printed in the United States by
Seaboard Lithograph Corporation
Bound in the United States by American Book—
Stratford Press, Inc.

TABLE OF CONTENTS

INTRODUCTION TO THE ART OF THE STEPPES

The rich Scythian burial mounds of the Eurasian zone of the Steppes are now known throughout the world. They can be dated between the sixth and the third centuries B.C. Although by the time of the excavations most of them had been pillaged, they have revealed to us many remarkable objects in gold, silver, bronze, and pottery. These divide into two groups: the first comprises indigenous works in the animal style; the second consists of products, unique of their kind, which came from Greek workshops or from others in Asia Minor, but which were made for the nomads of the Steppes and were, in general, designed in accordance with their tastes.

Some of these objects depict the people for whom they were made, the Scythians, with various scenes from their daily life. The Greeks knew these people well, for they kept up constant economic and political relations with them. The Greek writers, especially Herodotus, have handed down to us information which, when married up with the archaeological data and the evidence provided by the monuments of ancient art, enables us to form a fairly precise idea of the early inhabitants of the southern part of the USSR, at least of the ones who lived within the field of observation of the Greek colonists settled on the northern shores of the Black Sea.

But the accounts of the country and its inhabitants left us by the Greek writers become more and more sparse and indefinite as we move farther away from the coast. True, the Greeks had some knowledge of the populations of Central Asia, thanks to information which they received through Persia; but farther away, toward the northeast, there stretched the fabulous regions of the bald Argippaeans, the one-eyed Arimaspians, and the griffins, watchful guardians of the gold. Nonetheless, the Steppes as far as the Altai Mountains were inhabited by Scythians or by Sacian tribes—Persian-speaking peoples of Central Asia, similar to the Scythians in their economic organization, way of life, and culture.

Searching for gold in the ancient kurgans (tumuli) became quite an industry in western Siberia, as early as the end of the seventeenth century and the beginning of the eighteenth. Some of the objects then discovered found their way into the *Kunstkammer* of Peter the Great and are now in the Hermitage Museum, where they constitute the collection of Siberian goldsmiths' work. It comprises more than two hundred pieces, including a magnificent dish whose decoration, representing wild beasts and other animals fighting, has remarkable expressive power. These scenes are closely related to the animal style favored by the Scythians of the Black Sea region, with the difference that Persian influences prevail over Greek and that the local animal species are fully represented.

At the end of the eighteenth century and in the first third of the nineteenth, an engineer, P. Frolov, gathered together a superb collection of bronze, bone, and wooden objects found in the Altai. The carved wooden objects have no equivalent in the Scythian treasures of the Black Sea coastal region. In and about 1860, V. Radlov discovered in the Altai, during the first scientific excavations organized in that region, the two large tumuli of Katanda and Bereli. The objects exhumed included, among other things, fur garments in good condition and carved wooden objects similar to those of the Frolov collection. It was believed for a long time that these were unique pieces, and people were astonished that they were so well preserved, for in general such objects made of organic materials, once buried, disappear without trace.

Systematic and scientific study of the large tumuli began in 1927, under the direction of M.P.

Griaznov. The expedition to Shibe resulted in the discovery of a large kurgan containing objects in metal, wood, and bone—a confirmation that similar objects in the Frolov and Radlov collections come from kurgans of the same type. But a still clearer idea of the ancient Scythian burials and their contents was made possible by excavations organized by S.I. Rudenko in five tumuli at the Pazyryk site in 1929 and 1949. Excavations were carried out later, also under Rudenko's direction, in two kurgans at Tuekta, and then in small tumuli, where the results of the exploration were more modest.

The excavations carried out by the Soviet archaeologists have enriched the Hermitage Museum with an altogether exceptional collection: objects in wood, leather, and felt, textiles of astonishing artistic value. These discoveries have taken us into an entirely new world, about which, until then, we had been reduced to hypotheses based on other documentary evidence derived from the same culture and period. The objects exhumed in the excavations have been published: here, without going into detail, we shall confine ourselves to a brief indication of their essential characteristics.

The tombs under the Altai gravemounds of the Pazyryk type are in the shape of a huge rectangular shaft approximately 592 square feet in area and between thirteen and sixteen feet in depth. The sepulchral chamber was generally constructed with two interlocking timber frameworks so arranged that on the north side, between the chamber and the wall of the shaft, a space was left that could hold the bodies of from five to twenty-two horses.

The sepulchral chamber itself was rather low—between three and one-half and five feet—though the height of the outer framework could be as much as six and one-half feet. The inner faces of the walls, the ceiling, and the floor were planed smooth and padded with felt. The body of the dead man, who was sometimes buried along with his wife or a concubine, was placed in a large lidded sarcophagus, carved out of thick larch wood. The sepulchral chamber might, in certain circumstances, shelter two small sarcophagi, one for each body. In one known instance two sarcophagi are entirely decorated with carved figures of animals. The other sarcophagi have figures—elk, cocks, ornamental motifs—cut out in leather or birch bark and then applied on the wood. The chamber also contained various objects of everyday use: small, low tables with carved feet, wooden cushion-shaped (birch and larch) and, on top of these, logs, over which the earth taken from the shaft was spread, and seats, receptacles filled with food. On the outside of the ceiling were placed several layers of bark then boulders. The size of these mounds—they could be as much as 118 to 150 feet in diameter and 13 feet in height—is significant, for it is on their height and thickness that the state of preservation of the objects in the sepulchral chambers depends.

At the time of the excavations it became clear that all the kurgans of the Altai had been robbed by men who completely understood their arrangement. The method used was always the same. After digging a tunnel into the mound, the robbers crawled in as far as the log roof and made a narrow hole in it, through which they penetrated directly into the funerary chamber; this was emptied of all its contents except the things that either had no value in their eyes or were too heavy. Sometimes the looters did not stop short of taking the gold ornaments of the harnesses placed between the walls of the frameworks; elsewhere they tried to penetrate into the graves where the horses were. For this purpose they pierced the side wall of the sepulchral chamber, but left alone the horses placed between the framework and the wall of the shaft, because to get the bodies of horses or any other objects out from under the logs would have been too difficult and arduous to be worth the effort.

It was also discovered that the tombs sheltered by the mounds were filled with ice. This had to be melted during the excavations, by pouring on it boiling water, which was then pumped away together with the water produced by the melting. It was noticed that this ice was not uniform: on top there was a thick layer formed, as a consequence of the opening of the barrow by the robbers, from water mixed with earth and other impurities which had seeped in at that time; lower down, there was a thin layer of perfectly pure ice, which had formed before the robbery as the result of a permanently frozen zone being set up beneath the mound of earth. In some of the tombs the funerary objects were imprisoned in this layer of ice, and the robbers had had either to leave them intact or to extract them with pickaxes.

The food placed beside the dead has decomposed, and nothing is left of it but small bones; the bodies of the buried horses have also been affected by decomposition. It may be deduced that a relatively short time went by between the burial and the formation of a frozen zone, but it is not possible to guage this interval precisely. Nor can it be said when the robberies took place and at what moment the tombs, invaded by the water and cold air let in through the channel dug by the robbers, became filled with ice.

The Altai barrows of the Pazyryk type are situated in a mountainous district, at a height of more than three thousand feet, but in a region where there is normally no permanent glaciation. In spite of the harsh climate of the Upper Altai, with its long winters, short summers, and relatively low yearly average temperature, ice would never have formed in the kurgans if they had not been covered with mounds of boulders. And, indeed, no such congealment phenomenon has been observed in the small kurgans of the same type. The stony mass, being a bad conductor of heat and permeable to air, has acted as a condenser. Within the mound and in the subjacent zone, a microclimate formed, distinguished from the climate of the surrounding country by having a lower temperature and being slow to respond to the warming in the summer. It was in this way that there came into being, under the mound, an area of permanent freezing proportionate to the shape of the mound—thicker at the center and becoming thinner as it neared the edge.

Because of this phenomenon, the woodwork, the bodies of the horses, and the various objects not carried away by the looters have reached us in fairly good condition. The state of preservation of the human bodies scarcely proves anything in this respect, for before being buried they were carefully prepared for mummification. Through incisions in the skin (later stitched together again with hair or sinews) the entrails and certain muscles were removed from the body, and the brain was extracted from the skull by trepanning. To make the body keep its shape, herbs of many kinds, sometimes also hair, were placed under the skin. All this fits in with the account given by Herodotus of the way in which the Scythians embalmed the corpse of their king.

The ethnic characteristics of the bodies buried in the gravemounds seem to indicate that most of them were of Caucasian type; but typical Mongoloids are also to be found, a fact which seems to show that here were two racial groups in close contact or even—more probably—mixed. The men had their heads shaved, either wholly or in front only; the women were adorned with plaits drawn back, and the men with false beards. One of the buried men has his skin tattooed with animals treated in the same style as the figures carved on wood. This tattooing must have been done quite a long time before his death, by pricking and with red pigment, on his arms, his chest, part of his back, and his legs from ankles to knees. Probably, in accordance with the customs of many barbarian tribes, it showed that the dead man held, when alive, a high position in the social hierarchy.

Because of the looting, it is impossible to make a complete list of the objects that were buried in the tombs. The bodies were found lying in disorder; some had disappeared; all were stripped of their clothes. In one sepulchral chamber the robbers beheaded two of the corpses, probably in order to get hold of their necklaces more easily; in the same barrow they mutilated a woman's corpse, severing the feet, shins, and right hand, with the aim, no doubt, of taking the bracelets and rings from wrists and ankles. They would even tear down the felt hangings adorning the walls, so as to take the bronze nails with which they were studded. Even so, what has survived, even in the form of fragments and debris, surpasses in wealth and variety all that it has been possible to find in the barrows that were not permanently frozen.

Costume, both of women and of men, is represented by a fairly complete set of samples. Apart from the shirts, which are of sisal or Indian hemp, the garments are of leather, fur, or felt, woolen stuffs not being used for clothing. Noteworthy among the men's garments are the narrow trousers made out of pieces of leather of the buckskin type, the felt buskins, the limp-soled topboots, the ample caftans with long sleeves, which were worn like a cape. On their heads the men wore a headband and a felt cap. One body had on its head a crown decorated with battlements arranged in steps—a design typical of Iran in the Achaemenid period (sixth to fourth century B.C.). The small boots with short tops that were worn on days of festival were adorned with glass beads and pyrite crystals even on their soles, because it was then the custom to sit with the soles of the feet turned outward. For ceremonial occasions the women wore, as their outer garment, a long-sleeved caftan with a small bodice over the bosom. Their hairstyles were more varied than those of the men: a skullcap of carved wood was worn on top of a complicated coiffure of which it was part. Several belts were also found, one of them decorated with silver plaques.

Only a few of the pieces of personal jewelry preserved in the Altai barrows have survived, although they existed in great number and variety before the looting, as is shown by the Siberian

collection in the Hermitage Museum. Here only a few objects can be mentioned: a pair of earrings, delicate jewelers' work with stippling; the fragments of a bronze torque in the form of a circular ring, adorned at each terminal with encrusted griffins which were carved in wood and horn and then coated with gold; also some gilt-bronze plates representing animals and sewn onto garments. To this list should be added glass beads, necklaces (mostly of turquoise), and various toilet articles—a horn comb and three mirrors, one of bronze with a short handle, another of silver with a long handle of horn, and the third in white metal, Chinese in style.

Very few weapons have survived. In one grave were found the remains of a sword and of an iron dagger, and in all the graves a rather large quantity of fragments of arrow shafts, from which the looters had removed the points. Among defensive weapons mention should be made of the shields of leather stretched over wooden frameworks, and of a wooden shield made in imitation of a leather one.

Various articles of everyday use were also found in the sepulchral chambers. Apart from the sarcophagi, mention should be made of a table and of various small tray-tables of wood, with short legs; also bedheads and headrests likewise of wood, wooden and clay vessels, felt pedestals for holding these receptacles, stone candlesticks, leather sacks, bags, purses and small cases, fur bags, carpets and rugs of felt and leather, horn drums, a musical instrument of the harp type, and some very interesting bronze cassolettes accompanied by conical wooden hexapods and small mats of felt or leather. The grains of hemp found in the same kurgans show that these implements were used for the smoking of narcotics, in the fashion described by Herodotus.

The objects placed in the graves reserved for horses are in much better condition, for they were usually spared by the looters. First of all, it should be noted that in many of the barrows the bodies of the horses themselves were found, very well preserved with flesh, skin, and pelt. They included, alongside small specimens, (which were stud horses), some large thoroughbreds. These were geldings, their ages ranging from two to twenty years and more, mostly saddle horses. They had their manes trimmed, their tails cut rather short, plaited and sometimes knotted. In some cases the horse wore a felt chamfron and had its tail covered with a casing. The animal was killed by a blow from a spike on the forehead or on the top of the skull. Usually its harness was taken off and laid in pieces on its body.

The bit was in two parts and was provided with rings, circular or stirrup-shaped, to receive the cheekpieces and the reins. The oldest cheek bars have three holes, the others only two. The former are to be found on the bits whose terminals are stirrup-shaped, the others on those with circular ends. The saddles were composed of two sewn cushions stuffed with stag's hair or grass and provided with a shabrack (saddlecloth), a girth, a crupper, and a breast strap. The height of the saddlebows was variable. The straps were fixed with bronze, horn, or wooden buckles. The cushions and shabracks were decorated with scenes of animals fighting, done by applying painted leather or felt. The sculptured figures were completed with incrustations in goldleaf or lead, the details being outlined in gold thread. Bridles and saddles were sumptuously decorated with figurative or ornamental motifs, usually carved in leather or wood and coated with gold or tin. The wooden figures adorning the pieces of harness must not be regarded as imitations, hastily executed for the funerals, of more solid metal objects: the traces of wear and tear, of breakages and repairs, show that these were objects in daily use, in which the brilliance of a thin gilding hides an inexpensive material.

The most remarkable objects found in the Altai barrows are the original masks which covered the horses' heads. The best preserved among them look like a sheath with large ears. One of these masks is crowned with big reindeer's antlers and has on its front, along the chamfron, the figure of a tiger molded in fur. Another has its top adorned with a winged, lion-headed griffin, and its front with a figure of a tiger mauling a griffin. On another there is an admirable sculptured goat's head with, on its backward-curving horns, a bird with wings spread. Other masks are in less good condition, but some of them show all the signs of prolonged use, proving that this element of equestrian caparison was not made specially for funerals, but was in everyday use.

In most of the kurgans parts of primitive wagons were found, their wheels sawn out of maple trunks, each with a hole to receive the axle. The considerable signs of wear on the axles suggest that these wagons were used for transporting the materials for the mounds, in particular the stones. At the same time Barrow 5 at Pazyryk yielded the scattered remains of a much more elaborate vehicle.

Also in Barrow 5 at Pazyryk were found a felt carpet with gold applications, and a shaggy woolen carpet which is now world-famous, it being the oldest known object of its kind. This carpet is certainly of Iranian origin. The same applies to some of the materials that have come from the Pazyryk kurgans: a shabrack showing women before a cassolette, a breast strap with a frieze of lions. Besides these Iranian objects, others of Chinese origin have also been found, notably the mirror mentioned above and a piece of silk stuff embroidered with plants and a phoenix. These objects admirably illustrate the close relations which the early inhabitants of Altai kept up with Iran and China.

As this brief account shows, the people of the Altai in early times used extremely diverse materials: while the Scythian barrows of the Black Sea coast have yielded us only objects in metal and bone, a great variety of wooden, bone, and fur objects was found in the Altai barrows; the use of felt, and also of birch bark and horsehair, was widespread. It is worth stressing that these different materials were often used simultaneously in a single object: for example, the horse masks, the details of which were treated with a pigment based on size, unite felt, fur, hair, leather, and gold leaf.

This variety of materials was inevitably accompanied by a diversity of techniques. Although woodcarving is the most typical, applications and incrustations of fur, leather, and felt are also very common. Some objects are veritable mosaics of pieces of fur, leather, and felt sewn together, and they present highly varied color combinations. Such is the case, for instance, with the bags which come from Barrow 1 at Pazyryk.

On almost all the objects, whether for funerary or general use, pride of place is given to decorative elements. Most of them are real works of art, using diverse techniques and various decorative motifs, in which animal forms predominate: elk, stag sheep, goats, tigers, as well as various kinds of birds, and of course those fantastic creatures of which the artist sometimes shows us the whole body (occasionally associated with other figures) and sometimes only a part of the body—in which case the design may end in some vegetable or geometrical motif.

These works of art are usually sculptures, in the round or in relief, and the body may be treated in relief, the head in the round. It is noteworthy that the sculptures were not all done in wood: the figures in the round, the swans for instance, were in leather and colored felt stitched together; similarly the griffin, cock, and sheep adorning the horse masks are in felt covered with leather. Still more often, these materials are associated with wood or horn, some detail or other of the figure being executed in softer materials: thus the griffin holding a stag's head in its beak is carved in horn, but the wings, back, antlers, and ears of these animals are in leather. The figures of stags with large antlers utilize both wood and leather. The figures in low relief were often carved out of leather.

Besides the sculptures, there are numerous two-dimensional figures done in a great variety of materials. Certain drawings of graphic character come into this category, among them the animals decorating a coffin from the Bashadar barrow. But it is more usual to find silhouettes cut out of leather or felt and stitched or stuck onto another material. This is the way in which the scenes of animals fighting were executed for the saddle-coverings, as also the cocks and stags decorating the coffins.

Polychromy is characteristic of the ancient art of the Altai. It was achieved by combining different materials, but also by dyeing the felt or leather, by applying a layer of gold leaf and tin, by emphasizing the outlines with gold thread, and by painting the objects themselves. Pure and lively colors predominate—red, blue, yellow, green—and strong contrasts.

The decorative motifs in ancient Altaic art have recourse largely to real forms taken from the fauna of the region. The fantastic figures are rather rare, and in every case certain features bear witness to their origin in observed reality. Most of the animals are easily recognizable. The stag, for instance, is distinguished by its slender body, short tail, harmonious head with small ears and characteristic antlers. The elk is more massive; its long legs ending in heavy hooves and its muzzle with the aquiline nose, beard, and long, flattened antlers distinguish it from the stag. The mountain rams are clearly recognizable by the accentuated curve of their horns. The most common wild beast is the tiger, and the artist never omits the stripes. The birds that appear most often are the eagle, the goose, the swan, and the rooster. However, besides the species taken from the local fauna, we do come upon animals unknown in the region, such as the lion, or fantastic animals, such as the eagle-or lion-headed griffin. These figures, like the scenes of animals fighting, are closely akin to the animal style dear to the Scythians of the Black Sea shores; in fact both of them have a common origin, and the locally derived subjects are treated in a common style determined by the decorative function of the art.

This style combines the dynamism proper to the figures with the strict balance of compositions that are rigorously closed in on themselves and with the grave rhythm of an inclusive symmetry. The

impression of impetuous movement is obtained by means of sudden curves, and especially by an original method which consists in reversing upward the hinder part of the animal's body. Very often the animal figures and their decorative motifs are treated as an S—the lines are incurved in volutes. The most prominent muscles are rendered by commas, half-horseshoes, or points, which stand out by contrast against the overall background of the figure—a method of which the encrusted polychrome figures of ancient Mesopotamia offer many examples. But in Siberia this method appears not only in the applique technique; it is also met with in the incrustations, particularly in the pieces of Siberian goldsmiths' work in the Hermitage Museum. The method that consists in giving the animals' hindquarters an upward twist is also a borrowing from the art of Asia Minor, where it had been used since Sumerian times. In the Scythian art of the northern shores of the Black Sea it makes its appearance only in the fifth century B.C. (the Seven Brothers Barrows), and this in figures derived from the Iranian style of the Achaemenid period.

For all its liveliness, the art of the Altai is nonetheless schematic. To begin with, the methods used are conventional ones; and secondly, this art knows only two positions of the figure—strictly frontal and in profile. However, one cannot fail to be struck by the astonishing diversity of the compositions which the artist obtained by combining a body in profile in relief with a head sculptured frontally, or with a sudden turn of the head in the opposite direction to the axis of the body—or again by combining the different possible positions of the head, body, and feet. The animals are depicted walking or leaping, with their forefeet drawn back and their hind feet outstretched, or again passively lying down with their feet tucked in; the position of the head can also vary considerably—outstretched at the end of a long neck, lowered, raised, thrown back.

The ornamental character of Altaic art appears with particular distinctness in the compositions executed on the principle of mirror symmetry, which was obtained by cutting figures out of pieces of leather or felt folded in two. This is how the pairs of roosters that have been found stuck on the edge of a coffin were produced. On the same principle wooden brackets were cut out, representing paired stags, birds, goats' heads, etc. Through their schematization these motifs tended to lose their initial figurative character and to end up as half-vegetable, half-geometric forms. A silhouette of a rooster with a high comb, for instance, leads on to a cutout figure with volutes, where only the juxtaposition of the two images makes it possible to recognize the initial motif. Besides the decorative motifs obtained by a schematization of figurative motifs, the art of the Altai includes forms related to decorative figures of foreign origin and vegetal character: such are the lotus and the palmette, which probably came in at the same time as other forms borrowed from Asia Minor, but are simplified and stylized in the spirit of the native art to the point where they become hard to recognize.

It has been possible to establish the chronology of the Altai barrows with precision, thanks to two methods of investigation whose results have reinforced one another.

On the one hand, study of the concentric circles in the wood, made possible by its excellent state of preservation, has enabled us to determine the *relative chronology* of the different kurgans—their time relation to each other.

On the other hand, the modern method of analysis based on the properties of radioactive carbon has enabled us to determine the *absolute chronology* of the same kurgans. The information obtained by this method—within a margin of error not exceeding ±130 years—has corroborated the results of the former method as regards the different ages of the different barrows.

The resulting chronology is as follows:

Barrow	Absolute Chronology	Relative Chronology
Barrow 2, Bashadar	c. 520 B.C.	0
Barrow 1, Tuekta		
Great tumulus, Katanda	c. 460 B.C.	+ 60 years
Barrows 1 and 2, Pazyryk	c. 390 B.C.	+ 130 years
Barrow 4, Pazyryk	c. 380 B.C.	+ 137 years
Barrow 3, Pazyryk	c. 350 B.C.	+ 167 years
Barrow 5, Pazyryk	c. 340 B.C.	+ 178 years

Thus, allowing for the margin of error mentioned above, the Altai barrows date from between the seventh and the third centuries B.C. Griaznov divided the barrows into three groups: the first, called the Mayemirskaya group, in his view made its appearance between the seventh and the sixth centuries B.C.; the second, the Pazyryk group, between the fifth and third centuries; and the most recent, the Shibe group, between the second century B.C. and the first century A.D. While admitting this classification as a starting point, S.V. Kiselev has added to it the Tuekta kurgans, which he explored with A.V. Adrianov, and has extended the dating of the first group down to the fourth century inclusive. He has, on the other hand, placed in the Pazyryk group the other barrows of the Altai, including those of Katanda and Shibe, and has dated them between the third and first centuries B.C. On the evidence from radioactive carbon analysis and the relative chronology as established by comparing the concentric rings of the wood, he agrees with the placing of the Mayemirskaya barrows in the second half of the seventh century, but dates Barrow 2 at Bashadar and the Tuekta barrows from the middle of the seventh century, Barrows 1 and 2 at Pazyryk from the second half of the fifth century, Barrows 3 and 4 at Pazyryk from the last quarter of the fifth century, and Barrow 5 at the turn of the fifth and sixth centuries. In his view Barrow 5 at Pazyryk belongs to the first half of the fourth century and is contemporary with the kurgans of Karakol and Shibe. In his view also, the most recent barrow would be that of Bashadar, dating from the second half of the fourth or the beginning of the third century B.C.

This classification, while not open to objections as a whole, does seem to go back rather too far into the past, if we compare the Altai monuments with those of the Black Sea coastal region. This applies to the most ancient group, that of Mayemirskaya. In point of fact, there have been found in the kurgans of this group some gold plaques which once formed part of a decorated harness carved in wood: these plaques show one of the characteristic motifs of the animal style of Scythian art—a wild beast turned on its back; in it we find all the features that appear on the Scythian monuments of the Black Sea coastal region in the first half of the sixth century. There is no ground for concluding that this style had its birth in the Altai or in any other region of Siberia. Along with the other elements of the Scythian culture, it was derived from the cultural heritage of the ancient East and originated in the peripheral regions of Assyria, among the Iranian-language tribes settled in the north of Iran. This style then made its appearance on the northern shores of the Black Sea with the Scythians of Herodotus—they had lived for several decades in Asia Minor—and spread, through the intermediary of the Sacians into Central Asia and Siberia as far as the Yenisey. In the Altai, after diffusion among the Guetshyes, an eastern branch of the Iranian tribes, it spread among the Huns of Mongolia and northern China. If we consider that the objects discovered at Ziwiye in Iranian Kurdistan—which date from the turn of the sixth and seventh centuries—are the earliest manifestation of this style, it is difficult to suppose that it existed in the Altai as early as the seventh century. The Mayemirskaya barrows are certainly more recent than those of Kelermes in the Kuban country. In artistic style the Pazyryk kurgans seem fairly close to the Seven Brothers Barrows on the Lower Kuban river, which date from the fifth and fourth centuries. In both cases it is possible to observe the general development of the animal style of Siberian Scythian art, with its gradual substitution of schematic decorative forms for realistic forms in the round; and, although there was never a complete identity between the art of the Altai and that of the Black Sea coastal region, the development of the art, both in the north and in the south, moved in the same direction and resulted in very similar manifestations, though Siberia was rather later than the coast.

As we have seen, because of the exceptional state of preservation in which their objects in organic materials have come down to us through the permafrost, the Altai barrows have shown for the first time how deeply art penetrated into the customs and daily life of the barbarians of Eurasia during the second half of the first millennium B.C., and how closely the culture of these peoples was connected with the more advanced cultures of Asia Minor and China. The brilliant and original art of the barbarians, which, in spite of certain borrowings, they developed in accordance with their own genius, expresses itself in materials of all sorts and in objects serving the most diverse purposes. It accompanied those men from birth to death and, while never ceasing to be an applied art, it expressed a certain way of thinking and contributed to the satisfaction of aesthetic needs. In this respect Scythian art is in no way different from the art of other peoples and of other historical periods.

THE BARBARIAN MODES OF EXPRESSION

Barbarian Languages and Foreign Languages

The city communities of classical antiquity invented the term "barbarian" to denote the foreigner—a person who was not Greek or Roman and who made a "bar-bar-bar" noise when he spoke, that is to say, spoke in so strange a way that it could be characterized by such an onomatopoeia. But the verbal image is used by all peoples and has to do with the form as well as the content of the concept to be expressed. Thus the Greeks regarded as particularly barbarian the natives of the Eurasian continent who had been given the name Hyperboreans—literally, inhabitants of the land "beyond the North Wind."

The ancients owed part of their meager geographical knowledge concerning these northern regions to the turbulent warriors and herdsmen who inhabited the Steppes, namely the Scythians. These said that they lived in a country where "feathers fell" in excessive quantity; but Herodotus, our source for this, notes that this must be an image for the fall of snowflakes. Even now the French peasants say, when the weather is snowy, that "God is plucking His geese."

Yet the perspicacity of the "Father of History" seems to have stopped there; for the fables which he proceeds to indulge in—fables told by the Scythians or other neighboring informants about monstrous creatures, half-animal, half-human, inhabiting those regions—show that he took literally a terminology which, like that for the lands and rivers, was obviously metaphorical.

Siberia, cradle of the nomad peoples, has indeed, throughout the ages, been described in various images. An old local etymology calls it "the sleeping land," which does fit well a country paralyzed by cold during most of the year. Marco Polo, thinking of the long winter nights in northern latitudes, described the region as "the land of darkness," while to the great explorer Nansen it was "the country of the future," that of "virgin lands"—as the Soviet pioneers also called it in their determination to make it productive—while journalists write of it as already "the rising giant."

For each, in function of his experience and way of life, has defined a Siberia in accordance with his own problems and needs, with the help of a word or a convention that in no way excludes the mnemonic device of metaphor, which is the best way of making a term assimilable between interlocutors.

And yet this country of the Steppes and Taiga will also be understood under its own name—though this be a barbarian word to the western European and plain to a Mongol—by two men looking at a map, at an aerial photograph, or at a bas-relief that symbolizes it clearly enough. And so Siberia takes us into the heart of an important subject: the respective advantages of, and the line of demarcation between, various human modes of expression, whether oral, graphic, or plastic.

Thus a language is a collection of agreed and structured signs—in this case oral—informing us of some fact. The same can be true of sign-objects. To Aegeus, when black sails were sighted, they announced the death of his son; to the sailors of the sixteenth and seventeenth centuries they meant the presence of a pirate ship. A signal is therefore a matter of convention between a sender and a recipient: it comprises the signified—which is its meaning—and a signifier—the subject of the convention, by which the sign is made manifest. Insofar as the signals are in themselves evocators (sign-objects, gestures, onomatopoeia, images, drawings, etc.) and therefore less abstract than their signs, two foreigners may manage by their aid to circumscribe some vague idea. If not, each of them sees or hears only a collection of unaccustomed signals which are incomprehensible to him and appear to him to lack order.

1

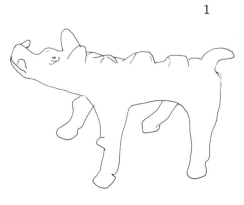

2

Herodotus, indeed, in a famous anecdote, shows how even realist symbols gave rise to opposite interpretations. Darius had received from the Scythians the following message: a rat, a frog, a bird, and five arrows. The Persian exegetes then translated these documents as meaning: the enemy was surrendering to the monarchy the lands and waters, domains of the rat and the frog, while the sending of the arrows signified that he would lay down his arms. But history ratified a different version, which had been suggested and rejected: the intention had been to signify that Darius should fly like the bird, go to ground like the rat, and hide in the marshes like a frog, if he wished to escape the murderous arrows of his adversaries.

These divergent interpretations, whichever version is the right one, exemplify two procedures characteristic of language—metaphor and metonymy: by one of them the proper meaning of a word changes in virtue of a comparison made in the mind; in the other, cause is taken for effect, the container for the content, the part for the whole. When a Frenchman says that a man feeling fear or shame—or, for that matter, a man taking cover from enemy fire—has "gone to ground like a rat" he is also recognizing that sometimes "fear gives a man wings." Across thousands of miles and across centuries these common metaphors linking the descendants of the Celts to their neighbors the Scythians provide, both in space and in time, an example of equality between peoples and races, one that has to do with their intellectual processes.

Other examples are available. In the case of recumbent figures on tombs, when the princes and warriors are given a lion crouching at their feet, and their trusty spouses a dog, the emblems respectively of prowess in hunting and of domestic fidelity, medieval symbolism is simply making use of allegories that are to be found, exactly the same, in far earlier arts. The sarcophagus of one nomad chieftain has, engraved on it, a procession of tigers pouncing on elk, rams, and a boar, while on a   225
Scythian plaque from Kul Oba a faithful dog is shown keeping company with the royal stag which is   104
shielding and protecting it.

In this last example, the grouping together of two animals that are so different may seem startling—though less so than the monstrous creatures of barbarian or prehistoric art which bring together limbs, paws, heads, and tails of animals of the most diverse species. Yet we use forms of speech quite as odd, and nonetheless full of meaning, as when we talk about "a wolf in sheep's clothing," meaning a person who cloaks a hostile intention beneath a friendly exterior.

Similarly, in all civilizations, military weapons and insignia are often decorated with animal symbols celebrating the powerful qualities of the object or of its owner. This is the point of the boar in the emblems of the German, Roman, or Gothic warriors, or of the bold pachyderm that denotes the "hero" in Mesopotamian ideographic writing.

3

On the painted ceiling of the Altamira cave Paleolithic man also depicted the wild boar bravely attacking cattle—no doubt also allegorical in view of the strangeness of the fight. And some twelve thousand years later a Frenchman still says, of some brave compatriot of his, that he "charges like a boar," that is to say violently, disregarding difficulties and injury. To improve his expression of the idea of impetuosity the Altamira artist also gave one of the painted boars some supplementary feet,   2
placed a short way apart from the others, as though in anticipation of a photograph in which the   3
speed of the photographed animal, being quicker than that of the shutter, conveys by superimposed impressions of the limbs the notion of their movement: this was a better way of depicting the boar starting from cover than the too direct device, used in nomadic art, of providing it with wings.   4

It is easy now to see why, on the famous gold ax from the Scythian kurgan of Kelermes, the pachyderm—unlike his worthy companions (ibex, stag, antelope, and the big cats) which are usually shown lying down—is depicted as "passant": in that barbaric heraldry the wild boar is always ready for some deterrent charge.

4

The Kakhovka pall is well known, with its many gold plaques repeating the figure of a boar with feet drawn in and snout down. On others from the same burial there are decorative themes which can be taken to signify a kind of dialectical opposition between pachyderm and a group of baying and leaping hounds. The imprecision inherent in a writing that is half art, half ideogram, does not admit of an exact translation, but conveys at most the symbolism suitable to the grave of a fallen warrior, in which the pose of the solitary man at rest finds its antithesis in the vital dynamism of the excited pack. Here again the parallel with language, French in particular, is easy to find: Saint-Simon describes Desmarets as "withdrawn into his lair," that is to say, as a man detached from the world of the living. At the same time the "pack" is a figure of speech for a turbulent troop of scouts or of men spoiling for action.

But the Scythian chieftain, just like Guillaume de la Marck who was nicknamed "the boar of the Ardennes," could be a ferocious leader of his people. Usually, in Eurasian art, the combativeness of the boar is quite directly the cause of its symbolic force. Indeed, several metal plaques represent the boar at grips with tenacious and relentless enemies—the bowman or the serpent. In isolation, the animal is even sometimes represented by its head alone, like a signature, to illustrate the concept of a masculine and brutal courage—differing in this respect from the language of Molière, where the boar's head is merely used to designate a shaggy, uncombed head, that of a "wild man of the woods," an image which still implies an active life.

The art of the Steppes shows a predilection for dynamic subjects with plenty of dash. Mobility is everywhere—it is so in the life of the herdsman and warrior, of course, but also in the decorative themes used for the environment and equipment of a Scythian man because of his liking for everything illustrating or symbolizing his own qualities of speed, agility, and endurance. The "Pegasus" figures produced by Greco-barbarian goldsmiths convey and unite these warlike virtues in the form of imaginary beasts, to be considered first as ideographic aggregates, whatever idealization and sacralizing the motif underwent later.

5

It is the same nowadays: automobile advertisements use such symbols as the mustang and jaguar to suggest speed and power; some air companies prefer the winged horse. Similarly, when the Greek artist wanted to show, on his vases, the superiority of a courser or its rider—that is to say, to convey it graphically—he placed an eagle in flight above the chariot, or even between the feet of the horse, wherever there was a suitable space for reinforcing that idea of primacy which a horse by itself could not convey, but which could be admirably evoked by the swooping king of the birds. (Birds of prey are the swiftest animals. Their speed can be as much as 110 miles per hour.)

Does it follow from these various examples that the many languages and other modes of human communication differ, in the last resort, only by the form of the signifier?

Conceptual Selection

Men's images of the surrounding world and the concepts to be expressed are defined differently by the different modes of expression proper to each ethnic group, because thought is always selective, approaching reality in function of the immediate problems with which it is faced. While the Eskimo possess about ten words to characterize the various states of snow, the Aztecs had only one to designate both ice and cold, though these are quite distinct phenomena: the greater or smaller wealth of the

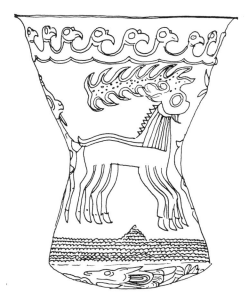

vocabularies and classifications used by each people is, in this case, explained by the difference between their climates. The image of the world which a man constructs for himself is always defined in function of the struggle in which he is engaged.

Art is no exception to this rule, for it too is a language. The repertory of motifs, the greater or lesser degree of precision in the depiction of animals, demonstrate how far modes of expression, through their semantics and morphology, reflect the way in which thought is directed by people's daily experience, by their general way of life.

For instance, where the arrangement of the teeth of lions, tigers, etc., is wrongly drawn, this lack of realism is necessarily a sign that the artist was not primarily interested in this detail. In worlds as distinct from one another as medieval western Europe, Pre-Colombian Peru, and China of the Chu period, the same error recurs as in Paleolithic engraving and painting—or in a modern advertisement: the misplacing of the canine teeth of the carnivores. The upper jaw is, in effect, represented incorrectly, set in the wrong way, as though jutting forward, whereas it is really farther back than the lower jaw. In contrast, in the art of the Scythians and of the nomads of the Steppes, the muzzle of the predatory mammal is usually equipped correctly with its forward canines the lower ones. The large number of felines in Eurasian art and this extremely rare accuracy in the representation of their teeth 225 combine to make of them proper hunters, in the real or in the figurative sense—that is to say, fit symbols for their biped rivals.

Indeed, some zoologists have tended to divide the vertebrates into two groups only—hunters and hunted; and the Eurasian artists, by the attitudes of the animals they represent, seem also to have been 45 conveying the same classification, devoting their main expressive effort to the most typical characteristics of each species defined in this way.

In the predators, for instance, that is to say the carnivorous mammals and the birds of prey, the 43 eyes are almost entirely frontal; the field of observation is always situated in front of the animal and is surveyed binocularly. The axes of vision intersect. The masticatory muscles, powerfully developed, 68 are located behind the eyes. The result is to give each animal of the cat tribe a rounded head with 70 striking eyes, a head that, with its lunar contours, is more characteristic when seen frontally than in profile. A Benin artist tends even to exaggerate the roundness of the face in his stylized representation 35 of the native panther, and the artist of the Steppes does the same for the Siberian tiger—as indeed does the illustrator of a children's book for our common cat.

We may therefore repeat word for word what Dr. Michel Rousseau has written about the treatment of these carnivores in Paleolithic art, since it is the same as that in the barbarian arts of Eurasia: "All the heads of felines have one otherwise very rare feature in common: they are made easily recognizable (if not more) by being drawn fullface rather than in profile. And, the neck being short, this head can be depicted in either attitude at the same place (or almost) to complete a body which is itself always in profile! . . . . This morphological peculiarity is bound up with a frontal vision like our own. It is rendered more striking by the two large eyes with their dominating gaze! . . . . "

The eminent veterinary surgeon stresses in this way, in the case of one species, a stylistic rule of expressionism that is applicable to extremely diverse arts. But while the feline, as represented in the scenes of fights by Eurasian artists, is an essentially dynamic animal, the Paleolithic depictions of it are, on the contrary, essentially static. In them, as far as is known, there is no representation of those spectacular scenes, typical of Scythian decoration, in which the lion and the Siberian tiger attack some quarry and set themselves up as rivals or models for the human hunter. No allegory of hunting is legible in the Paleolithic paintings, engravings, or sculptures of felines, unlike in the art of the Steppes.

6

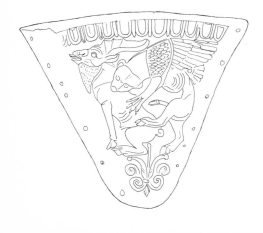

This greater or lesser insistence on the cruelty and violence of the predator implicitly reflects very different ideologies and social relationships in the two types of human society under consideration.

It is the same with birds of prey. In the Trois-Frères cave (Ariege), a Paleolithic artist has left us an engraving of a family trio (parents and chick) of one of the nocturnal species, and they look entirely devoid of ferocity, as if the monogamy of the birds was the most important concept to be stressed; but in the iconography and symbolism of the Scythians and related peoples it is the bird of prey that is emphasized, either alone or taking part in suitable hunting. The essential organs of the winged predator are therefore exaggerated, the better to express the part they have to play in the allegory. The hooked beak, firmly anchored in the rock of the skull, is a master tool—simultaneously ax, stiletto, pincers, and club; its upper mandible is the more formidable, massive, and trenchant of the two, and it emerges from a wad of thick skin, which the scrupulous artist reproduces faithfully. Behind it, the eye, exposed fully to the light, is protected by the arched brows that resemble eaves or a visor, shading the gaze that darts from its round and protruding pupils. Wide open, the eyes of a bird of prey have an exceptional volume, in the case of the royal eagle even surpassing a man's: they bulge and dilate with greed, and often the plastic artist even exaggerates their dimensions, the better to represent and accentuate their essence. As for the wings, the forward feathers, or primary remiges, stand out with an outline rounded at the ends, which is typical of the plumage of winged predators, from the sphinx of antiquity to the hunting eagles of the Scythian goldsmiths.

But, since a bird cannot lift a weight greater than its own, the kinds of spoil that can be carried off are limited. A cap-clasp in the Hermitage Museum shows an eagle with its wings spread, its feet thrust forward, and its claws hooked as it seizes an ibex; the fanned-out tail of the bird has just braked its descent, and its gaze is still riveted on its prize. A gold plaque from the Seven Brothers Barrows in the Kuban likewise shows the bird slaughtering a hare, which it will have no trouble in carrying off. On the other hand, in spite of the uncertain outcome of the rivalry between the two predators, bird and feline, for possession of a yak on one of the Altaic gold plaques, it is clear that the bird will, if it gains possession, have to devour the prey on the spot—so clear, indeed, that the craftsman has not conveyed by the slightest detail any impulse to fly off with it. The eagle has simply swept down in a storm of wings and is gripping the neck of the victim with its beak.

The yak is one of the hunted, the herbivores, and has its eyes placed more laterally. Their fields of vision are very extensive to either side but do not intersect. Even though they embrace most of the horizon, they still have two dead angles, opposite to each other along the axis of the body when the animal is moving straight ahead. Therefore, although it is difficult for an enemy to get near the hunted because of the largeness of the field surveyed, the whole cleverness of a swooping or pouncing attack consists in approaching within one or the other of the dead angles. This is exactly how the predators (eagles, lions, other felines, and griffins) depicted by the Eurasian nomad artists operate: the carnivores even seek to break the neck of their prey and thus paralyze it at a blow.

The hunted are obviously uneasy creatures. To survey their environment more effectively, they often turn their heads at an angle of 180 degrees. Many depictions of them in Eurasian art show them like this, especially when fighting. Such is the case with the ibex attacked by a griffin on one of the Pazyryk saddle yokes, or again the herbivores pursued by carnivores on a phalera (ornamental plaque) from the Black Sea coastal region. Already in Paleolithic art, does and fawns sometimes have the same uneasy attitude. And every leitmotiv has its own rules.

Seeing that the animals depicted by the nomads of the Steppes fall into two clear-cut categories, hunter and pursued, it is not surprising that the expressionism employed, the more vividly to situate

7

each animal within one or the other of these categories, also leads to those so-called conventional techniques of representation characteristic of the Eurasian artists. The fact that in Scythian art there are practically only two positions of the face—strictly frontal or in profile—and that the compositions combine a relief body in profile with a frontal head in the round or with a head completely turned in the direction opposite to the body's motion, is not the whole story: in fact we notice that essentially it is the felines who have the head at an angle of ninety degrees to the body and the herbivores who have theirs turned completely about,—that is to say, each in the position best representing, respectively, the carnivore and the anxious quarry.

The exceptions prove the rule. On a ceremonial ax from Uzbekistan, dating from between 1000 and 800 B.C., an ibex is depicted being seized by a tiger whose own hindquarters are being attacked by another beast: while the ibex has its head turned right around to recognize the feline tearing at its flank, so has the tiger, to see what treacherous assailant is behind it.

Many of the stags in Eurasian art turn their heads into the same prudent and fearful position; but, on the other hand, the old stag with its ears stretched back (that is to say in a combative attitude), 102 its head pointing forward, and its muzzle thrust out—though at the same time the feet drawn in under 100 him indicate confident and serene expectation—is signaling the courage and assurance of which he is also capable on occasion.

A similar point might be made about the feline shown by certain anthropomorphic artists on ancient works of art from the Near East: their lions with "their tails between their legs," illustrating 123 literally a metaphor still widely used to express the humiliation of a captive. And a writer of fables might describe a prisoner as being "as ashamed as a fox caught by a chicken."

The Motivation and Convention of Sign-Images

Thus the function of animals in symbolism, fables, and caricature is to give a more concrete and accessible expression to the qualities, defects, and social relationships of the human species. In addition, 295 even technical language commonly makes use of animals, or of their organs, so that the tool, form, or 10 function which the signifier is designating may be shown by a more easily comprehensible convention. 112 Inversely, when a tool, form, or function is thus graced with an animal terminology, its artistic treatment tends to reflect the process of expressive nomination, because hand, thought, and thought's form—language—combine in the work of man. And man, once liberated from hunting and harvest, uses other objects, including some of his own making, to enrich his modes of expression and the new names he has to find. From "lion" the hero becomes "sword" and then "bomb."

In other words, the fact that on prehistoric slings, harpoons, or assegais there are animals leaping 44 like ibex, flying like birds, running like horses or elk, or even gliding through water like fish, should not surprise us. French classical sculpture sometimes treated the *cul-de-lampe* (lamp bottom) motif with crude realism. And just as we speak of a "table leg" or the "foot of a vase," the Eurasian artists 179 did not hesitate to transform the supports of their dishes and receptacles into legs or feet. 113

In the case of vases, it is easy to demonstrate the same thing the other way round. In current French the pot is often used as a humorous symbol. A short, stocky man is called a *pot à tabac* (tobacco jar), while *pot de fer* and *pot de terre* symbolize persons whose strength is ill-matched, since the earthenware pot breaks if it collides violently with the saucepan. The expression *pot sans anse* (pot without a handle) describes a helpless person, while *faire le pot à deux anses* denotes an exaggerated sociability. The pot owes this anthropomorphic application to its rounded volume. So, in our own time, the plump part of a vase is known as the belly and a man with a protruding stomach is called

8

potbellied. This same idea of a spherical and containing form recurs in the French word for head, *tête,* derived from the Latin word for pot, *testa,* which itself comes from the word for a shell. This dance of meanings continues in modern slang, in which a silly, fatheaded person may be described as being 90 "potty." No wonder, then, if a piece of painted pottery dating from the third millennium B.C. is described as "head-shaped" when the concentric circles decorating it represent eyes and the vertical handle a nose.

20 - 26   Since a woman's form, with its roundnesses that are increased in pregnancy, is less elongated than a man's, the Russian word *baba,* which is used not only for a stocky peasant woman but also for the snowman that children build, could be used to denote those round-bellied vases which the Neolithic 95 potters made and, as if the resemblance needed stressing, adorned with a pair of breasts. On this subject the great Siberian excavator Griaznov writes:

The study of pottery may give us some idea not only of some of the decorations on the materials, but also of the style of the ceremonial clothes. Among many peoples, both ancient and modern, receptacles made of pottery are anthropomorphic, above all the ones used in religion, and especially for funerals: these are urns and other vases representing a figure, a head, or a whole human body. Anthropomorphism extends even to the terms applied to them, for the different parts of a receptacle bear the names of different parts of the human body: lip, neck, shoulder, or belly. It is very possible that the richly decorated pots of the Andronovo culture give us the decorative scheme of the clothes. The lip and neck, like the collar of a cloak, have simply one or two lines round them; the upper part of the belly is decorated with a broad band with a complicated geometrical pattern, or with four large festoons like the ones with which the shoulders, front, and back of sumptuous robes are adorned; lastly, at the base of the belly, we find a narrow band of ornaments pointing upward, as we do along the edges of robes, at the hem of a cloak, and at the ends of the sleeves.

9

Pottery was often women's work, at any rate originally, as it still is in the Near East or in North Africa. According to the few Mesopotamian texts mentioning the work of pottery, the goddesses play a decisive part in the creation myths, in which the creative powers of women are exercised in giving birth and in modeling clay. One may therefore ask oneself whether this sexualization—by the attributes of the female sex or the costume belonging to it—was not a brandmark, which fitted in with the metaphors to which the forms gave rise. Such a hypothesis is evidently more secular than the one which systematically transforms all ancient receptacles adorned with breasts into exclusively religious objects dedicated to some "Great Goddess," whose worship still awaits proof.

However that may be, what we have said above certainly applies to another part of the vase: 89 when this has a spout, the French say that it has a *bec-versoir* or a *goulot* —that is to say, the names of 94 animal organs—the bird's beak, and the mouth and throat of other vertebrates—are used in common terminology to designate a feature whose function is to pour or regurgitate.

Such verbal images being common currency, it is not surprising to find so many nomad or barbarian pots whose spouts or lips are developed into ornithomorphic beaks, and so many rhytons 32 (drinking horns) with necks made to look like the foreparts of animals. A medieval sculptor would similarly treat a gargoyle jutting out from the roof, so as to throw the water from the gutters clear of the building's walls: this too is a zoomorphic forepart, with mouth wide open, eyes starting, and feet braced against the wall so that each detail may convey the effort of getting rid of the water, well away from the entrails of the block from which the motif springs. Sometimes, also, the orifice of this drainage system is not a mouth: hindquarters, extended for a scatological release, make the water from the gutter "piss." Even modern fountains sometimes spew their water out through animal mouths or through a manikin's penis.

In many other cases also a function brings with it a specific decoration. One thinks of a certain spatula from northern Iran, now in the Louvre: this is an earpick, whose top is decorated with a small figure of a deer at rest, with his feet folded under him and a small bird on his crupper. This theme of a bird perching on an animal to rid it of its vermin surely corresponds to the object's function, besides suggesting the stillness required of the patient.

There are many other examples. The words "eye," "eyepiece," "eyelet" denote holes or rings (for instance, the eye of a needle or of an axhead) into which other mechanical parts or fastenings can be introduced: they are part, that is, of a technical terminology with a biological origin. Why, then, should it be strange to find the bridle of a nomad harness threaded through the eye-socket of an ornament in the form of a head of a bird of prey?

Lastly, there are other analogies between the two human modes of expression. Thus the information contained in a sound or written sign is not equally distributed within it. While in a spoken word there is concentration around the phonemes of the accented syllable, in a written word it is the first letters that carry the largest amount of information. A contemporary human being, during his visual analysis, spends most of the time examining the left-hand half of the motif represented, and this is the half with which he starts his detailed observation; the examination of the rest takes place afterward, in a clockwise direction. In other words, one half of the field observed has a greater immediacy as regards possibilities of expression.

In this connection, the relationship between writing and graphic or plastic art is obvious. In both modes of expression abbreviations occur. In the one, we retain and put together the initials of the words or terms that are joined—as in FBI, BBC, USSR, etc. In the other, we often see an animal reduced to its head or to its front half—that is to say, it too is limited to its most important extremity, even though the tail, by its form or attitude, might be a feature no less characteristic of the species and of its temper.

This itinerary of our gaze is regular. It may be consequent upon an education governed by the reading of written language. In any case, it shows that the form of the expression does not necessarily correspond exactly to the morphology and lines of force of the image. Reciprocally, the impact of the information would be at its maximum where, and insofar as, the structure of the imaged space fits in with the angle and the position of attack that are specific to the observer's gaze. In other words, two symmetrical images do not necessarily carry the same significance.

Let us consider, for instance, the animal motifs on a sword-sheath found in Barrow 16 at Elizavetovskaya (Lower Don). Depending on the starting-point and direction adopted for describing the sequence of the protagonists, so yielding symmetrical images, the description will at once steer their interpretation toward opposite meanings: the meaning can sway in divergent directions, between a title like "boar preceding lions" and another like "lions following a boar," through the very fact that the accent is not placed on the same elements in the hierarchy of the parts of the message. In the former case, the subject could be some kind of social precedence illustrated by a theriomorphic allegory; in the second, simply a pursuit in a hunt. What is signified varies according to the place given to the boar, and the signifier has to be read in a determined direction.

There are quite a number of compositions of Greco-Scythian art, as also in Paleolithic art, that depict sequences and assemblages of animals which do not live together in nature, so that their grouping must be admitted to be symbolic rather than natural. A gold plate found at Vettersfelde (Witaszków) brings together deer, lion, and fish strangely in single file. On another gold ornament from the same site, troops of equally ill-assorted animals (fishes, a bearded marine sphinx, a falcon, felines biting the hindquarters of a boar and of a buck) seem to be playing follow-my-leader.

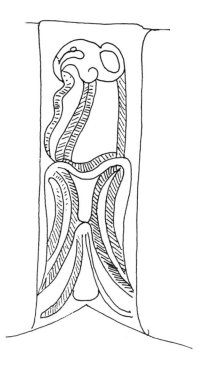

10

But in these examples, though the directions of movement are not identical, analysis is not much affected, even if, for us, writing has still further lateralized our way of seeing, and even if the training of our eyes (by language, through writing) no longer allows us the same freedom of composition, in a work of art, that prehistoric man had—at least on the graphic plane. This is indeed one of the things that makes it less easy for us to understand the ancient messages, when these combine several ¹¹ signifiers: often they are not trying to follow the kind of thread of discourse or of thought that is expressed in words and conforms to their structural sequence; and the direction of the "writing" is unknown to us.

Nonetheless, this relative accessibility of the work of art, as compared with a proposition or a written work, comes precisely from its difference from linear modes of expression in space and time, modes which lead to rules of reading that are restrictive because of the very fact that they have to be learned. The work of art, on the contrary, because of the syntactic and multidirectional bonds between each of the elements in the puzzle constituting it, has less need for being approached and read from a determined starting-point and in a particular direction. This freedom of approach is one of the causes of its success.

The immediate legibility of a work of art comes also from the fact that it uses sign-images or sign-copies, which facilitate a close correspondence between the signifier and the signified. Thus, as Griaznov stresses, the undulatory rhythm of the volute is sometimes by itself sufficient to lend ⁶³ dynamism to the motifs in Altaic art: whether an animal is represented by its whole body or by a part, the alternation of rhythmic curves in an S-shape, in whirlpools, and in undulations helps to suggest the idea of movement and of petulance, even when the pose seems forced and somewhat unnatural in its exaggeration. There is here a beginning of convention. For a difference of degree between art and writing or language comes from the fact that the former is a system of unlimited signifiers, while the latter, by its internal structure, is a system of symbolic figures that are limited and capable of serving the composition of word-signs—themselves already much more conventional than sign-images.

In fact the S-symbol, upright or horizontal, conveys the idea of movement so effectively that in electrics it is the code sign for alternating current and in typography for the transposition of words or lines. The use of such a sign in the art of the Steppes tends, therefore, to become picto-ideographic. We are plotting, approximately, that point of no return at which visual art and writing as such—in their present-day acceptance—would arise from the divergent paths they would then take, with only the second ending up at conceptual symbols independent of context.

In other words, there are more particular relationships between the reality of a serpent and its figuration in Scythian, Greek, or Celtic art than with the word "serpent," even though this has in its phonemes an onomatopoeic sibilant conveying the characteristic hiss given by a snake when disturbed: the oral term is in fact, to a greater degree than the graphic representation, a conventional sign, independent of the size, age, and sex of the animal. The French word for boar—*sanglier,* from the Latin *singularis* (solitary)—has, at least in its sonority, nothing in common with the pachyderm of the Taiga or the Ardennes: the term has meaning only within the framework of a certain system, a certain language. This makes the word *sanglier* barbarian for anyone who is not French—because the motivation is of an ethological order and the appellation owes nothing to any onomatopoeia, unlike, for instance, the word "cuckoo"; but a picture of the wild boar is assimilable by any human being who knows the animal.

The free play enjoyed by the artist, free as he is to specify, by a stroke of the pencil or engraving tool, the particularity of a concept that is highly personalized because necessarily understood and drawn in accordance with his complex individuality (for which reason a mechanical reproduction of a work of art is usually no more than a sugared and impoverished imitation), has to be paid for by difficulties and shortcomings in other ways. The word, because of its relative abstraction and its generalizing rigor, leaves more room for variations, by the very fact that there is less of a one-to-one correspondence between the oral sign and the thing than there is between the sign-image and the object. Syllabic writing makes a return to particularized realism impossible, because it conveys the word, on the graphic plane, in a still more conventional fashion and sways it irrevocably in the direction of complex structures. The logical conclusion of writing is called algebra, with mathematics becoming that "universal language" which no barriers or linguistic difficulties can stop—and, what is more, the one relied on for communication with any possible extraterrestrial intelligent beings.

While, then, spoken and written language is often a more effective means of communication than other systems of signs, this is because it is "hierarchized." In other words, it is made up of bricks, which are the phonemes forming words—of a handful of figures constantly rearranged in fresh order and enabling us to construct a great many signs without much trouble. Indeed, Swift, in *Gulliver's Travels,* describes the mistake made by the wise men of Laputa when, giving up oral language, they decided to converse by means of objects. But the number and size of things made the attempt a vain one; even should the interlocutors try to express themselves more economically by means of word-images, they would still need thousands of these and the time to find them in huge dictionaries; and they would still lack the whole gamut of abstract words, difficult to symbolize by concrete representations. The experiment was in fact carried out a long time ago by protohistoric and Chinese man, through their picto-ideograms.

Unable to free itself from particularism, plastic and graphic language is useful in other directions. To begin with, it paves the way to picto-ideographic writing—indeed there often seems to be no discontinuity between the two. Being highly evocative in its form, it is the least abstract of the modes of expression, and therefore the least "barbarian" in the sense in which the Greeks used this word, meaning an incomprehensible language. More than any other mode of expression, art seems universal because it often uses not only the same elementary structures but also identical symbolic signifiers. As with a diagram, plan, or model, its proper specificity, which is expressionist in its way (two-or three-dimensional according as it is in one plane or in the round), renders it irreplaceable—complementary to the other modes of expression as soon as, in practice, it becomes more competitive as a means of exploiting certain types of message.

Such at least, are the essential characteristics of primitive, barbarian, and "savage" art.

Examples? The talker of slang and, say, the Harvard professor, when expressing in quite different ways their admiration for a member of the fair sex, often do so by emphasizing one of the primary or secondary sexual characteristics. To the first, she may be just a "piece of ass" or "tit"; the second may be led by his classical education to speak of her "callipygian beauty," meaning, in plainer terms, that she has fine buttocks, because scientific etymology provides him with these chastely roundabout expressions of which the coarse-mouthed knows nothing.

If the user of words stylizes, distorts, eliminates, or exaggerates this or that detail of the female form in this way, the user of another mode of expression has a perfect right to do the same in his own code. Thus, using a language of gesture, the straightforward man defines the feminine outline which he prefers by producing with his hand in space two inverse curves, continuing them until they have conveyed the rounded contours of bosom and rump. The artist is no less explicit, direct, and schematic in his expressionism. Among other prehistoric examples, the latest female statuettes discovered in East Germany resemble those of the Eurasian area: descriptions of them stress their "posterior outline," taking account of the exaggeration of the buttocks which form the only element that structures and outlines the human form with sexual definition on the small ivory plaques or pebbles from Oelknitz. The ivory wands found at a Magdalenian site near Nebra-am-Unstrut are scarcely more realistic: the curves of the breasts suggest the sex of the figures, which is essentially conveyed by the exaggeration of their rump on one side and, on the other, the cavity of the groin.

127   But why should any chance motivation be assigned to the Paleolithic statuettes from the Ukraine,
128 in which the buttocks are transformed into the hindquarters of a bird? Have we, linguists apart,
129 forgotten that the Greek word πυγή (which has given us "callipygian") and the Latin *nates* (whence the word "natiform") were used, both of them, for the rumps of birds as well? In French, the rump of a bird is called *le croupion,* a specifically biped variant of croupe (English croup, crupper), which is reserved for animals—although, in France, men do not disdain its use when they speak of the buttocks of a *poulette* (chick) who is to their taste as a *croupe arrondie.* The girls at the Casino de Paris, even when in extreme undress, do not hesitate to adorn their bottoms with a few ostrich feathers, a device that

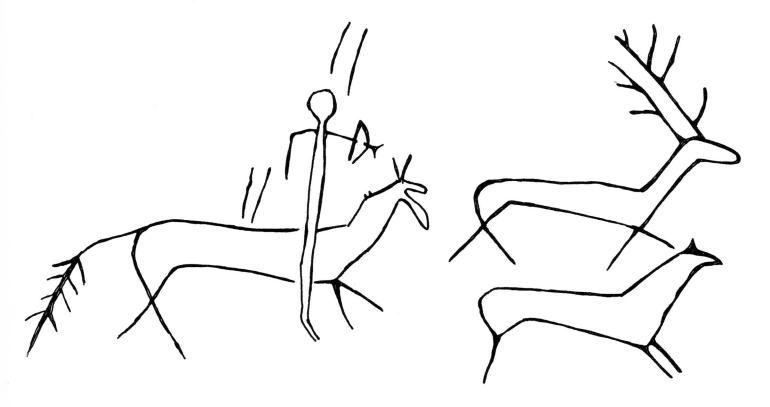

11

12

accentuates and magnifies the haunches, as fashion is constantly seeking to do by various means: it did so, for instance, in the time of the crinoline. Certain attitudes and steps in modern dancing, often of African or South American origin, compel the stomach to be curved inward, so thrusting the thighs somewhat backward and projecting the bust forward (whether stooping or still straight), in a general profile that is distinctly birdlike, at least as regards the back.

Possibly indeed, the mere exaggeration of the buttocks, in some cases with the suppression of the breasts on an almost plain bust, indicates the younger members of the fair sex—they are represented in this way on purpose, without the opulent maternal bosom of the full-fledged matrons. On the other hand, the latest discoveries at Gagarino, close to the Upper Don, are yielding us statuettes of women who are clearly pregnant. And, in the West, the Venus of Tursac, in whom the part of the body above 22 the waist forms a flattened appendix without even the sketchiest arms and breast, is also depicted with a belly which descends to the knees, as though she were about to give birth. But there are still many uncertainties about the meaning of some stylizations, and these must be taken into account.

It is clear, however, that verbal and plastic language and the language of gesture exaggerate the essential and atrophy or eliminate the incidental. Yet, although the terms "callipygian" and "tit" denote femininity as clearly as do the rounded breasts and buttocks, of the Ialangach-Depe statuette 28 or of the "Nanas" of Niki de Saint Phalle, it is right to stress certain obvious differences between the verbal and the plastic modes of expression in all historical periods.

Spoken or written language makes use, in fact, of redundance of sounds and letters, in the word as well as in the sentence, and does so not out of clumsiness but because repetition and plurality of conventional signals guard against a slight error being disastrous for the understanding of the message: what has to be prevented is that a single wrong letter may radically transform one word into another, since already in the case of homonyms there is need for a sometimes considerable accompanying context to make plain their exact meaning. But in figurative art the value of the image as a whole is not too perceptibly modified by the Scythian artists' correct drawing of canine and feline animals and the Greek artists' incorrect drawing of them. Given this fact, repetition in a plastic mode of expression would be clumsiness, because here a useless precaution would tend to brake and encumber the clear reading of those multivalent bonds which connect spatially the different sectors of the form represented—which also make possible some instantaneous and unmistakable shortcuts.

And so, on account of the multidimensional syntax characteristic of a work of visual art, the plastic artist is now subject to the same restrictions as the writer or speaker. These, because spoken or written utterance is highly linear in space and time, find that a wrong word is often only detectable when it comes into direct contradiction—which is not always immediate—with the rest of the text.

Finally, oral and written language, because of their unidirectional nature, tend toward long statements, when it is necessary to go back in order to make clear all the many elements and aspects required for a good description. For instance, in human beings symmetry is only approximate as regards the nervous system, the distribution of the organs, and the dimensions of the limbs: it was perfectly easy for a Bronze Age artist to show—as is the case with most women—the left breast as larger than the right; this went naturally with pictorial representation. But a term like "tit" contains no such 42 precision as regards this asymmetry in the female body and leaves room for alternatives.

On the other hand, the rules of writing allow no such initiatives in the notation of words, except in the case of ideographic writing, which retains an evanescent trace of its pictorial origins. In the hieroglyphic system, expecially, the direction of the reading is still relatively independent, as we have found it is in barbarian art, because the orientation of an ancient Egyptian text is bound up with that

13

of the ideograms representing imperfectly symmetrical living creatures: the inscription is read in the direction corresponding to that in which they are turned. Again, in China calligraphy was considered as an art, like music, archery, or chariot driving, because its characters left complete liberty to the writer and to his artistic feeling in their execution, apart from certain tacit and conventional rules.

Nonetheless, modern typography, even with syllabic writing, does not escape from the demands of progress in the modes of graphic expression. While a speaker imposes his utterance willy-nilly on his interlocutor, the written sign and the motif in visual art must, if they are to be read and looked at, excite and capture the attention of the person to whom they are directed—who has in any case to make more effort to take them in because of this business of reading them.

14

Thus, in the composition of a page of this book, as in a Scythian artist's depiction of a panther, there are different levels of signs. The shock elements come first: in this case the titles, in the other the
35 characteristic or even caricatured silhouette of the feline predator. The middle elements appear on the second plane and in the second visual analysis: such is the function of the subtitles in the one case, in the other the spots, shaped and accentuated by stylization so as to stress the specific pelt of the beast. Lastly, the accessories and explanations are placed in the background: these form the body of the present text and, in the animal motif, the details showing age and sex—such as the animal's teeth, the
232 more or less senile dip in its back, and its pregnant belly or its sex organ, exaggerated for the sake of legibility.

But is this expressionism—in speech, writing, or visual art—something independent of materials and tools, (in which case the barbarian art of the Steppes, for instance, would be anonymous and unoriginal compared with its equivalents in other civilizations)?

The Handwriting of the Artist

Every kind of graphic expression is in fact traced on a support by means of a more or less skillfully handled instrument. The morphology of the signifier varies according to whether the material is stone, fresh clay, palm leaf, papyrus, or paper, and according to whether the tool is a needle, a pen, or a brush. Thus the use of pliant materials has produced free and more cursive forms of writing. In China, the use of the brush and the discovery of paper brought about a transformation of the characters, in many of which there is no longer any realistic drawing of the objects represented by the ideograms.

15

It is the same with plastic and graphic art: they are subordinate to their own materials and tools. Thus the character of the ornament in Altaic art establishes itself notably by those symmetrical motifs
52 53 which were obtained by cutting out shapes in pieces of leather or felt and folding them in two. The
116 pairs of roosters which were found stuck on a coffin are a well-known illustration of this art of cutting
87 out, which includes also certain wooden brackets representing paired stags, birds, goats' heads, etc.
86 Like all geometrical morphology, symmetry results in giving the motifs an abstract style in which the
122 real subject is sometimes difficult to make out, at any rate in assemblages of reversed figures. The orthogonal web of the tapestries tends likewise toward a specific style by decomposing the curves of the
210 objects depicted.

More often than not, the Siberian artist treated even his depictions of animals and of their fights
16 as silhouettes, cutting them out in felt or leather, sometimes brightly colored, assembling the elements
310 of the puzzle into polychrome mosaics, and then sticking or stitching them onto a ground whose color and material might be either similar to them or contrasted. These methods create varied plays of tex-

ture and color which, for the understanding, are as effective as is modeling with shadows and lights. But are they sufficient?

For, although Eurasian nomads did try to create low reliefs sculptured in laminated leather, the animals inevitably, through the insufficient volume of the material worked on, remain expressed by figures either frontal or in profile, chosen with regard to their efficacy as signs. The dynamism of the animals is nonetheless rendered by the combination of those two aspects, stressing that limb or organ which seems the most significant in one way or another as regards the attitude to be represented. Even when the material is wood or metal, which would have allowed of a fully sculptural treatment of the motif, the Eurasian artist limits himself to expressing the essential by means of a few lines of force and conventions. In the case of the tigers on an ornament belonging to a bridle found in Pazyryk 2, the schematized hindquarters are turned at a right angle, in a typical position sometimes adopted by a feline in repose—that is to say, with the two hind legs stretched out together on one side at an angle of ninety degrees to the axis of the body, the front part of which remains symmetrical with the forefeet as a kind of prolongation of the head. Again, on one Altaic plaque there is a wolf gazing at its hindquarters which are twisted upward, the torsion being depicted entirely in the plane of the figure, with no perspective foreshortening: the whole motif may therefore be looked at without top or bottom, in any of the attitudes a nomad herdsman might adopt in the course of a ride or a violent struggle. And this complete torsion of the depicted animal has not brought with it the sensible play of volumes which might have been expected from a work executed in wood, a material that lends itself to sculptural treatment. Except in works of Scytho-Greek inspiration, the nomads, though they made abundant use of metals, did not draw from them all the technical possibilities which these new products offered. The Hellenizing exceptions are, indeed, generally on anecdotal subjects: realism for its own sake, though always particularly seductive in the case of metalwork and gems, seems to have found little favor among the men of the Steppes for their native themes.

The goldsmith's art, including that of working precious metals in general, owes its prestige not only to the aesthetic and commercial value of gold and silver but to their exceptional visible qualities. Gold is incorruptible, ductile, and so malleable that one ounce is enough to coat a wire a hundred miles long. Silver, tougher than its rivals, retains an elasticity sufficient to make it easily pliant to all the forms one wishes to give it. Both of them can be carved in the mass, melted, forged, hammered. All pieces of goldsmiths' work are finished with the help of more or less soft and fine files, mallets, carving tools, and chisels. These metals being heavy, precious, and expensive, methods of working designed to be economical or quick, such as repoussé, cloisonné, and the soldering together of separate fragments, are often adopted to produce diverse textures and specific surfaces in the works of the goldsmith, in harmony with the material and technique in current use. Often, indeed, gold and silver are used as inlay, filigree, or plating, to decorate or cover awkward materials, the brilliance of a thin gilding being sufficient for the desired impression. (Some of the gold leaf used as plating was only fifteen to twenty microns thick.) Thus the bridles and saddles of the nomads of the Steppes were decorated with motifs in leather, felt, and wood covered with gold, silver, or tin.

But above all, the malleability, ductility, and density make possible a boldness of which the other materials do not allow. The goldsmith does not, like the carver of stone or the potter, have to worry about stabilizing his work with supports, struts, and large pedestals. He need not, like the carpenter, take account of the grain of the wood, nor does he have to think of precautions against future distortions, splits, and shrinkings in clay, bone, or timber.

And yet barbarian art—like all others, especially Greek art (with that repeated modular con-

16

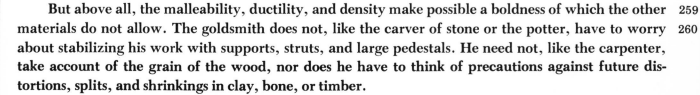

struction which takes away all scale from architecture)—is not exempt from formalism, and it too shows evidence of the ideological superstructures lagging behind the economic and technical infrastructures. The Scythian artist, even though metal sets him free from certain constructive and morphological rules inherent in other materials, still, in his purely metallic transcriptions of traditional themes, mechanically repeats certain "canons." Fashion and habit, in place of reflection, result in some of his finest pieces of goldsmiths' work containing uneven surfaces which, though certainly inevitable when the material worked is wood or bone, are quite unnecessary in the case of molding or any other way of working metal. The same is true of ceramics. The fineness of Scythian goldsmiths' work reacts on the forms of the pottery: in the clay vase from the Scythian treasure of Ziwiye, the lip takes the form of a bird's beak, which is copied from examples in metal; though the solidity of metal allows of such imitations, they are extremely fragile in earthenware or terra cotta.

These examples illustrate how modes of expression have signifiers whose morphology is closely bound up with the history of the code itself. Like art, writing shows its form lagging behind its technical means—and this even in anomalies that persist in our day: fountain pens and ball-points, by allowing the hand to remain resting on the paper and making easier the writer's ligatures and gestures, have brought about, in spite of the reservations of expert calligraphers, a decreased use of the types of writing that are too slow (round hand, slanting, Italian hand) but which were still very much favored in the nineteenth century; yet these have not completely disappeared.

Again, the Siberian or primitive artist's choice of materials itself bears witness to the expressive function which the plastic mode originally possessed. In a single work these artists combine and juxtapose, without any purist scruples, the most diverse materials—hard (bone, wood, metal) and softer (felt, fur, leather, colored hair). Looking at the celebrated and successful pieces from the Altai might lead one to believe that this marriage of materials is exclusively a characteristic of the art of that region; but as early as Paleolithic art objects appear which must have been completed with perishable materials—as is the case also in works of present-day Eurasians, Africans, Indians, and Polynesians. The reason why barbarian art does not aim at homogeneity of materials is that to these artists "any wood is fuel," because to them the effect mattered more than the means. If the expression, caught by diverse means, produces a clear image, to hell with the virtuoso vanity of getting the most out of a single material! The work is not signed! As yet, nobody was trying to detect in it the personality and mastery of its creator. There was no artist's introspection: the one purpose was to get the message across. Finally, the handwriting of the artist depends on skill: in Paleolithic art, for instance, the iconography includes more clumsy works than masterpieces, and it is probable, if not certain, that no body of specialists then existed, any more than it does in the communities of Australian aborigines, where everyone in some way practices the graphic arts. But when, as with the nomads of the Steppes, a high artistic standard in regard to the motifs that are produced appears, the artist, like the calligrapher, exhibits his craft, his specialization. This does not mean that he may not place his talent at the service of a faith or a proclamation; but the perfection of the work done does imply for art, under the influence of various catalysts, the possibility of becoming, through its refined and individualized form, a means of approaching the author as well as the message itself—or at least of rendering this message so personalized that its conceptual value is directed toward particular aspects. Production, having become "artistic," reciprocally creates for the work of art an eager recipient, a solicited public, in due course rendered sensitive and artloving.

17

Graphic Art Transformed by Writing

The parallels between such different modes of expression as the oral sign, the written sign, and plastic art can obviously not be presented with mechanical neatness. Each is the result of an intrinsic dialectic and has its own history. The aim of a work varies in time and according to the society from which it comes.

While it is easy to show that art, originally, is a means of expression, it is no less easy to prove that the love of work well done, its author's skill, and the market value of the product became essential factors which bent art away from its initial purposes. This problem will be resumed in greater depth in the chapter dealing with the relations between art and social life and its economic bases. But in considering "barbarian" art (that is, art produced by societies described by that name), there are many 276 proofs that it was not an affair of aesthetics. For instance, as early as late Paleolithic art, the represen- 278 tations of strange groupings of animals—which are static and stereotyped rather than naturally 243 dynamic—suggest proto-ideographic and ideological schemes. Even when, as in Scythian and related art, the animal pictures lay stress on movement, the pride of place allotted to the predatory species necessarily confers on them a symbolic value.

Finally, this animal art of the ancient world, with its fundamental difference from the sophisticated, carefully considered, scrupulous, and finished works—marked, in fact, by an academic realism—of such great men as Géricault, Décamps, or Barye, conveys by its writing that its aim is not so much realism for its own sake as expressionism, and that what it seeks is the fact in itself—conceptual—rather than any attempt at a total representation of the object. This means that such art is indeed language, and the study of an object with the special purpose of depicting it fully is the result of an intellectual activity within a much later socioeconomic context. In early art, drawing was certainly not valued as a means of revealing the artist's sensitivity, but for its stenographic effectiveness. The enormous canines of the Siberian tiger, the frightening strength of the beak of a bird of prey, and the nobility of a fully grown stag are depicted from memory, not from life or on an easel: the essential features alone are reproduced, stripped of all anecdotal details that would not contribute to the message.

In Egyptian drawing, also, we find this conceptual function in the hieroglyphs, which are really images for reading. But such an orderly translation of the quintessence of forms appears already in Paleolithic art and continues in that of the barbarians, who were still "unlettered." Yet it was not a congenital ignorance that prevented the artist of those times from, for instance, representing perspective correctly, or that made him show the muzzle of an animal in profile and the horns frontally (as Picasso would later do), but it was first and foremost a determination to make a synthesis of the most 24 important characteristics: the artist was depicting not exclusively what he saw, but what he intended 27 to say.

18

This, in the last resort, is the proof that, in prehistory and then in protohistory (our examples here being taken from those of the Eurasian continent), art is a system of conventions in which, nonetheless, the speaker retains a considerable liberty, and in which the logic of the code results in this having a determinant share in the signifier; and this works, paradoxically, both to the advantage and to the disadvantage of the signified, producing at one and the same time more punch and less strictness than other, more conventional, modes of expression.

When we turn to the stammerings of correct perspective and realism, we are reminded of the well-known observation that man never sets himself problems that he is not going to be able to resolve.

Truth in the representation of the thing seen makes its appearance along with the great empires and
364 urban civilizations of antiquity which practiced writing. The peak of realistic representation was at-
362 tained by Greek art and by the arts related to it—that is to say, precisely when writing had finally and
363 completely renounced its picto-ideographic character in favor of syllabic and alphabetic writing,
which was both highly conventional and fertile in potentialities. Art was immediately set free from the
necessary script conventions which had marked its origins. Its nature, form, and content changed ac-
cordingly. The way of realism was opened to it. In the choice of themes for the graphic and plastic arts
of civilization expressing itself about itself, animals and fantastic composites yielded pride of place to
man.

Such is the irrevocable process and dialectic history. We will let Marx and Engels do the summing
up, in a distillation of their notes about art: "The eye became human when its object became a
human, social object, coming from man and destined for man . . . . The eagle's sight is much longer
than a man's, but the human eye notices more in things than the eagle's eye does . . . . The tradition
of all the dead generations weighs very heavily on the brain of the living. The training of the five senses is the work of the whole history of the world down to the present day."

In consequence, "is the Iliad possible in a world with the printing-press and rotary presses? . . . .
A man cannot become a child without falling back into childhood. But does he not rejoice in the
naivety of a child, and must he not himself aspire to reproduce this truth on a higher level?"

19

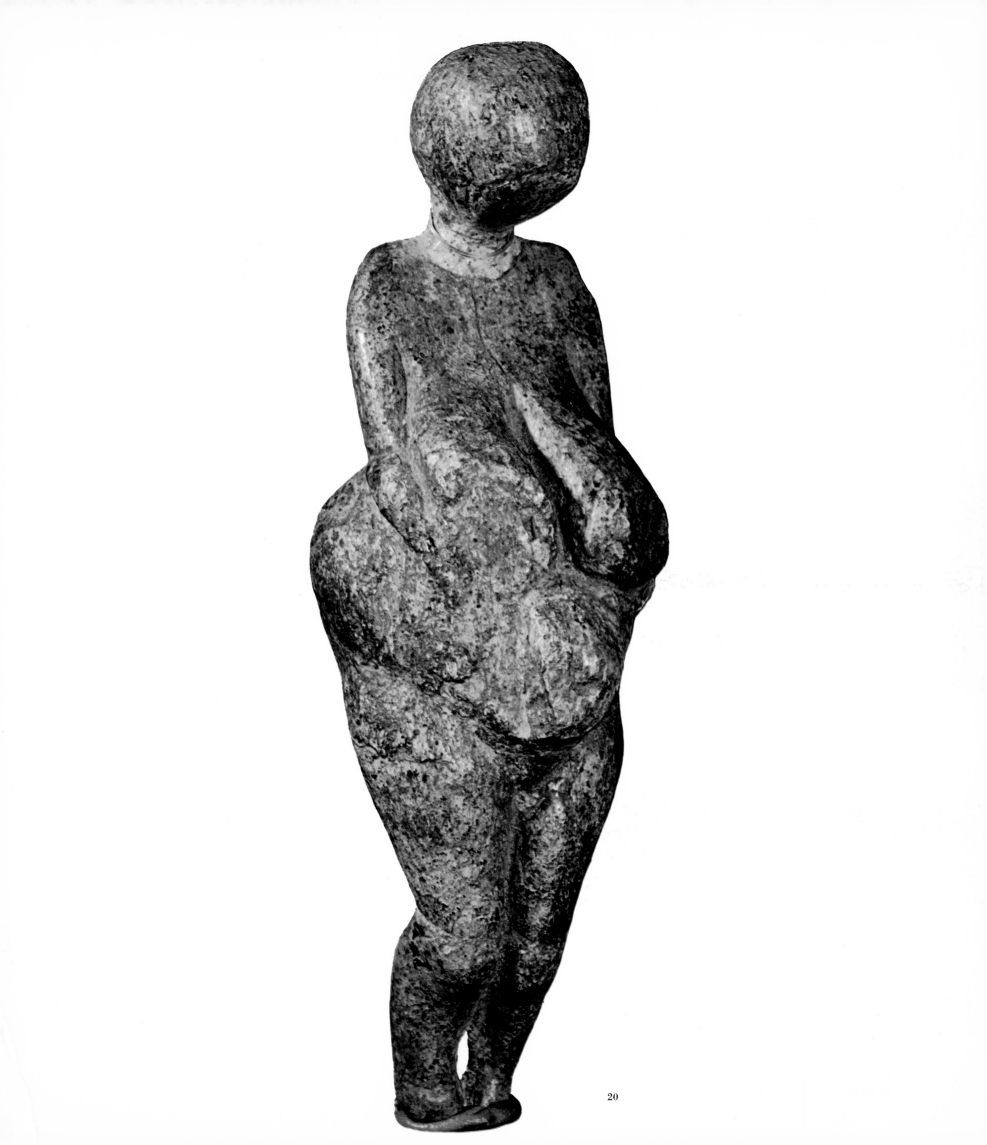

21

23

22

25

24

26

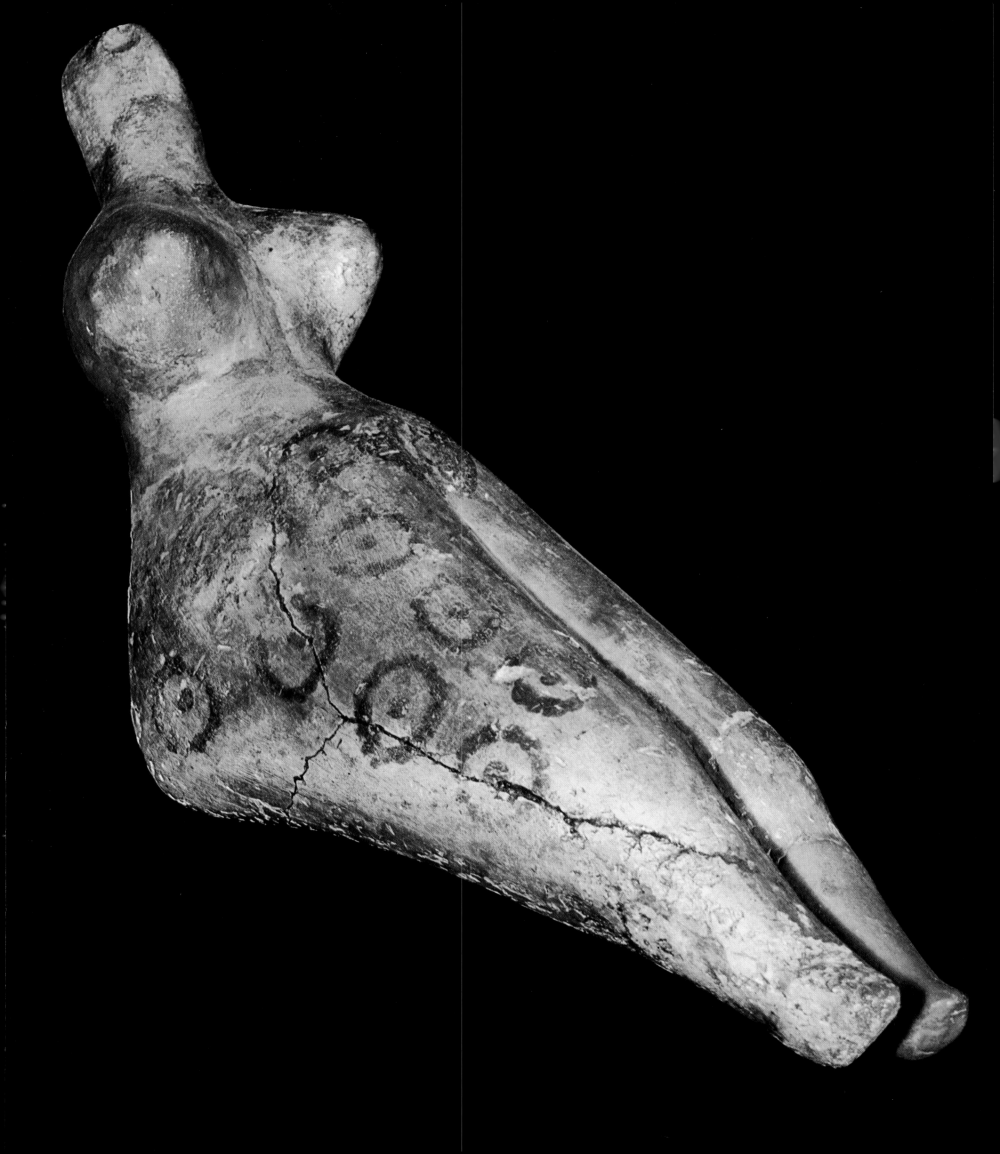

29

30

31

32

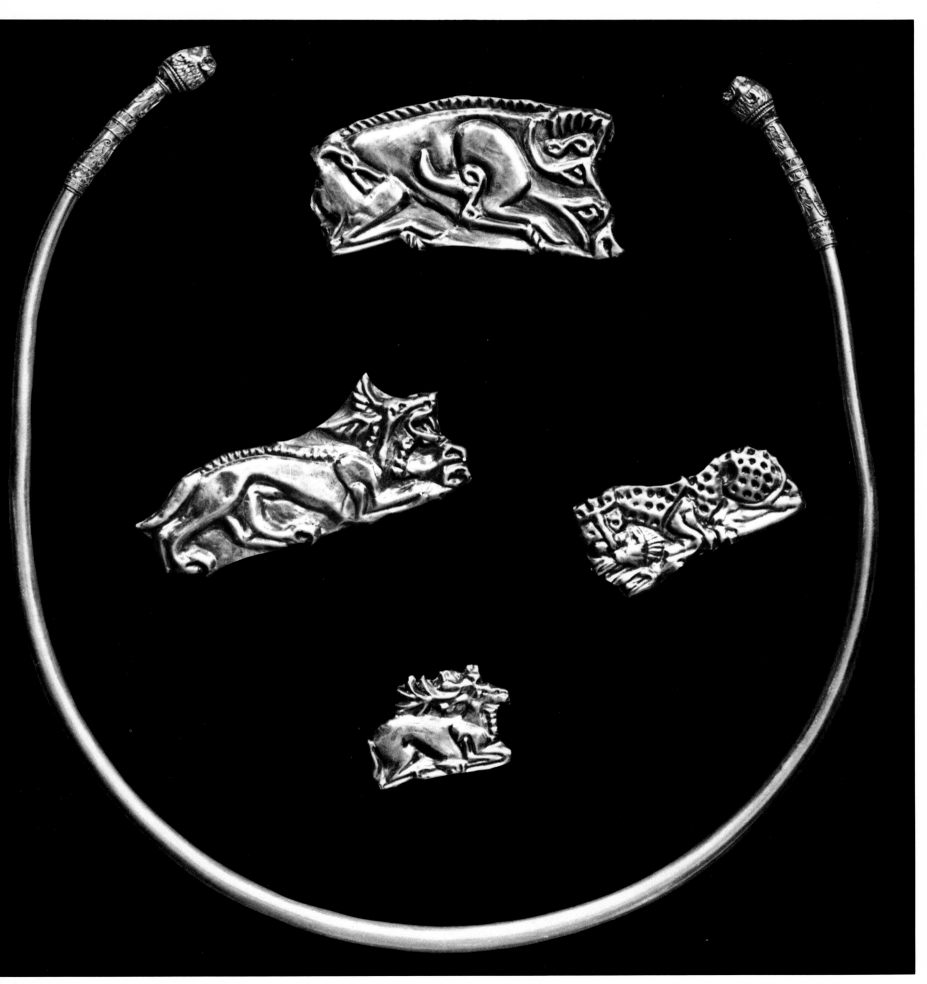

38

39

40

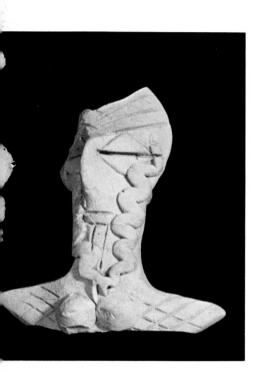

41

42

43

45

46

44

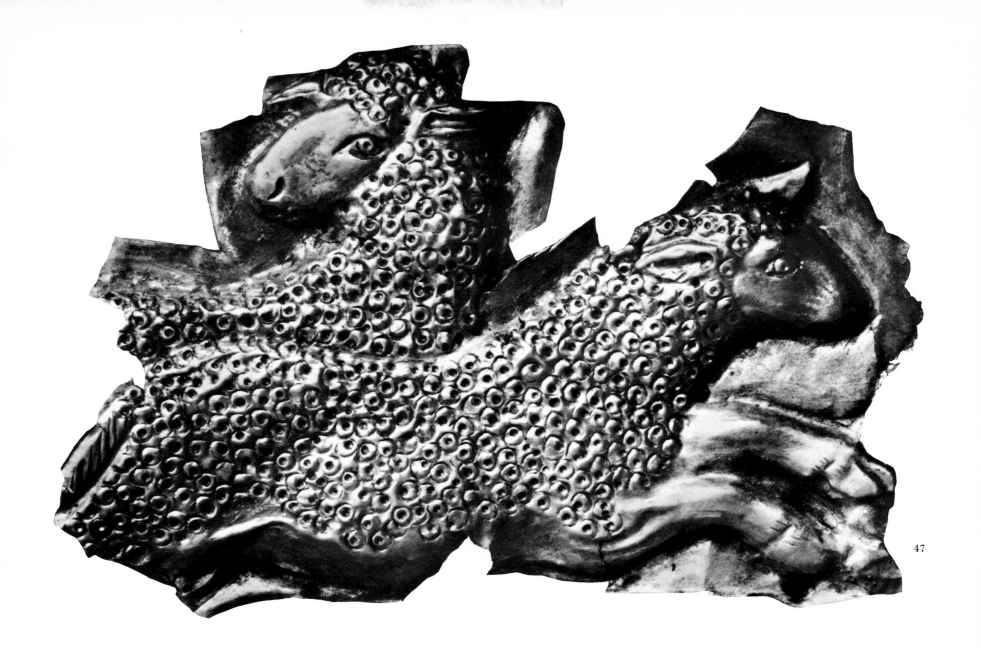

47

48

49

50

51

52

53

54 ▶

55

56

58

59

57

62

63

64

65

67

66

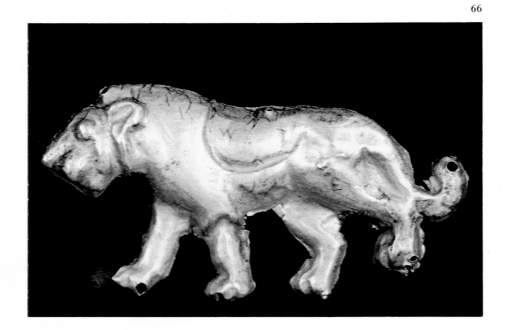

68

69

70

71

72

73

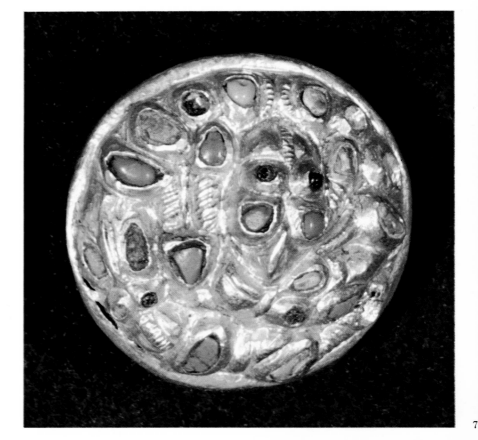

7

75

76

77

78

79

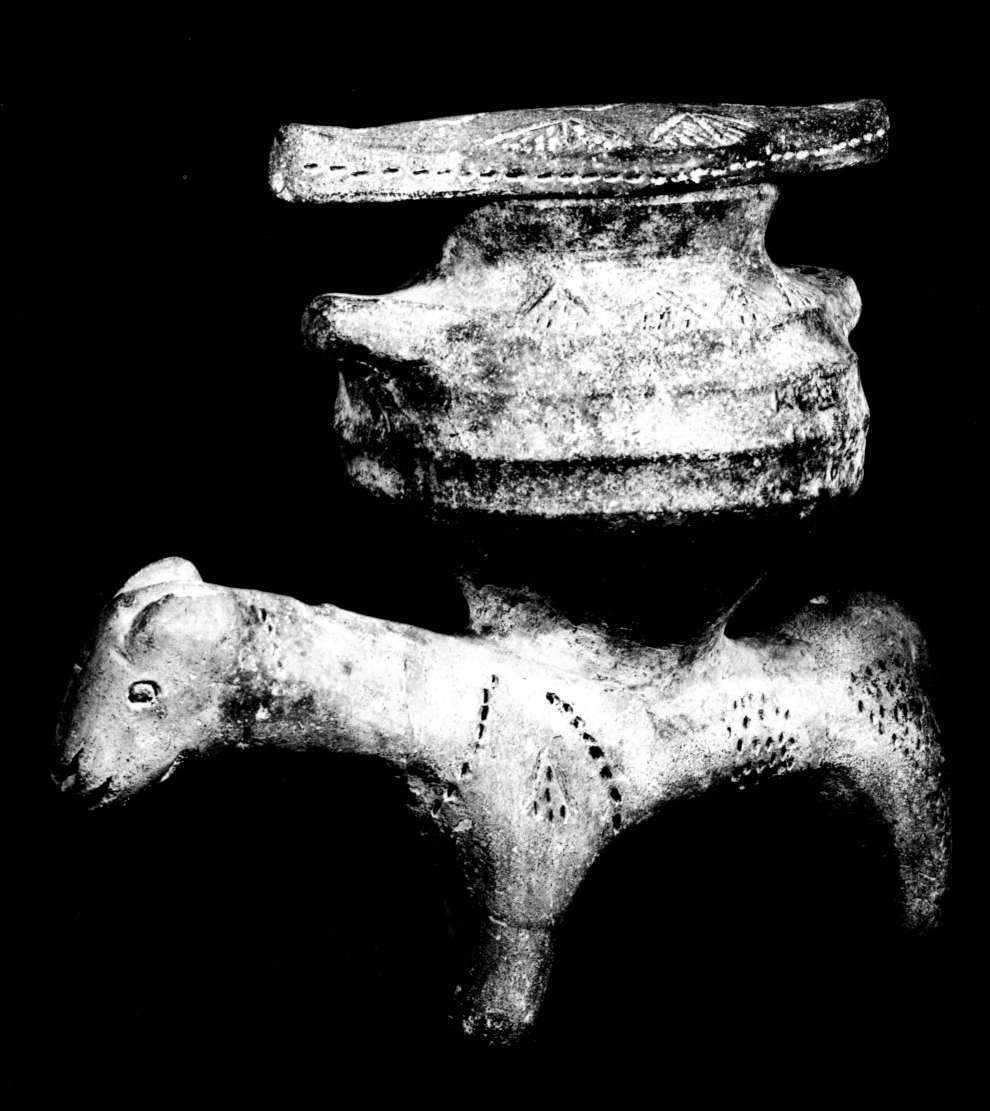

84

86

85

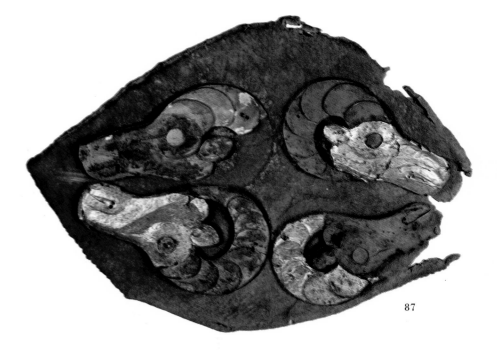

87

89

90

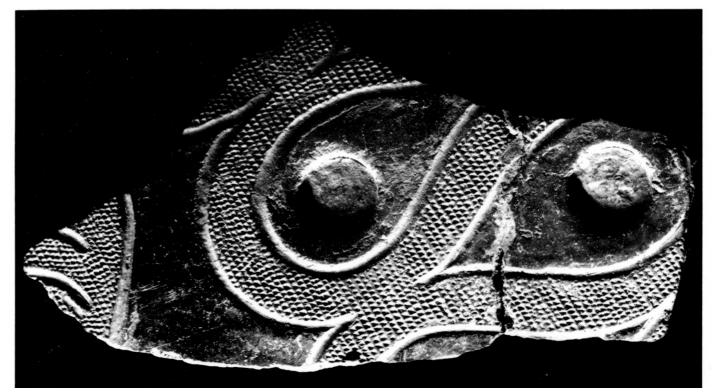

91

92

94

93

95

98

96

97

99

100

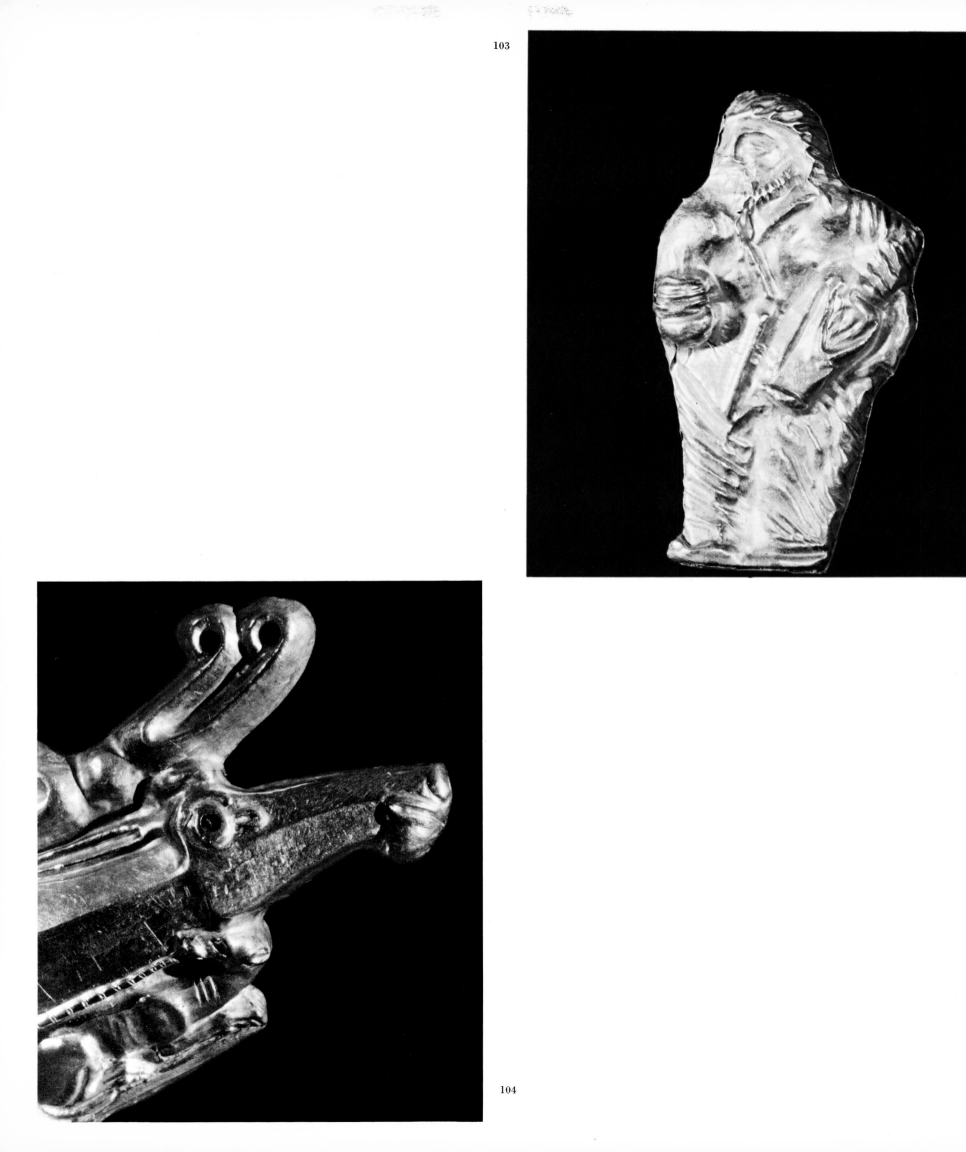

103

104

105

107

108

106

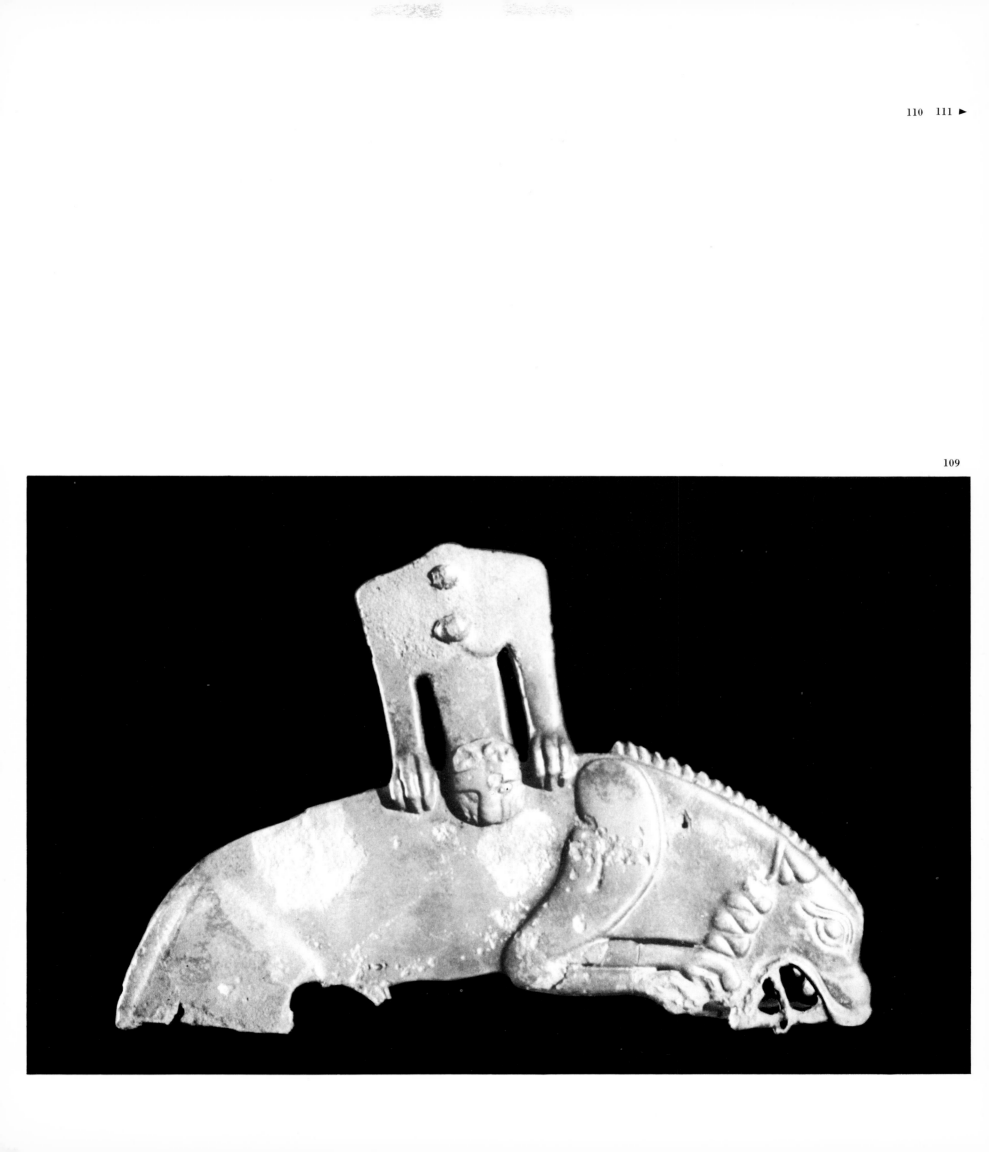

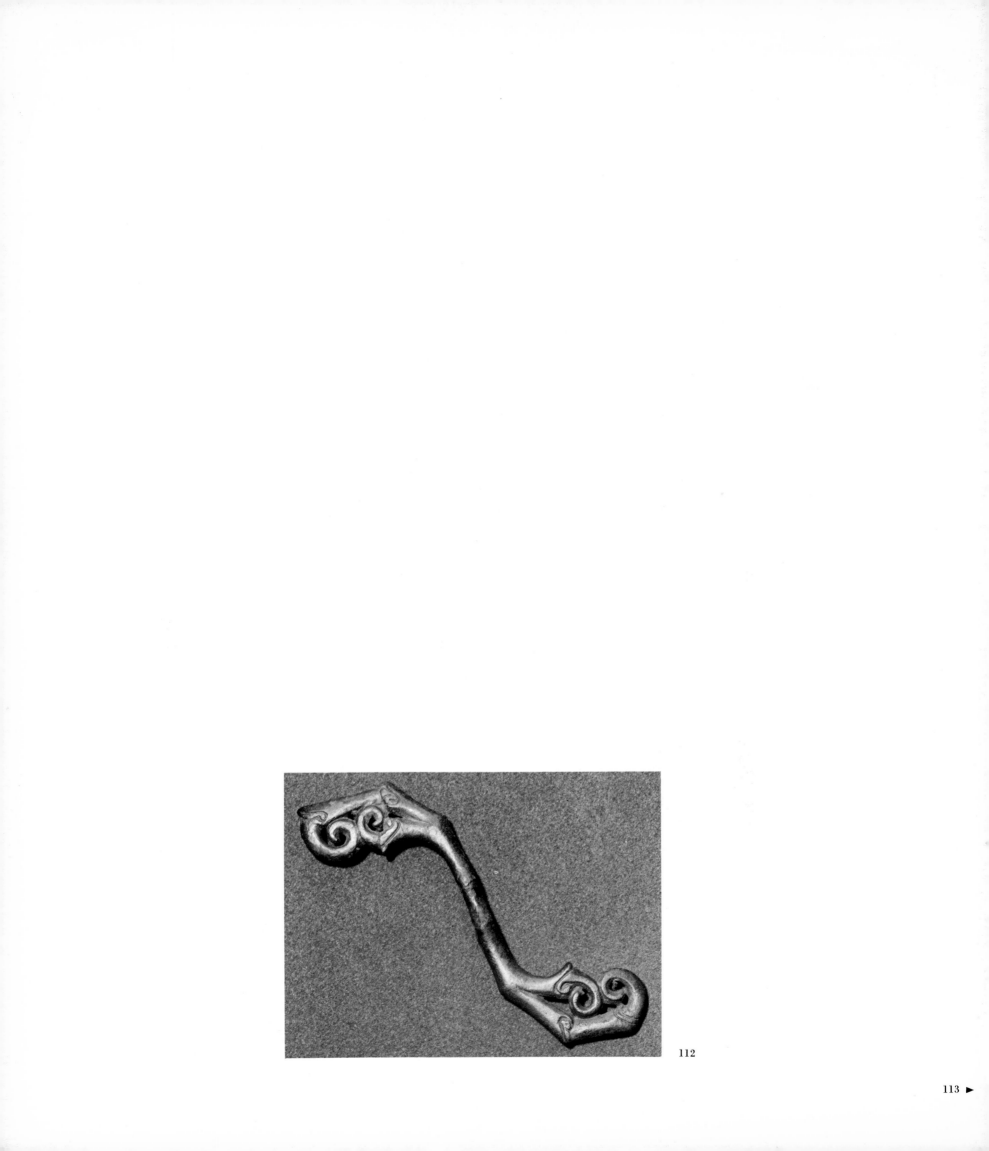

112

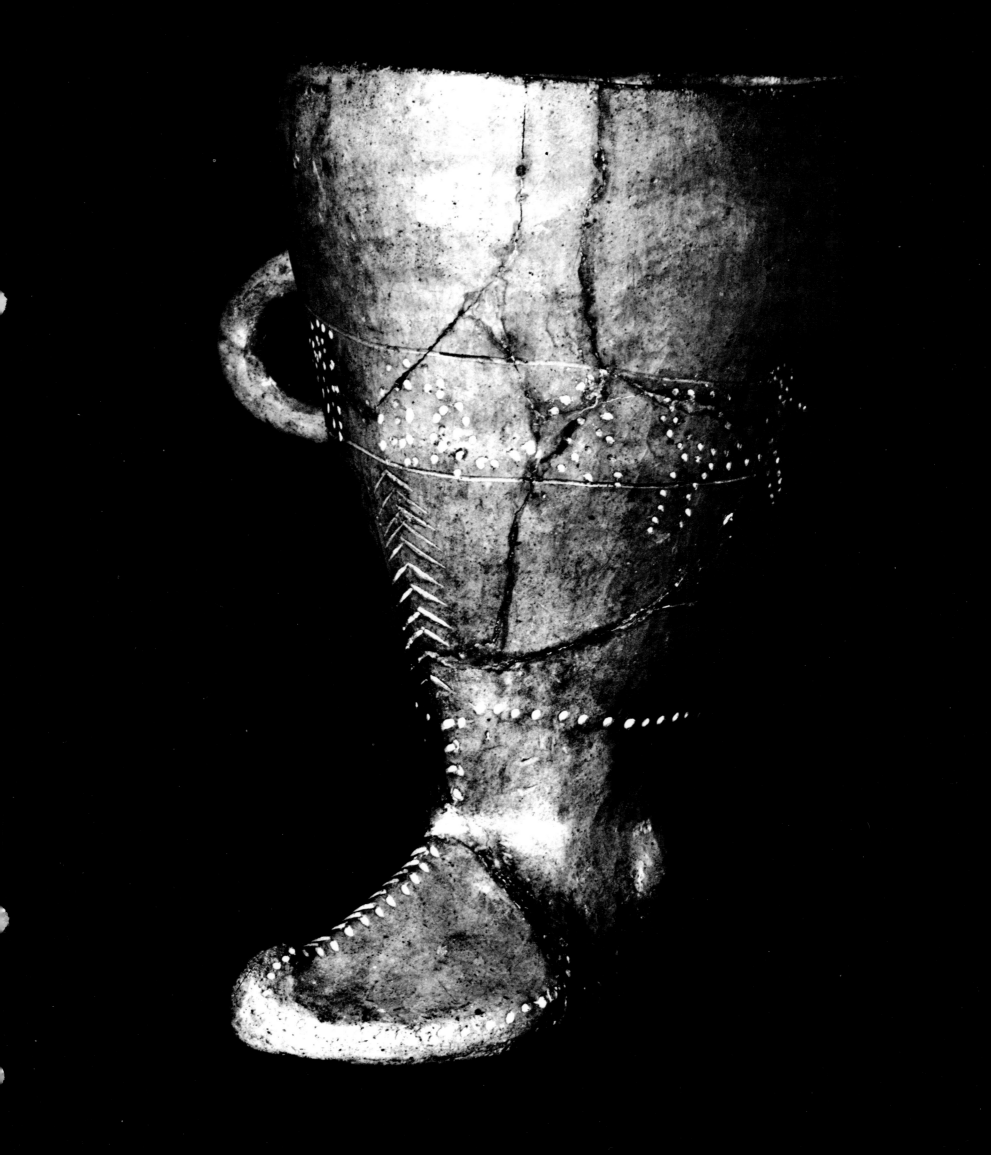

114

115

116

117

118

119

120

121

122

ART DEMYSTIFIED

The Known Divinities

The existence of a religion is demonstrated by rites and beliefs, but unfortunately archaeological excavations are often unable to reveal these. To approach the most ancient religions (insofar as comparative study can throw light on them) it is necessary to begin with those about which written evidence has come down to us.

To judge from what the Scythians said, as reported more or less faithfully by the ancient authors who Hellenized the barbarian gods, their peoples had as their divine ancestor Zeus, who was called "papaios," or the Great Pope, the father par excellence of all the Indo-European gods and men, those who were using a single original language some two thousand years before our era.

Zeus, or Jupiter, was a Don Juan with innumerable feminine conquests. In southern Russia, for instance, he had seduced the daughter of the River Borysthenes, the present Dnieper. She was a creature half-woman, half-serpent, who gave birth to a fully grown king, Targitaus according to the barbarians, Hercules to the Greeks. This offspring of the gods in his turn had three sons, for the gods like males and the uneven number. Soon a gold plow, a yoke for harnessing it, and a golden battle-ax and cup fell from heaven. Only the youngest of Targitaus' sons was able to lay hands on these object-messages, his brothers having been prevented from doing so because the gold burst into flames at their approach. So the youngest was his father's successor, since he had proved able to take up the symbols of sovereignty over the farmers and warriors of the Steppes.

But the Scythian pantheon, as described to us by the Greek and Roman writers, has no great specific originality. Its gods are anthropomorphic and assimilated to Jupiter, Diana, Apollo, Hercules, and Neptune. They had, however, no consecrated temples, no votive or venerated statues. In this the gods of the Eurasian nomads resemble not those of the Greeks but those of the Iranian shepherds, who were scarcely less mobile than their northern neighbors.

Yet Herodotus does note that for the Scythian Ares, god of war, a square platform was constructed on billets of wood and a sword was planted on it, before which cattle, horses, and prisoners were sacrificed. A sword was often represented among the Sarmatians and the Huns, though whether it was an emblem or a fetish is no longer known. Battle-axes which seem to be too thickly covered with zoomorphic decorations to have been used as weapons have been found at the sites and burials belonging to the herdsmen and warrior peoples of Eurasia. But such an ax may have been like the double ax in Crete, a princely symbol—or even a sign of divinity, seeing that it is brandished by the king of the Hellenic gods in his fight against the giants, though this does not mean that there is evidence for hoplolatry (the worship of weapons) having been a practice among the Cretans, still less among the Scythians.

Apart from the barbarian Ares or Mars, the most important, and certainly the most often depicted, of the Eurasian divinities is Tabiti, who clearly resembles the Roman Vesta in being goddess of fire, but also perhaps in virtue of the animals that accompany her in some representations. Yet it is not certain that she is in fact the winged divinity shown on part of an engraved silver mirror from Kelermes. This figure suggests an Anatolian Cybele holding two frightened lions, with their tails between their hind legs—an expression of taming common in the art of the Near East. An iron mounting from Alexandropol similarly shows her grasping two animals whose front parts flank her on either side. One is reminded of the painting on a small Corinthian bombylios belonging to the Louvre: a Persian Arte-

81

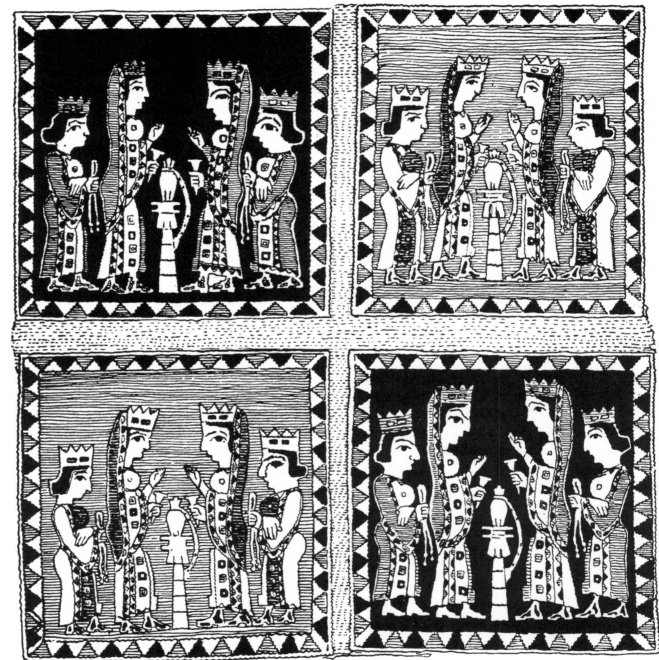

mis with the wings of a bird of prey is depicted grasping Anatidae (aquatic birds), one in each hand.

Is Tabiti also the opulent matron adorning a Sarmatian phalera found in Bulgaria? She has the heavy tresses worn by the Eurasian women, and birds, possibly ravens, seem to be whispering in her ears. Images of this type are also common in Celtic art: birds of the crow type spoke to the gods of Gaul. And this is less strange than it at first seems, since members of the crow family are good at imitating the human voice—as for instance the famous bird belonging to Augustus.

But the dark bird is also a symbol of fire in many mythologies, and so it emphasiszes the igneous attributes of the Great Goddess. For the ancients the raven signified fire-carrier, because his blackness is the consequence of his zeal in stealing terrestrial fire at the cost of burning himself. And in fact these birds' propensity to flutter in the midst of embers is real and well attested: the eminent British zoologist Maurice Burton has published some astonishing photographs that show the bird enjoying the pickings it finds among flames and smoke. This mania is the origin of the Celtic name for the raven, "bran": the word comes from a common Eurasian root that, from the British Isles to Russia, is found in words for "fire," "burning" and "embers," and denotes by extension blackness, insofar as this is an attribute of charred objects. Moreover, the ancients accused birds of the crow type of setting fire to their harvests, and this complaint now seems justified by the recent discovery that the crow is fascinated by embers, as well as by its notorious kleptomania. In the wheat-growing plains of the Ukraine the danger was a real one and must have made the crow seem an appropriate symbol for the goddess of fire.

125

But besides being a robber and master of fire on earth, the raven or crow in the ancient Chinese cosmologies is also an inhabitant of the sun's disk: it is related to the celestial fire whose source is the sun, and it builds its nests facing the sun, in order to enjoy, just as humans do, a beneficent warmth. In addition, crows are migratory birds and follow the rhythm of the seasons governed by the sun: in winter they leave their Eurasian homes for more clement and southerly skies. These reasons converge and explain why the Roman Apollo borrowed the solar raven from his Delphic neighbor. Herodotus in his Fourth Book, which deals with Scythia, reports that a certain Aristeas—whose name oddly resembles that of Aristaios, son of Apollo—was so possessed by Phoebus that he accompanied the sun god in the form of a raven. Accompanied him where? To the Issedonians and the Arimaspians, northern barbarians who doubtless lived to the east of the Scythian and Sarmatian territories. And this migration from west to east is surely the same, in direction, as that of the springtime migratory movements of the Corvidae.

So far so good. But is the crow sufficient to cover all the attributes of the Great Goddess of the nomads? It has been remarked that, before their time, she was present at the prehistoric sites, notably the Bronze Age ones from the Urals to the Dnieper, along the courses of the Bug and the Donets. The terracotta statuettes that are said to represent her strangely resemble those many centuries older, which have been found in Elam, in Babylonia and also among the Neolithic populations of the Steppes. In the Crimea, for instance, she is said to have made her appearance in about the ninth century B.C., depicted standing and holding a child in her arms. It was perhaps the persistence of this maternal form that enabled the Greek colonists settled on the shores of the Black Sea to develop, in an autochthonous medium the cult of Demeter and her daughter Persephone, as this emerges in the ornaments of the kurgans belonging to the mixed art of the fourth century B.C., both at Olbia and in the Taman peninsula.

211
212

126

But are these really divinities? It seems possible that statues of venerated ancestors might have been made without any attempt at likeness and individualization, because their attributes would have been a better memorial to them than personal characteristics, which the living would have forgotten in the course of generations. One hesitates between the strong hypothesis—that of goddesses—and the weak hypothesis—of ancestral female guardians of the fire, a few aged babas singled out for honor and depiction within the framework of a matrilinear genealogy, but acquiring divinity only in the long run, with the development of the ancestor cult.

This indeed is the process that seems to have taken place in the Minusinsk Basin. Let us examine,

127

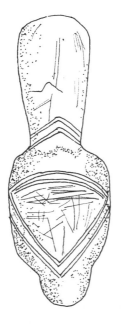

128

for instance, the statuettes of the Okunev culture, which date from the beginning of the second millennium B.C. They are small steatite wands, whose upper part represents the head of a woman 180 with Mongoloid features, hair worn loose, and earrings: these heads probably completed the bodies of 181 dolls made of some flexible textile substance. As many as five heads of this kind were found in each 183 tomb. They could, therefore, be portraits of the "grandmother": grandmother worship went on until quite recently, in similar forms, among many Saiano-Altaic tribes. These sacred dolls were transmitted from mother to daughter because they were considered as ancestors and protectresses of the family. The fact that several were found in each tomb argues in favor of the "grandmothers" having been renewed as the generations succeeded. This redundance may equally well be proof of a propitiatory religious prudence, or a sign that the figures simply marked the succession of generations—so that deification is reduced to one hypothesis among others, and there is no a priori ground for a preference.

In any case, it must often have fallen upon the women to maintain the continuity of the hearth 210 within the family unity. A woolen tapestry recovered at Pazyryk shows several women gathered about 124 an altar with a fire on it and having a censer similar to the one that is placed close to the royal throne in one of the Persepolis reliefs. In a kurgan at Chertomlyk an electrum appliqué has been found on which the central figure is probably, in view of its size, a goddess ceremonially enthroned: on her left there is an altar from which a flame is rising, and on her right a Scythian apparently worshiping. This is without question the most plausible representation of Tabiti as the divine mistress of fire.

There is clear evidence that she was worshiped among the Mongolians and Tatars in Siberia, as well as earlier in ancient Persia and Vedic India. Here Agni, the god of fire, seems to have brought ecstasy and a feeling of immortality to the faithful, who, however, in order to experience this, had first swallowed *soma,* a drink in which hemp was presumably an ingredient in view of the hallucinations that were obtained. And in central Russia the Galich statuette, seated and with a halo of flames, 209 provides evidence from the second half of the second millennium B.C. of what may have been the worship of such a god. But here also proof would be needed that this was not simply a metaphorical representation of a piece of newly introduced metal, a piece of freshly smelted bronze possibly being depicted as a person who is "all fire and flame,"—to be classed with the many and various secular images in which fire expresses ideas less concrete than its immediate reality. In present-day Ossetian stories, of archaic inspiration, the heroes, whose bodies are metallic, are brought to white heat by the blacksmith god who then, to harden them, tempers them both really and figuratively in sea water or she-wolves' milk.

Whether religious or not, the Galich object corresponds to the introduction of metallurgy into that region of central Russia. Although there is not always anything to be gained by looking for logic in a field that is irrational, it may be observed here that religion, as an ideological superstructure, bears traces of reflecting the development of economic life. For the appearance of Hephaistos, Kurdalaegon (the smith god in the Ossetian mythology), and other male blacksmith gods is bound up with the success of a new technique and its effects on production: to melt gold, silver, copper, and bronze, temperatures of more than one thousand degrees centigrade have to be obtained, temperatures far in excess of those of the early domestic bakings. The baking of pottery, already achieved by specialists in the Tripolye culture, brought with it the appearance of the male sex as the master of kilns, perhaps along with an increased idealization of fire as a producer of wealth. But in various places the encounter of pastoral and goldsmith nomads with more settled farming communities must have resulted in peaceful compromises including the new cults, and in theogonies in which the possible Neolithic fire goddesses sometimes retained their original attributes, if not their nudity.

191   In any case, the Tabiti of the nomads seems austere and savage. The leaders owed allegiance to
192 her, if this is the meaning of a ceremony reproduced on a wall hanging from Pazyryk, and if one is to
believe Herodotus. On various applied ornaments she is a stiff-necked matron with wings; on another,
from Kul Oba, she appears with a vase-shaped basket and with the lower part of her body swathed in
serpents and griffins. The goddess is brandishing a sword, and in the other hand she carries a severed,
bearded head, and is like some young Sarmatian girl who has scalped her first enemy.

Elsewhere again the depiction of the Great Goddess as holding in check a terrified feline in each
of her hands, and, finally, as having wings, presents her as a queen. One thinks of the emblem given to
the Sumerian god Ningirsu to show his omnipotence—a majestic lion-headed eagle with wings spread
and an animal in its claws. The stele of the vultures at Tello (Lagash), the Tell Obeid relief in the
British Museum, and the silver vessel from Entemena in the Louvre show that, during the first half of the
130 third millennium B.C., one current semantic or plastic theme consisted in visualizing the power of a
133 leader or divinity over men by thus combining the forms of the king of beasts and the king of birds.

There is evidence, indeed, that in the Indo-European and Indo-Iranian languages of Persia and
Anatolia the word for prisoner-of-war signified literally that he was "taken in hand." Our word "captive" has almost the same sense, being derived through the Latin *capere* (to take) from the root *kap,*
which in Sanskrit yielded *kapati,* meaning "the two fists." But as the language of Cicero and modern
languages remained insufficiently explicit, expressions came into being like *manum dare* and "command" whose etymology reflects the original metaphor. And to denote political power there are still
current expressions such as "to have the situation well in hand" or "holding the reins of power," and
one speaks of "falling into the clutches" of someone and of being able to "recognize a lion by his claws."

What is significant in the stele of the vultures is that Ningirsu, the Herculean but agricultural god
of Lagash, is holding in one hand a club, which renders intelligible the monstrous symbol brandished
in the other. And the relief shows the logical sequence of the allegory—the capture of prisoners-of-war
who are caught in a net and will no doubt make excellent slaves to work on the land.

One may therefore wonder if the omnipotence of Tabiti is purely spiritual or if the similar attitude in which she is shown has not some relation with the captives made by the Scythians in the
course of their raids. In this case the prisoners, with their feline form indicating their deep-rooted
hostility, would be falling into the power of the "Queen of the Scythians," or under the guardianship
of the woman whom she symbolizes, to be put to manual work. Thus domesticated, in the real and
figurative senses, the ex-enemies would now be merely "tamed lions."

The Louvre indeed possesses a piece which strikingly evokes this idea, already underlying the
above-mentioned examples: a creature in human form, wearing a robe that comes down to its calves,
has its head surmounted by horns curving inward, and is holding, one in each hand, two lions that are
still trying to use their claws. One thinks at once of a well-known piece from the Altai in which a tiger,
also horned, is holding two Anatidae. Whether male or female, the allegory seems always to be one of
215 seizure, of manhandling.

It becomes clear that there is a glaring difference between the archaic and extremely uncertain
prototypes of Tabiti and these final, severe representations in Greco-Scythian art: paradoxically, the
nearer we approach to the great Quaternary glaciations, the more the female figures are practically
naked, whereas their protohistoric representations stress social attributes which relegate the carnal
ones to the second plane. Yet any statement that this difference of treatment corresponds to different
motivations would still be hypothetical; for, as improvement in clothing followed general develop-

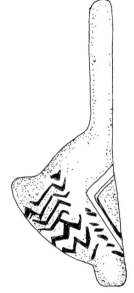

129

130

131

ment and the division of labor, specialized costumes and adornments for men and for women became a convention sufficing to identify the sex, age, or social class of a figure. In some cases, clearly, it is better for the purpose than nudity is: there is, for instance, no striking bodily difference to distinguish a young father from a young unmarried man, or a newly married woman from a confirmed spinster, either among men or among gods. In consequence, modern Russian writers have taken to describing the prehistoric figurines prudently as "female statuettes," in the absence of any evidence as to their social function or religious value. The insistence with which the early artists asserted and exaggerated the primary and secondary sexual characteristics of women is first and foremost the sign of an expressionism stressing that they were meant to be regarded as mothers. The Lespugue or Ialangach-Depe statuettes, in spite of the atrophy or disappearance of the arms (but because they are works of art), thus seem to defy anatomical good sense, in spite of their provocative feminity.

And in some cases where realism has led to facial features or details of clothes and hairstyle being depicted (for instance, the Malta and Buret statuettes, or those from Kostienki with belts), it may be that these elements, which today might seem to us merely anecdotal, were expressing what it was then essential to express. But more often the feet and heads (in the Paleolithic) and even the arms (especially in the Neolithic) disappear—so much so, sometimes, that one might doubt the female character of the subject, if the "breasts" and "wand with breasts" from Vestonice, or the breasts carved on the tympana of the *allées couvertes* of western Europe were not there to remind us to what degree of spareness stylization can be carried—when by good luck it remains realistic enough to be still accessible and comprehensible to us.

Thus one general tendency in the development of Paleolithic art—and one that recurs in the Yenisey region and in the southwest of France—is, starting from realism, the schematic simplification of the female body, in which the anatomical details (including, very exceptionally, the breasts) are neglected in favor of exaggeration of the buttocks. In this respect, the stylized figurines of Mezin are more recent and simplified than those of Kostienki and Gagarino, and the same applies still more clearly to more recent ones, those from Pekarna and Krasny Yar.

The same concern with impact, where detail without interest is neglected in favor of what is significant, recurs in the so-called Venus statuettes of Neolithic art—female figurines whose charms are as much asserted and denuded as those of their Paleolithic opposite numbers. And this gives them also a modern air, because the early artists also aimed not so much at a scrupulous "photographic" realism as at making the language of forms effective, immediately striking, like a punch in the face.

132

The stylization of the female body, whatever its local rules, therefore surely had little to do with either the canons of feminine beauty in prehistoric times or a savage eroticism: exaggeration of the secondary or primary sexual characteristics was meant simply to make the pictures more striking. Given this expressionism, it seems legitimate to think that only the more accurate and insipid statuettes were provided with appropriate clothes, so as to render them more functional on the symbolic plane.

Whether clothed or not, were these figurines cult objects? Did the Neolithic figures from the Danubian basin, for instance, make concrete the myths of the farmers of the Tripolye civilization? In the middle of the dwellings where they were found there was a clay platform, at most nine inches high, but cruciform and decorated with incised lines or with painting. This is said to have been a ritual element whose large and rounded cross-arms have a strange resemblance to the form of the Minoan altars at Mallia in Crete. In the Ukraine, at any rate, the domestic character of these "shrines" and the fact that the statuettes were sometimes found close to ovens make one think of the cult of the hearth in general, or of more specific cults of fire forerunning that of the Goddess Tabiti. And since gods are represented more often than their servants, and their symbols rather than their worshipers, these figurines may indeed have represented some theophany. Still, in the absence of attested rites, there is no proof of their divine usage.

Nonetheless, the collector of atrocities and savageries will find his fill in Scythian religion. Perhaps he would be tempted to see in it confirming evidence of a barbarian society, as opposed to a civilized one. It would be the height of presumptuousness to leave out of account such things as the Massacre of Saint Bartholomew, the pogroms, the Inquisition, the vandalism of Saint Martin. It would be as bad to ignore the fact that Greek civilization—that model for the humanism of our time—also had its original matrix of abominations and superstitions and was sullied by sanguinary excesses like the death of Iphigeneia, attested by Aeschylus and Lucretius. Perhaps it was because the believers in classical Greece were offended by such barbarian rites that a less abominable version of the story claimed that the girl was in Tauris, having been saved by Artemis, who made her a priestess, with the duty of sacrificing all foreigners disembarking on Scythian soil. Such in fact were the rites practiced by the savage Taurians who inhabited the Crimea, as described by Herodotus, who identified the princess with the Goddess herself.

Hashish and the Scythians

The Scythians were no more objective and tolerant in matters of religion than their neighbors. When they had caught their king Scyles in Greek costume, taking part in the bacchanalia at Olbia, the nomads in their fury had put him to death: they regarded his action as treason and mistrusted a god whose cult produced such madness. Capital punishment was also visited upon Anacharsis, the uncle of one of their kings, who had been seen practicing the rites in honor of Cybele.

Yet the ecstasies and trances produced by intoxication among the adepts of Bacchus, and the delirium of the Corybantes when they celebrated the Great Goddess of Phrygia and Asia Minor, had their equivalent in those provoked by Indian hemp in the vapor baths in which the Scythians indulged. Herodotus, in Book IV of *The Histories,* tells us that all who had taken part in the Scythian funeral ceremonies had to clean themselves afterward: "On a framework of three sticks meeting at the top they stretch pieces of woolen cloth, taking care to get the joins as perfect as they can. Inside this little tent they put a dish with red-hot stones in it. Then they take some hemp seed, creep into the tent, and throw the seed onto the hot stones. At once it begins to smoke . . . . The Scythians enjoy it so much that they howl with pleasure . . . . " (Translation by Aubrey de Selincourt. Harmondsworth, Penguin Books, 1959.) This passage, to which little importance was customarily attached, received confirmation when, in 1929, the remains of a tent as described by Herodotus and a caldron which contained stones and some grains of wild hemp were discovered in the Pazyryk tomb.

Hashish does, as Herodotus relates, produce a characteristic exhilaration: the nerves and muscles controlling laughter are incapacitated, and it is hard to stop laughing. But the effects of the drug are not limited to this.

The story of the "Old Man of the Mountain" is well known; it is no mere legend from the *Arabian Nights* but has a basis in fact, and concerns a sheikh of Persian origin who fought against Saint Louis and against the Mongols. First he would take young men when they were in a deep sleep caused by a massive dose of hashish, and would have them transported to delightful gardens, worthy of the celestial paradise. The young men, on awakening, found themselves in idyllic and enchanting

133

134

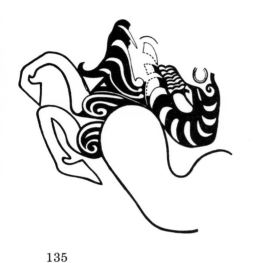

135

surroundings, which were still further enhanced by the illusions produced by the hemp. In the course of another sleep the soldiers-to-be were then removed from this Muslim Eden and returned to contact with harsh, everyday reality. This made them impatient to fight and to brave death for their chief, convinced as they were that this death would bring them a deliverance they longed for, taking them once more and without delay to the lost paradise.

Thus the "herb of the fakirs" proves that a clever use can be made of the hallucinatory and anesthetic properties of hemp to assure the power of chieftains or pontiffs. Kaempfer, a doctor employed by the *Compagnie des Indes,* has told how in Malabar, under the effect of a perilous mixture of hemp and opium, many virgins taken from the Brahmin temples used to adorn themselves richly and would dance and leap, shouting, contorting their limbs, foaming at the mouth, and showing the whites of their eyes, while the priest read calmly from the sacred writings; then an antidote was administered secretly to the hallucinated girls, and the faithful were tricked into believing that a god had exorcised them and had restored them to reason by his intervention.

Were the Scythian leaders equally crafty? There is no means of telling. But in some of the nomads the abuse of hemp may have led to those signs of degeneration which the ancient authors, in particular Hippocrates, noted in the Scythians. They were, we are told, afflicted by a tendency to obesity—"these men who are more like eunuchs than anything else." Their sexual indifference, sometimes going as far as complete impotence, was something that struck foreign observers. It is known that hashish can not only sometimes diminish sexual appetite but can produce great hunger and thirst, which in turn can lead to obesity through overindulgence in meat and drink. The softening of the flesh of the face must have helped to give some of the nomad hashish-users the typical appearance of the eunuch, with his flabby, pendant cheeks and characteristic paunch. From generalizations based on these, it was but a short step to denigration.

For all these dangers, which have led to its being excluded nowadays from use in hospital treatment, hashish seems, in the Scythian funeral ceremonies, to have been relatively prophylactic, amounting to a risky palliative for the stress and affliction caused by the loss of a precious human being, and to a means of easing the attendant cruelties. For, considering the sinister practices customary at these ceremonies—at which the human sacrifices of his household necessarily strike us as religious aberrations—the living certainly had need of such tranquilizers. Herodotus's description of the long and bloody funeral ceremonies of a Scythian king has been fully confirmed by the discoveries at Pazyryk. The body, after being emptied of its entrails, was stuffed with aromatic herbs and sewn 178 up again, then placed on a cart. This was followed in procession by the members of the tribe, with their heads shaved and one ear cropped, weeping and howling, tearing their arms and faces, and digging arrowheads into their left hands in sign of mourning. (The mother of Totyradz, in the Ossetian legend, also tears her face and strikes her knees at the death of the young hero.) After being thus accompanied for forty days through the whole territory, the dead leader was placed in the tomb, on a bier at the four corners of which standards or posts bearing rattles were planted. One or more of his wives and his chief servants—butler, cook, groom—followed him in his death and to his last dwelling place. All of them were dressed in their finest clothes and jewels. Each had his allotted place in sepulchral chambers arranged close to that of the master, who was surrounded by his furniture and by sumptuous vessels filled with his favorite food and drink as provision for the life beyond. Only his horses, in magnificent harness, reposed in a carefully observed order outside the main part of the tomb: their number was variable, but amounted to several hundreds in the tombs of the Dnieper and Kuban regions.

The Scythian belief in an afterlife seems proved by some of the details; for the motive for such hecatombs was surely not so much the desire to prevent anyone else from taking possession of the victims as the hope of a future life, in which the leader would enjoy all his usual luxuries—servants and concubines included. The way in which the wife's body was set out in a tomb discovered near Kerch in 1846 proves that, while the king was anxious to be accompanied into the next world by those whose duty it was to look after his mounts, he also counted on finding more erotic pleasures there. On the threshhold of the tomb there was a small glass lamp with an evocative scene in relief, showing the woman and the man enjoying quite earthly pleasures.

136

Herodotus adds that, after the raising of the mound, it was customary to let a year go by before a further ceremony, in which, as he says, "they take fifty of the best of the king's remaining servants, strangle and gut them, stuff the bodies with chaff, and sew them up again. . . . Fifty of the finest horses are then subjected to the same treatment." The horses were impaled and arranged in a circle, with their legs dangling. The fifty servants were placed on them, held up by stakes supporting the spine. "When horses and riders are all in place around the tomb, they are left there and the mourners go away."

Similar slaughters in some districts of central India, where religions equally costly in human life have been practiced, show how the use of the local hemp made the victims undergo the sacrifice voluntarily. There, after the wife had chosen the day for the holocaust, a particularly strong dose increased her courage and guarded against any shrinking: in an ecstasy she would go to the altar of her own accord. One may therefore wonder if it was not the same with the sacrifices forming part of the great Scythian funerals. For neither Herodotus nor the excavations suggest that there was ever, even in the last moments of life, any violent natural defensive reaction on the part of the men and women who had to follow their lord and master into the tomb.

The anesthetic properties of hemp might also be the explanation of the relative ease with which the Scythians in the funeral processions were able to undergo the physical torments that were considered obligatory and seemly. During the last century it was the same at the Indian festivals of the ferocious goddess Kali: not only did an impressive number of drugged fanatics throw themselves under the feet of the sacred elephants and under the cutting wheels of the chariots of the gods, but others, from devotion, mutilated themselves horribly; religion and the drug combined to produce such apparent derangement.

137

The numerous experiments carried out by artists, writers, and scientists have helped provide precise information on the nature and effects of drugs—from the wine used by the Biblical Noah to the alkaloids and stupefacients of modern chemistry, all of which can produce illusions and excitement of the senses, while their abuse leads to moral and physical decline. In drunkenness or in the use of stimulants of vegetable origin, man has sought release and euphoria as a temporary distraction from sufferings, cares, or depression whose real solution lies in more radical remedies. But there is nothing fundamentally religious in this procedure, unless it be the flight from the punishing struggle which is really incumbent on man throughout his life.

Modern drinkers try to justify their excesses with a statement that they are "drowning their griefs" in wine. It was the same in the East with the use of hemp. Diodorus Siculus writes that the Egyptian women of Thebes dissipated their pains and their anger with this herb. It is even thought that hashish may have been the remedy given by Helen to Telemachus to make him forget the desolating losses of life which the Greeks said they had suffered at the siege of Troy, more than a thousand years B.C., in the course of their real or mythical colonization of the Dardanelles region. But already the Indian Vedas and the Zend-Avesta in northern Iran—that is to say, the oldest literary works of the Indo-European world, to which the Scythians belonged—sang the praises of hemp because of the laughter and happiness it provokes.

The other signs of intoxication are the dilating of the pupils, the contraction of the jaws, the need to lie down. The recumbent griffins decorating a necklace found in the kurgan that contains an apparatus for inhaling hemp would seem to give a true image of all this: hilarious faces seen through a distorting hallucinatory prism which unites the real and the fantastic, man and beast, in agreeable fantasies. 195 193

For in Scythian art also there is such a debauch of forms and colors, such a quantity of singular fantasies verging on madness and revealing so clearly the use of hemp, that it is hard to believe that its use was exceptional and confined to the function of a tranquilizer during the funerals. The saddle-coverings found in Barrow 1 at Pazyryk carry fantastic scenes of fighting between griffins and ibex, whose bodies, instead of being modeled by the classic play of light and shade, are expressed simply in appliqués with vivid colors quite unrelated to the natural tints of animal pelts: greens, yellows, and reds are dominant, and one is reminded of the pictures and statements of that colorist of genius and eventual madness, Van Gogh: "I would like to paint men and women with something eternal . . . . which we seek through radiance itself, by the vibrancy of the colors we use . . . . I have tried to express with red and green the terrible human passions." But also: "How beautiful yellow is!" 369 370

To the delirium of colors Scythian art added that of forms. In Barrow 5 at Pazyryk, a felt hanging represented a fight between two fabulous creatures, half-human, half-animal, whose limbs and extremities expand into mad, many-colored arabesques. Similarly, the bodies of the dead, in Barrows 2 and 5, were adorned with extremely complicated tattooings, whose motifs are fantastic ones, all derived from animal forms. One specialist has written that they are "so living, so full of energy in their conception and execution, that they easily take their place among the finest in Scythian art." Antlers gradually take on the appearance of huge outbursts of blossom, and the tails of the animals depicted describe circumvolutions or fold themselves elegantly under the legs of the protagonists, to end in equally flowery or leafy appendages. It is rare to find designs that give such an impression of rapid, almost frenetic movement, with the bodies interlaced, twisted, coiled, dislocated, in such unexpected postures that they sometimes lose all similarity to life. It is a fantasy of forms and colors, in which the variations on a given theme do not come from simple observation of nature. Hashish is as evocative as this—even more so than all the other modifiers of the mind, at least the natural ones known in the world of antiquity: it opens to the artist the gates of a magical paradise in which jostling and unstable forms offer themselves to his exalted sensitivity, his intelligence, and his taste. It is lucky for us that a painter and poet like Théophile Gautier should have experimented with hemp, for every image in his account can be illustrated by the strange bestiary and the treasures of the Eurasian nomads. He wrote: "I saw quite clearly in my chest the hashish I had eaten, in the form of an emerald from which there darted millions of little sparks. My eyelashes grew longer and longer, curling like gold threads around small ivory wheels which were turning of their own accord with dazzling speed. Round about me precious stones of every hue were trickling and crashing down, and continually renewed floral designs, which I could best compare with the play of patterns in a kaleidoscope. I still saw my companions now and then, but changed in shape, half-men, half-plants, with pensive airs like an ibis, standing on one foot like an ostrich, beating wings, such strange ones that, in my corner, I writhed with laughter." 14 274 138 139 51 100

The intoxicated vision of the hashish-user was not continuous. The writer notes also the

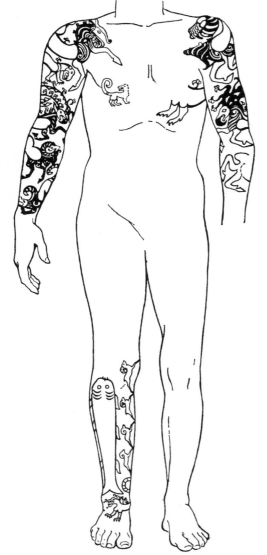

138

following: "In a confusedly luminous atmosphere there fluttered, in a perpetual swimming movement, myriads of butterflies whose wings rustled like fans. Gigantic flowers with crystal calyces, enormous hollyhocks, gold and silver lilies arose and blossomed about me." One might be listening to the archaeologist writing on the subject of Altaic art: "We are here in the field of dream and fantasy. And what colors! Always gentle and delicate, they recall, especially when they are being used to paint birds and flowers, those large Chinese compositions set in a dream landscape. There is one extra-ordinary embroidery, found in Barrow 5 at Pazyryk, a Chinese silk tussah which has a border of pheasants with immense fanned-out tails, treated in extremely delicate colors, rose pinks and greens, dancing on the branches of a dream tree with unreal leaves and flowers: monstrous pistils, immense petals . . . ."

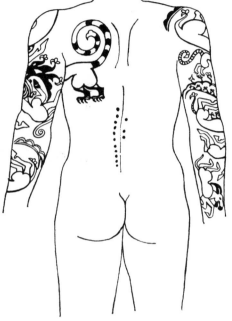

139

The same marvelous transformations take even clearer form in Théophile Gautier's third vision, which could equally well be of barbarian inspiration: "Caprimulgidae, cocklicranes, bridled goslings, unicorns, griffins, nightmares, the whole menagerie of monstrous dreams was trotting, leaping, flut-tering, yelping . . . . The visions became so baroque that I was seized with a desire to draw them, and in less than five minutes I did the portrait of the doctor as he appeared to me, sitting at the piano, dressed Turkish fashion, with a sun on the back of his jacket. The notes are shown escaping from the keyboard, in the form of rockets and spirals capriciously corkscrewed. Another sketch bearing this in-scription—an animal of the future—represents a living locomotive with a swan's neck ending in a ser-pent's head, waves of smoke spurting from it, and having monstrous feet made up of wheels and pulleys. Each pair of feet is accompanied by a pair of wings, and on the animal's tail one sees the an-cient god Mercury admitting defeat in spite of his winged heels."

Besides superimpositions of objects and motifs and the transformation of things and creatures (particularly at their extremities), all of which are phenomena and processes that recur in Scythian art, the taker of hashish undergoes other visual and psychic illusions. He becomes inclined to imagine himself as a superman, or as a god gifted with immortality and with extraordinary physical capabilities that enable him, for instance, to fly in an atmosphere made to his measure. His hallucinations then become peopled with Pegasus and other horses, with griffins, or winged mam-mals. These fantastic aggregates—which belong within the context in which the modern hashish user lives, as is clear from Gautier's vision—are such that necessarily each ethnic group makes them its own, in spite of their common features. This seems to be the case with the arts of Eurasia, central Asia, and the Himalayas. So the Scythian decorations, like those of the Tantric Buddhists, often con-vey the unreality of the perceptible world in which they are placed, in spite of their being constituted with the help of concrete elements: forms that are more or less fabulous because composite—human and zoomorphic at the same time—seem to be floating in space or twisting about in it for mysterious purposes.

140

Before invoking religion as an unaided deus ex machina to explain all these fantasies, it is worth-while handing over the pen once more to another famous taker of hashish, to Charles Baudelaire who, in his *Paradis Artificiels,* relates how, in the intoxication produced by hemp, "you glide in the azure of the immensely magnified sky . . . ." And the poet adds: "Since it is also certain that the memory of the impressions survives the orgy, the hope of using them is not unreasonable." For, "your innate love of form and color will at once find an immense pasture in the early developments of your intoxication. Colors will take on an unaccustomed energy . . . . The sinuosity of the lines is an implacably clear language in which you read the agitation and longing of souls . . . . Absurd objects take on monstrous appearances. They reveal themselves to you in forms unknown till then. Then they become deformed,

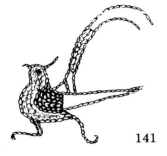

141

142

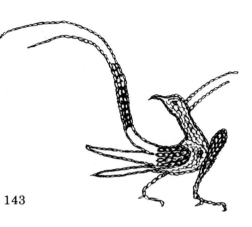

143

transformed . . . . "

But it is a specialist in Scythian art whom we shall quote next:

The nomad sees everything in the form of design and motif. It is no more difficult for him, starting out from an animal form, to turn it into a geometric design than it is to turn a geometric motif into an attribute of an animal. The variety of all these forms issued from the animal world is impressive. Real or imaginary, these animals, fighting and confronting one another, mingled or interlaced with such an exuberant and cruel abandon, open to us horizons giving on a new world . . . . The love of decoration is expressed elsewhere at Pazyryk. Arrows expected to serve only once are painted with meanders and spirals as eloquent as the motifs embellishing objects of more permanent use. The bridles are adorned with designs in the form of diamonds, stars, hearts, crosses, rosettes, palmettes, lotus flowers, and petals. The saddle-rugs are true carpets.

144

145

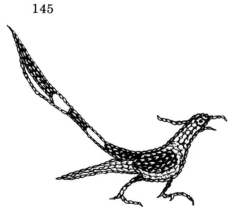

146

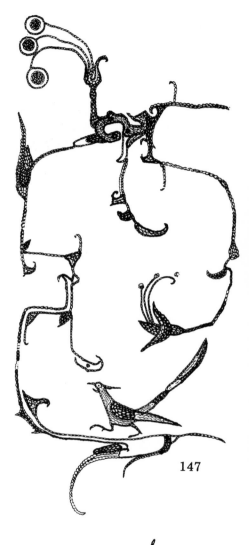

Even when the human head makes its appearance—and this occurs so rarely as to require explanation—the Scythian artist cannot resist the temptation to distort it or to attach it to some nonanthropomorphic element. For everything is a pretext for the play of decoration: chamfrons, harness, and bits for horses, soles of boots and shoes, plaques decorating bridles, table-rugs, weapons, tools, and gourds—nothing escapes ornamentation, as though every form suggested and implied this.

The mirrors found in the Scythian tombs are no less decorated. But what is intriguing is their number, as also the fact that not only the tombs of women but also those of men are equipped with them, as if those rough warriors indulged in secret coquetry. The hypothesis seems so farfetched that it has been suggested that these objects came into the tombs because of their magical power. Is this a sufficient reason for denying to the barbarians a taste that is confirmed by their adornments and jewelry?

In fact the shamans still use copper mirrors to catch souls and to light up the path to the lower world. Under Chinese influence the mirror has become the object of a complicated symbolism among

147

148

149

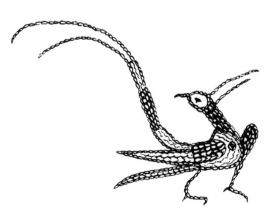

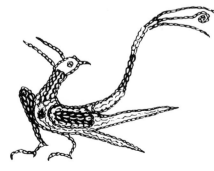

151

152

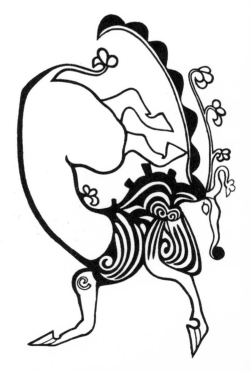

the Siberian peoples. This is chiefly due to its function as a reflector: since it produces an image that is at the same time like the thing reflected and psychologically opposite (the object's right becomes its left), the mirror does illustrate the immateriality of another world by its reflection of the real. The phenomenon is by itself enough to nourish the myths of eternity; but when joined with the intoxication produced by hemp, this immaterial image surely allows of more fantastic mirages.

Another of Baudelaire's notes on the hallucinations produced by hashish gives one pause for thought: "Mirrors become a pretext for that dreaming which resembles a spiritual thirst." So the poet's analysis leads to this important and often confirmed conclusion: hashish merely develops beyond measure the existing personality in the circumstances in which it is placed. The illusions, starting from the real, vary and come to rest in the patient's preferred field, according to his nature, his tastes, his artistic or literary tendencies. The essentially plastic and colorful account given by the painter Gautier would not be the same as that given by a Scythian nomad—or even by the author of *Les Fleurs du mal,*

153

154

155

156

157

158

159—160

though he was an excellent draftsman and art critic. For Baudelaire, as a writer, found in the hashish trip enjoyments of a literary order, which he thus describes: "It sometimes happens that people not at all adept at wordplay improvise endless successions of puns, utterly improbable combinations of ideas such as to bewilder even the virtuosi in this absurd art . . . . Understanding of allegory takes on in you proportions of which you yourself had no idea . . . . Words come to life again, clothed in flesh and blood."

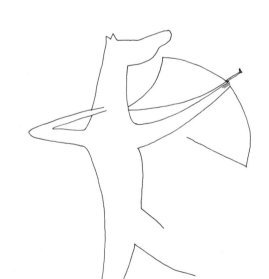

162

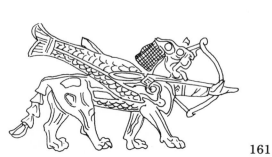

161

163

Myth in the Context of Symbolism

The lesson seems applicable to Scythian art: its bestiary, however fantastic in style because its forms are explained by a kind of embroidery whose origin is hallucinatory, nonetheless corresponds to a type of thinking which uses specific symbols—more precisely, zoological ones. But the fact that the newcomer may not understand them or may be bewildered by their form does not suffice to confer on them a restrictive religious motivation.

164

A gold sword-sheath found at Melgunov supplies a useful example. It is decorated with a succession of monsters, some of which, although they have animal bodies and their heads are in some cases zoomorphic, are bending a Scythian bow with their human hands and arms. Superimposed on each of these strange and warlike protagonists, all moving in the same direction rhythmically and in the same style, there are fishes, which all have a similar posture and are at equal distances: these accentuate the rhythm of the martial procession, being each placed above the shoulder of the combatant. One of these, for instance, is a lion, complete with four feet and a scorpion's tail, plus two 161 human arms bending his bow in the native Scythian fashion, while a fish—as though in a hashish user's vision—forms what is very like a fantastic wing added to this singular aggregate. One thinks of the kudurru (boundary stone) of Nebuchadnezzar on which there is also an archer with the body of a 162 scorpion and the feet of a bird of prey. 163

But it seems doubtful that a nomad trained in warfare ever believed in such monsters being capable of using an instrument whose handling is so complex and difficult. And indeed, on the celebrated gold sheath from Melgunov, the artist has mixed up human and animal details with a profound contempt for any zoological probability: in this respect the carnivore's head is characteristic—like a human one, it has its tongue hanging out in its concentration on the task in hand! To bend a bow and take good aim while marching requires of the archer a high degree of attention: he must therefore, in common parlance, be "as silent as a fish," keeping his eye on the target "like a cat watching a mouse," and fix it with his "eagle eye." Such expressions, along with the hallucination produced by hemp, or even simply with a little imagination, but necessarily with artistic sense, lead quite naturally to an ideographic translation that gives the archer the characteristics of the predatory species—human, feline, or raptorial—and may even add to them, as signs of silence and discretion, the few distinctive marks of an aquatic vertebrate.

But, while giving the fishes their due place in the decorative context of the sheath, we have also seen that they were above all a means of reinforcing the idea of a disciplined troop. This word "troop" is indeed incongruous in relation to its Indo-European root, since it is akin, through this, to "trouble" and "turbulence." In its Latin origin (turba) it denotes a crowd in movement without any order. A shoal of fishes is an apt image for migrants and other nomads, human or animal, moving from place to place in accordance with the established rules respected by them all, for the fishes of a shoal are, in spite of their different ages, of roughly the same size, and are all oriented in the same direction: they all move at the same speed, change direction at the same moment, and maintain a constant distance—characteristic of the particular species—between one another.

The procession of fishes on the Melgunov sheath recalls that of salmon, those typical migrants, depicted on the Lortet wand (a famous decorated Paleolithic object), where they are moving in the opposite direction to a herd of stags: they are swimming upstream to their spawning place while the stags, also in a group, have likewise perhaps given up the individualism which separated them during the mating season. These troops, not being warlike, are less disciplined, but the underlying allegory remains the same: the idea of the cohort is their common denominator, though it does not exclude others.

The religious exegete will find these semantic interpretations disappointing, because they give, even to hallucinatory visions, a springboard of reality—the symbolism, the language of a predatory man, speaking to others in a language of images about the problems and activities within a particular social and economic context. Thus the strange animal bending a bow in the barbarian manner may, in the last resort, merely represent a nomad spending his day in the saddle, as though one with his mount. This is the origin of the Greek concept of the centaurs, the horse-archers, which at the same time shows how, between Homeric times and the classical era, reality changed into fiction—how a living enemy became mythical or legendary. The hesitations of the Hellenic artists betray an uncertainty which is symptomatic. The depictions of centaurs are not standardized. Sometimes the whole front part of the body, including the legs, is human and clothed; or they are turned about, like the Parthians, on the point of shooting their enemy.

165

The Greeks similarly associated the Amazons with the Scythians, having perhaps confused them with their neighbors the Sarmatians, among whom the young girls could not marry before they had killed an enemy in battle. In this connection we should mention a tomb which was found near Tiflis—that of a woman buried in a crouching position, with her weapons within reach. She was probably a girl warrior who fell in a fight against the Scythians. These women, with their masculine and warlike courage, and who also rode on horseback, are often depicted in battles against the Greeks, for example on a frieze of the temple of Apollo Bassae. They come into Hellenic mythology as the descendants of Ares and Aphrodite, through the intermediary of their daughter Harmony, another serpent-like divinity,—that is to say, in relation to fables which must have been, in more ways than one, akin to those of the Scythian pantheon.

But if the Greeks thus mystified and denatured a perfectly simple reality, how can we be sure that the nomads themselves did not, in the long run, do as much to their own imagist concepts by idealizing them? This problem leads us, then, to the gnoseological sources of religion.

Magic, religion, and mythologies are in fact the convenient "holdalls" for anything in the semiotic or archaeological harvest that appears strange and without function, for the inexplicable is quickly classed as irrational, therefore religious. The motivations assigned to the ancient, barbarian, and primitive arts do not escape from similar simplistic demonstrations. The trouble about these is that they lead thus to the overestimation of the influence of such aberrations over prehistoric man, to his being described as crushed by gods, monsters, and rites—in short, to his being represented as at every moment subjected to constraints forged by himself, these constraints being the explanation of his too slow emergence from the savage condition. This leads also to the postulate of an innate religiosity, and tends to misrepresent the true causes of the social relationships which, however, every religion reflects in its themes and rites.

On the other hand, the religious message itself finds its expression, as does the secular, through sign-objects or sign-words—oral, pictorial, plastic, or gestural—whose very form is primarily a convention between utterer and recipient. True, the convention is often eloquent and imagist—mnemonic, one might say—but the form itself is by no means always explicit about the real nature of the statement being communicated, the less so since the analyst who has to translate it a posteriori into symbols of his own lacks knowledge of the referential context which gave birth to a specific language, to a particular code.

166

So let us imagine an archaeologist of the thirtieth century A.D. coming from another planet and discovering, in the grave of a twentieth-century Soviet citizen, as the one and only cultural index, the sign of a hammer and sickle. With that deformation which consists in extending the religious field to cover any and every surprising find, we might expect the perplexed scientist to say that, a thousand years before his time, there was a worship of tools. He might even see in it a spiritual and custom-consecrated heritage, that of the funerary adz, that mattock with the broken outline whose strange image was to be found already in the graves of some of the Roman legionaries and colonizers in the Balkans, who used it for making their trenches and ditches. Better still, almost a thousand years B.C., the tombs of Eurasian nomads contained axes so profusely decorated that some have considered their ceremonial use a more plausible hypothesis than their function as real tools. According to the above-mentioned reasoning—and it is a common one—these objects became immediately and exclusively cult objects, whereas they are first and foremost descriptive.

Functions and Content of Funerary Customs

At this rate religious preoccupations would also always account for the secular ensign, which may be a military one, to distinguish a unit and act as a rallying point, as was the case with the standard or the sword of the Scythian warriors to which Herodotus alludes. Yet expressions like "to bury the hatchet" or "to ax" an official are sign-facts or verbal images that speak to the mind and have nothing mystic about them. Under their ornaments, the royal scepter and the episcopal crosier merely convey the civil and moral authority of wands of command such as are entrusted to princes of the state and of the church. And to die for the flag, the cross, or the hammer and sickle can only turn into a fetishism of these emblems when the death of combatants and propagandists no longer contributes anything to the idea that is being defended, to the galvanizing value of the sacrifice. Idealism can, it is true, lead to such aberrations; but this does not mean that every object not directly utilitarian is therefore a fetish dominating its creator, or is a sign of irrational beliefs.

In the tombs of the Asianic—Asianic being used to refer to Asian peoples of non-Indo-European origin—occupants who inhabited the space between Russian Turkestan and the Persian Gulf and used carboniferous pottery with lozenge decoration, the dead man was buried with arms and utensils which are said to have been meant for his use in the next life. This hypothesis does indeed seem almost certain when, later, the Scythian tombs—confirming the evidence of Herodotus—show that not only 348 the dead man's possessions but also his wife, servants, and horses were buried with him, being killed 331 and then arranged so that their lord and master might find and enjoy their company on his awakening in the next life. Yet the burial of the dead congener already appears among animals, and so could not by itself be evidence of religious feeling, any more than this is implied by mourners leaving to the dead 349 man his clothes, arms, and tools, his insignia, jewels, or personal playthings. Some people have 332 nonetheless, when miniature objects were found (such as the models of wagons discovered in a Bronze 333 Age burial in Azerbaijan), interpreted these as merely substitutes for expensive objects denied to their 334 deceased owner, who was thus forced, in his supposed life beyond the grave, to content himself with these little clay replacements.

By the same reasoning, a speculative mind of the future would represent the Russian communist whom we mentioned above—and who was perhaps not a manual worker at all—as an agricultural laborer whose relatives laid hold of his tools at the time of the funeral, though the qualms of conscience made them replace these with some trinket marked with the hammer and sickle so that the dead

167

man's soul might use this imitation in the gardens of paradise. The point of this absurd hypothesis is to make us cautious about assigning a religious function to many nonutilitarian objects which come to light in archaeological excavations. A critical attitude toward a systematic "mythism" does not, however, exclude the possibility of there really having been such strange aberrations.

Objects, rites, and customs can, therefore, be either secular or sacred. The same applies to the public monuments whose use defines their precise nature more than do their tenuous traces. Thus the dolmens of the Caucasus, raised by the sedentary inhabitants in the third and second millennia B.C., prove—as elsewhere in Neolithic or Chalcolithic western Europe—merely that the dead received worthy burials. In the USSR the best known megalithic vaults are those of Gelendzhik, Beregovaya, Dakhovskaya, Storozhevaya, and also those of the Novosvobodnaya barrows. But—and this applies both to the Soviet examples and to those of Brittany and of southern France—the hole, with which the entrance tympana of the burial chambers were sometimes pierced, in itself still leaves, even when surrounded with engravings, too much room for uncertain and divergent interpretations: it may have been merely a practical orifice for ventilation, a ritual hole for the escape of the soul or for bearings taken on the stars, a hatch for offerings necessary to a life in the next world, etc. All these are hypotheses, some of which imply, but do not prove, a worship of the dead far removed from mere practical preoccupations or from marks of natural feeling and regret.

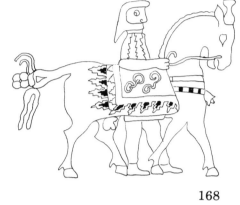

168

No more conclusive—in, for instance, the French *allées couvertes*—are the pillars or jambs decorated with a female figure, which is sometimes reduced simply to its sexual or ornamental attributes, indeed sometimes without a mouth, probably in order to convey a semantic link with the silent world of the dead. But even this symbol, conveyed thus by an image, does not necessarily reveal its essence or nature, any more than that of the female form as a whole: she may have been a goddess of death, a matrilinear ancestress honored after death, an image enjoining retirement upon women and visitors—many suppositions are possible, all equally gratuitous, though too often grounded on religious motivations.

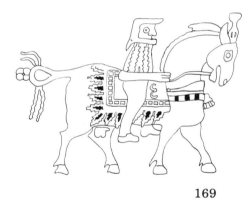

169

Apart from the lines of menhirs connected with the funerary barrows of the great nomad chieftains, there are in the Minusinsk region some curious stelae of stone that belong to the Karasuk culture. Carved in the form of sabers, they have their faces decorated with human heads and have motifs of radiating lines that may show Chinese influence. On some of the stones one can make out—clumsily carved—a belt, with weapons attached to it, while on the lateral walls there are several designs of stags. These stelae were originally placed near tombs, and must have had some connection with the warriors buried there.

170

Does the same vague deduction apply to the earlier stelae of the Okunev culture, found in the Yenisey basin? The principal representation is always of a woman's head, which in some cases is completed by a bosom, shoulders, arms, and even the belly. The face is framed by various attributes, in rare cases comprehensible to us (horns and animal ears), or is surmounted by a crown. On the upper part of the monolith is engraved the head of an animal (ram, carnivore, or other), or else a second woman's head—differing therefore, both of them, from the first head, and implying some symbolic link with her, perhaps a genealogical one (of clan or some other category); yet there is no proof of any sacralizing of the motifs and figures.

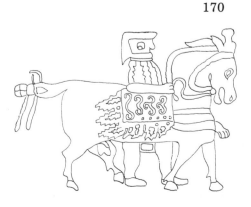

Right up to the twelfth century A.D., what are called "stone babas" were erected in Russia, especially in the Asiatic part of the country. These, placed near the barrows, are statues of warriors armed and holding a vase, and they are connected with the ancestor cult among the sixth and seventh-century nomads. At first, their legs were not represented. Then, in the following century, subjects ap-

190

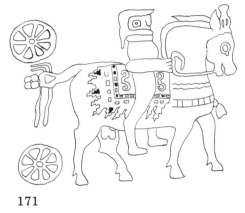

171

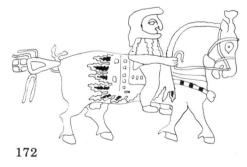

172

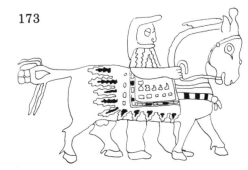

173

pear that are more complete and realistic with regard both to their lower limbs and to their clothes. At the same time there are more representations of female figures. In the tenth and eleventh centuries, these statues are associated with the kurgans of the Volga steppes, which were inhabited chiefly by the Petchenegs. These various examples remind us somewhat of the statue-menhirs of Corsica and of protohistoric Aveyron. There are noteworthy examples also in the Gard and Hérault.

But the fact that all their figures are either masculine or feminine—that is to say, personalized and humanized by their social or sexual characteristics—by no means always implies definitely or conclusively that such monoliths were considered as the sacred images of divinities and of already deified ancestors, or as the statues of idealized dead people—even perhaps already as receptacles for the souls of the dead or, still more simply, as memorial stones. Otherwise all the representations of Lenin, Pushkin, and Peter the Great could be arbitrarily included in the arsenal of cult objects or talismans. And so we are back to the uncertainty, already noted, regarding the exact function of the prehistoric "Venuses" whose attractive title keeps up the mystery!

Even that part of funeral customs which has become in the long run a traditional ritual has not necessarily an origin in magic. Certainly there is something surprising about those funeral ceremonies, which were carried out in several phases, possibly to allow the flesh to decay: the rite which consisted in powdering the skeletons in the tombs with red ocher—a rite which prevailed in the early pastoral cultures of the Altai, of the upper Yenisey basin, and of southern Russia—is not less surprising, even though many Eurasian burials show that it already existed in Paleolithic and Mesolithic times. There is, in fact, a classic type of late Paleolithic burial—a trench in which the body has been powdered with this ferruginous oxide, whose colors range from yellow to violet. This has been found in seventeen cases out of twenty-seven, ranging from Great Britain to the USSR. And yet, more recently, when, only a few centuries ago, the very human skeletons of Saint Gervasius and Saint Protasius were discovered, their bones, dyed red, were still considered as sufficient evidence for their sanctity!

One sees here how, even when absolutely nothing is known for certain about the original purpose of a custom, its centuries-old, mechanical practice has ended by giving it a sacred status. Was this use of ocher always ritual, in the religious sense? Is it, that is, evidence of a practice that has stiffened into convention because emptied of all symbolic or utilitarian content, and this from the most ancient times, in which case it would certainly push back the first human religions a very long way? Many writers seem to take as their starting-point the assumption that our ancestors regarded ocher as an allegory of blood, ensuring that the vital liquid of the body remained present in this static form in the permanent world of the Beyond. According to this view, magic could be the cause of these applications of ocher, and flint-using man, having sampled the blood of the meat he ate, was able to confuse it, when dried, with a common clay. And yet a more secular function of ocher is perfectly well known: the Papuans embalm the corpse of their chieftain in a mass of red ocher, which enables it to be preserved long after burial; the product is in fact used to prevent the vermin from propagating and to neutralize vile odors, even those from dead bodies.

Ocher is a peroxide of iron, anhydrous when it is red; more precisely, it is a sesquioxide containing, for a given weight of metal, half as much again of oxygen. The peroxides, whose general formula is M_2O_2 (M denoting a monovalent metal like iron), decompose in contact with water or with diluted acids and form oxygenated water or oxygen. Some of them are used in pharmacy—oxygenated water, ectogan, hopogan, and the well-known colcothar or peroxide of iron, known as English red (an ingredient in the Canet ointment for ulcers of the limbs). Modern pharmacy also includes iron sesquioxide as a disinfectant. At the same time manganese, with its well-known antiseptic properties, and whose black peroxide was also used by prehistoric man for painting walls (and bodies?), imparts a brown or purple red to certain ferruginous ochers, which makes it a considerable aid to them in their aseptic functions. Thus, in its various forms, ocher provides a good and even cheap protection to the calcareous bones of skeletons, against bacteria or against acids diluted by rainwater after it has filtered through the surface soil. So the practical use made of ocher by the Papuans implies that its use by prehistoric Eurasians had no exclusively religious or even ritual purpose. For if sixty-three percent of the skeletons preserved were treated with this product, its mere value as a preservative may well be enough to account for so high a percentage, without the method having been followed and generalized for religious motives. The disinfectant function of such oxides would also explain, better than any magical purposes, why most of the late Paleolithic strata were impregnated with these powders, of which a pound spread over on hundred square feet gives the soil of these sites a sustained reddish color.

Even when there is clear evidence of rites, as for instance from the direction in which the bodies were laid (toward the midday sun in most of the Andronovo tombs), is it possible to state that they bear witness to celestial and cosmic cults? To observe the anniversary of a death when writing does not exist—and Herodotus provides evidence of this in the case of the Scythians—is only possible with the aid of mnemonic devices or of sign-objects enabling people to establish the recurrence of astral positions (moon, sun, planets, risings of the sun or moon or constellations), that is, by the direction in which bodies and tombs are laid out or by alignments of stones, the practice in itself not being in the least religious.

And the more archaic a society is, the less its architectural programs are diversified, and in such cases the monuments are essentially monuments of the whole community, the expression of all its acquired and accumulated skills, including those of building and astronomy. Excavations by no means always make it possible to delimit exactly what is due to calculation based on knowledge of the calendar, and what to astrological aberrations.

Like us, the ancient peoples had traditional ceremonies and collective festivals, taking place at determined cyclical dates, these being no doubt consecrated as much by convenience for memorizing, and by social or productive life, as by myths. Herodotus has recorded that the Scythian plowmen used to celebrate a springtime festival: the nomads said they had preserved the gold objects sent by Heaven to one of the sons of Targitaus, and at these festivals of the sacred gold, which were accompanied by large-scale propitiatory sacrifices, the annual custom was, in particular, that one of the Scythians should mount guard over these divine gifts in the open air during the whole of the festival. Woe to him if he fell asleep; but in exchange for a vigilance on which he staked his life, he was given as much arable land as he could encircle in the course of a day.

174

This anecdote is all that we know about the Scythian calendar. Are we any better informed by the famous carpet from Barrow 5 at Pazyryk, which is roughly square, measuring seventy-one by seventy-nine inches, and is considered by Rudenko to illustrate cosmic themes—which nothing, however, obliges us to call religious? Its central field is rectangular and is made up of twenty-four squares, each decorated with a star motif. The decorative band surrounding this has, as its theme, griffins: there are forty-two of them. Next, as we move away from the center, comes a peripheral composition of twenty-four staglike animals proceeding from right to left; then, surrounding this there is a band of sixty-nine floral motifs, similar to the ones in the center, and then a frieze of twenty-eight horsemen who are circulating from left to right, on foot or mounted. Lastly, the outermost decorative band resumes the theme of griffins, to the number of about eighty-nine, plus or minus one or two.

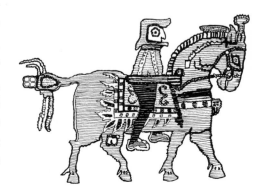

175

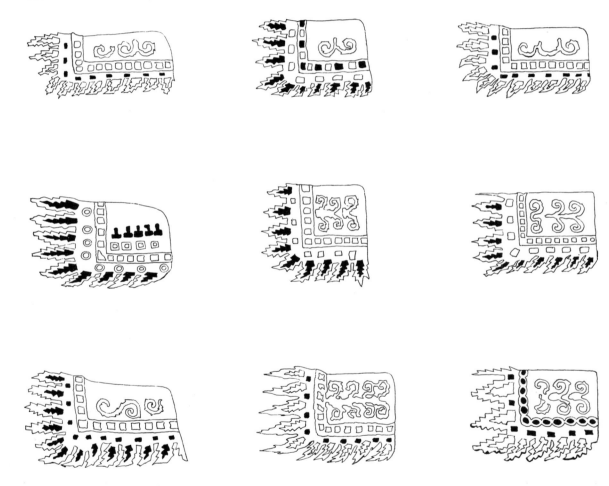

There are some signs which suggest that this carpet was not only ornamental. As if the number of motifs in each sequence was essential, the composition of the carpet was complicated, having to pass from an almost square exterior shape to an inner rectangle. In some of the sequences also, certain signs indicate a definite starting-point, which implies, as the work moved to its conclusion, a repeated 171 reduction of the elements forming the bands. More generally, these concentric processions of motifs in opposite directions suggest the regular and ample courses of the eternal stars, which move on their way as surely and calmly as the stags and horsemen shown on the carpet. But the heterogeneous sequence of the horsemen is perplexing.

Should one wish to find in the numbers of the objects in each circuit astronomical correspondences of which one could be sure, the correlations would be few. Eighty-one, not eighth-nine, is the number, according to the ancient Chinese, Hindus, and Chaldeans, of synodical lunations yielding a whole number of solar days, sixty-two being the number of those same lunations in a cycle of five years as observed by the inhabitants of ancient India. The number of the compartments and divisions of a lunar zodiac used by the Vedic, Chinese, and Arabic astronomers is twenty-eight. Finally, twenty-four is the number of half-lunations which more or less make up a year of twelve months, and of the k'i (breaths) which divided the solar year of the Chinese peasants as early as the period of the Warring Kingdoms.

But whether the carpet be an image of Elysium, a calendrical picture, or even evidence of some game (as has been supposed), the fact remains that its secular or sacred use is not explicit. Within the framework of archaeological knowledge as it stands at present, the best and most realistic approach to the question of the ideological superstructures of the Eurasian nomads is still to keep coming back to the brief report by Herodotus, the father of history, on the cults which they practiced, and especially on the veneration with which the barbarians surrounded their dead. To Darius, when he was in search of a battle front and of contact with his enemies of the Steppes in order to defeat them, the King of the Scythians sent this message: "I have never yet run from any man in fear; nor do I do so now from you . . . . Fear of losing a town or seeing crops destroyed might indeed provoke us to hasty battle—we possess neither. If, however, you are determined on bloodshed with the least delay, one thing there is for which we will fight—the tombs of our forefathers. Find these tombs, and try to wreck them, and you will soon know whether or not we are willing to stand up to you . . . . As for your being my master, I acknowledge no masters but Zeus, from whom I spring, and Hestia the Scythian queen."

The passage quoted makes no mention of a mythical bestiary or of a religious cosmology accompanied by rites. But it is to be feared that the tomb of that leader, buried like his fellows with his rich treasure, may one day be taken by excavators for that of an adept of the cult of Bacchus or of Epicurus, while his contemporary, the Scythian soothsayer, whose skeleton may perhaps be found without any great abundance of impressive belongings, will remain silent about the beliefs which encumbered his gray matter. The constant confusion between the symbolic manifestations of secular life and those of religious life often renders the problems inextricable, because it has helped to set them out wrongly at the start and to head them in the wrong direction.

176

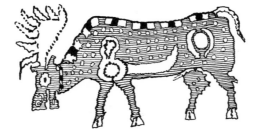

177

178

179

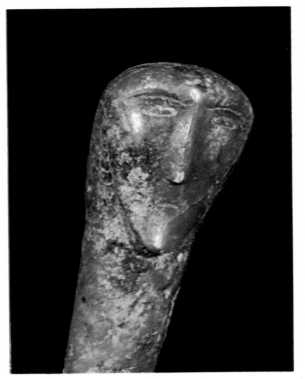

180

181

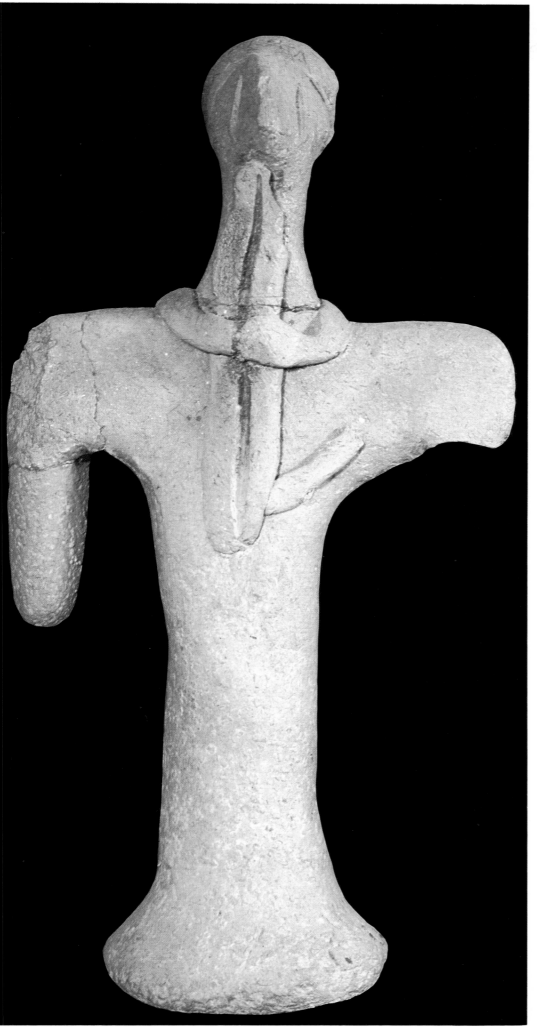

182

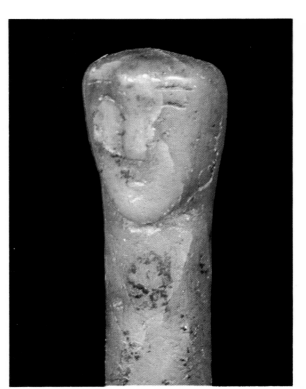

183

184

188

189

190 ▶

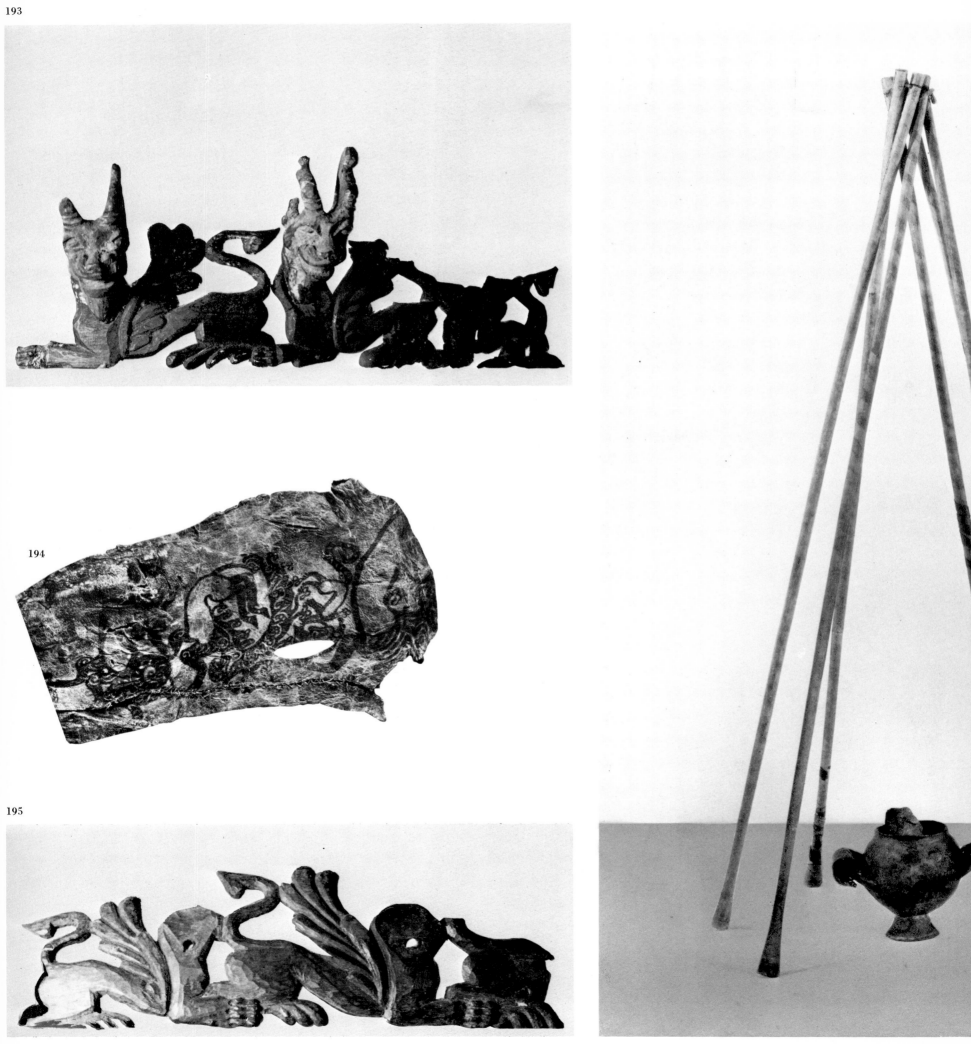

193

194

195

197

198

196

211 212

213

214

215

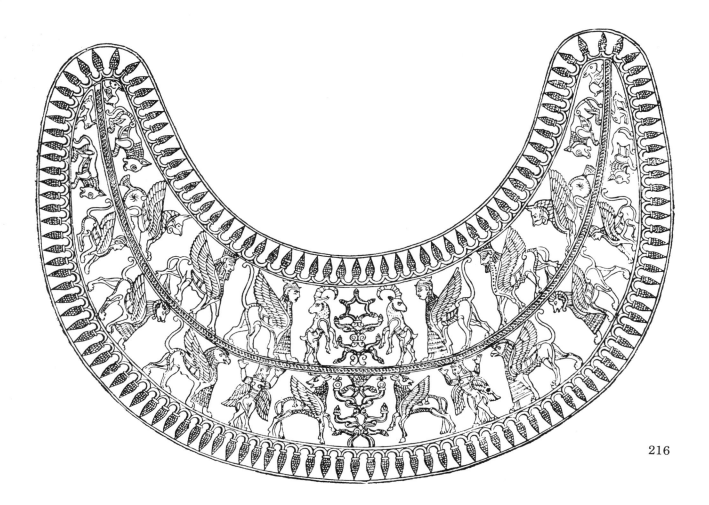

216

The Female Monsters

279 Another sign-object or sign-word which is interesting to examine because of its strangeness and its
216 richness in possible interpretations is the bird-woman, sphinx, harpy, or siren of antiquity, both barbarian and Greco-Roman. She still appears on some twelfth-century Russian pendants, having had a
long past as a motif of Eurasian art. Sumerian art also had winged women, whose bodies were
faultless except that their legs were too elegant for their bird-of-prey feet. The harpies of the infernal
regions had similar feet. Far earlier, the Paleolithic artist of the Ukraine, in particular at Mezin, carved female statues so stylized that the part with the buttocks is rather like the hindquarters of a bird,
and the neck suggests the long neck of a goose. Lastly, the siren of Greek mythology, whose singing
troubled voyagers by sea, has passed through the Latin language to become the audible signal of our
factories, besides giving its name to the serin (a small European finch related to the canary) —much
more melodious, although modern imagery prefers the nightingale to which to liken a singer whose
voice is pure and flexible.

281 But, in spite of the similarity of form that unites these bird-women, whether their whole body or
only their wings and claws are birdlike, nothing is less certain than that their symbolism is identical.

217

218

219

The Paleolithic woman with a bird's hindquarters may be simply an expressionist rendering of a big-bottomed wench—*poulette*—whom the artist has provided with a long neck, more feminine than the thick masculine neck, graceful and slender like a swan's. Whether this is a happy initiative of the artist's, or purely and simply a translation of verbal images that were current at that period, is hardly relevant here.

For in language, whether verbal or plastic, such methods as metaphor and metonymy, schematism and exaggeration, remain on the whole parallel and complementary means toward an immediate and approximate understanding of the type of woman represented. What is involved is not a headless, fabulous, or mythical monster combining bird form and human form, but a stylized evocation of the female body. Whether the theme itself has a religious motivation becomes therefore even more problematical, or at least remains to be proved.

The Anatidae (ducks, geese, swans, etc.), as we all know, are not distinguished singers. But many sedentary or migratory birds both of Eurasia and of Mediterranean Europe make it easy to understand, by reason of the clear note characteristic of them, the expressive image that often transforms birds into women and vice versa. The metaphor, whether graphic or verbal, renders the convention of the sign more effective, with a closer relation between signifier and signified. Anyone can understand it.

So the allegory of the sirens, like that of the Muses, concerns their song. It seems to have been well understood by the artist who created the ring worn by one of the female skeletons in the Great Blisnitza Barrow on the Taman Peninsula. The creature on the bezel is a woman holding a lyre—the characteristic instrument of the Muses; but the player's body is transformed gradually into that of a grasshopper and ends in a griffin's head. As is well known, the insect that animates the great plains with its chirping was given by the ancients the name "muse of the fields"—a well-justified image which must have been known, indeed used, by the dead barbarian woman and her Hellenized entourage, in view of the Greek influences that are evident in the decoration and funerary furnishings of her tomb. In spite of the figure's generous bosom, the body is certainly that of a male orthopteran, because in the species of the Acrididae or Locustidae it is only the male that produces anything like a song. Even for someone who did not know that the lyre is a musical instrument, the whole form of this female musician would be there to evoke her function. In this case the meaning is more important than the sex!

But does this explicit motivation allow of any certainty as to whether the instrumentalist is secular or mythical? Caution still incites us to say no.

And what of the woman with the bird-of-prey's claws? If she had those of a lion she would become a sphinx, of which there are so many in Greek, Scythian, and Assyrian art. And the French chansonnier Georges Brassens sings of yet another member of this ominous type, whom he describes as a "pretty cow disguised as a flower." Translated into a pictorial or plastic form by some ideographic writing, the poet's image would be that of a monster, half-cow and half-flower, of which the perplexed archaeologist, that innocent from another planet whom we have conjured up, would say that it illustrates an imaginary sacred being from the complex mythology which still animated . . . . the first men to visit the moon!

This seems reinforced by the appearance of such female monsters, in sphinx form, on the black pottery of *bucchero* type in Iran as early as the first millennium B.C. A Greek artist in about 500 B.C. even decorated the tomb of the Persian king Xanthus with harpies: they are shown holding up the souls of the dead and children. But let us beware of confusion: harpies, sirens, and sphinxes, though all sinister, were not identical. The scenes with black figures decorating the lid of the terracotta sarcophagus from Clazomenae show Sumerian horsemen in battle against Urartian charioteers, under the patronage of sphinxes and harpies, collaborating in the carnage but clearly differentiated. The choice of birds of prey for these frightening protagonists is indeed appropriate, in view of their well-known predilection for the flesh of corpses. True, they are not the only predatory vertebrates to like carrion, but the birds of prey also have a form that makes them immediately apt for female allegories of this type: in this animal species the females are generally bigger and stronger than the males. (We should bear in mind the Kirghiz legend in which the hero Töshtük has to fight the female eagle-giantess.) So it is easy to understand why the sphinxes had, in addition to their woman's nature, wings of birds of prey attached to a leonine body. Also, in the family of the king of beasts, it is the lioness that is the more active and attacks the prey which her mate, more idle, is content to head off. As a result, in our metaphors the terms "lioness" or "tigress" are at least as suggestive of combativeness and cruelty as the terms denoting the males. Thus sphinxes of all kinds and countries were equipped with attributes appropriate to their sex, in terms of their animal specificity and of the aggressive function they had to fulfil.

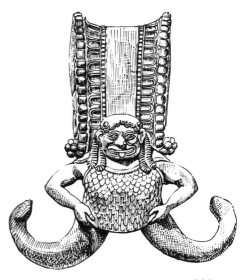

220

There is another of antiquity's female monsters which had a clear success in Greco-Scythian art, no doubt because it had more than one affinity with barbarian symbolism. This is the Gorgon, which appears time and again on a gold cup from Kul Oba or as the masks of the Medusa from the same
247 barrow. This sinister head also decorates a magnificent bronze breastplate found at Elizavetinskaya
217 and the gold plaques which come from the Seven Brothers tumuli. Lastly, she figures on the handles of
221 the large ancient mixing-bowls of Macedonia, Gaul, and southern Russia.

Aeschylus, in *Prometheus Bound*, locates the home of the Gorgons in the fields of Kisthenes, which extend behind the southeast coasts of the Black Sea, at the foot of the Caucasus. And when one recalls that at one time Zeus and at another Hercules had dealings with serpent-women in those parts, his information seems to be corroborated at least on the mythical plane—so much so that in Scythia a variant religious myth united Hercules with Echidna, Medusa's serpent-formed granddaughter. The Greco-Scythian artists represented the Gorgon with serpent-like tresses and similarly equipped the Great Goddess of Kul Oba with ophidian excrescences. But the handles of the ancient European mixing-bowls are even more explicit: often each of the Medusa's hands rests on the body of a serpent which emerges from the base of a scaly corselet that reinforces that snake analogy. On the splendid example from Vix, as if the reptilian character of the whole were still not sufficient, the artist has arranged under each arm a small serpent ready to strike, thrusting out its triangular head and darting a thick and pointed tongue.

221

To the Greek and Roman writers the Gorgons were winged virgins, at whom no man could gaze without being "medused"—that is, turned to stone: Persues decapitated the only one of the three who was mortal, but still did not dare to look at her. Ancient iconography and art have reproduced her moonlike face surrounded by its terrifying tresses. The eyes are round, fixed, and insistent, the tongue
189 hanging out. The mouth is wide, distended, exhibiting two rows of impressive teeth. The canines look like fangs, with nothing human about them, and extend far beyond the teeth of the other jaw, and the whole hideous maw is surrounded by extremely narrow lips.

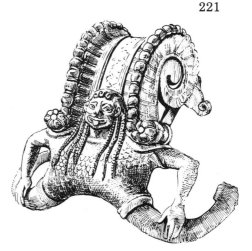

If this description of the head of Medusa were not treated plastically in anthropomorphic fashion (and sometimes with tresses that recall the Eurasian women) one might think it was applied to a female serpent (if this is what classical images and myths suggest by more than one feature), possibly as an esoteric transcription—or one resulting from imperfect understanding or memory—of a

222

perfectly natural reality.

Serpents in fact have eyes that appear fixed because their lids are transparent. And since these reptiles are also good at lying still and melting into their surroundings, they habitually exercise a real fascination, over birds for instance, and capture their attention: instead of escaping, the prey is insensibly drawn into staring at the snake, or rather at certain of its organs which appear strange, intriguing, and excite curiosity because they resemble food. The serpent's tongue, too, is definitely specialized as an organ of fascination: not only does it emerge in a unique way, like a dart through the rostral orifice of the closed mouth, but it is curiously colored and executes strange contortions. It is then like an insect that lures birds or squirrels, their attention being absorbed by the strange organ while the predator glides toward them. Needless to say, once the prey has been pricked its immobilization and paralysis become real. The poison-injecting organs are often grooved hooks, situated in the front part of the upper jaw, as fangs and canine teeth would be in mammals and human beings.

Being carnivorous like the eagle, wolf, or feline and having, in addition, a specific mimetic equipment and an immobility that extends to apparent fixity of gaze, the serpent has the air of some sentinel always on the watch and able to pass unperceived. This makes it often, in many religions or legends, a natural watcher; it can also serve simply as an emblem, sign, and symbol for a warlike ideology, or even a pastoral one, insofar as the vigilant herdsmen must protect their herds from its stealthy enterprises. One understands better why the serpent was the attribute of the war god of the Celts and of the goddesses who guarded and protected crossroads. But in Crete and in Greco-Roman antiquity its divine or symbolic virtues appear more rustic and homely: there it was the *genius loci*, sedentary and mouse-catching, the protector and guardian of the hearth. When introduced among the nomads of the Steppes, more or less at the origin of a symbolism that was to become lost in the Greek version of the Medusa, the monster must have awakened many memories or associations. Since the Hellenes said that Perseus had given the Medusa's head, which he had cut off, to Pallas, so that the Athenian goddess might then fix it on the pectoral part of her tunic or on her shield, the mask of this Gorgon consequently appears on the Elizavetinskaya breastplate, in the center of the chest of the valiant warrior who wore it. A feat of arms like that of Perseus was bound to attract the Scythians, 247 who were also past masters at scalping and who gave the severed heads a preservative treatment which made them into trophies.

The serpent's changes of skin and its ability to survive the loss of its tail also enabled it to be associated with allegories of resurrection. This is clear in the case of the Gorgon, of whom it was said that some of her blood could bring the dead back to life, rescuing them from that nocturnal and chthonic world where serpents slept in winter—or, that is, an infernal world, an inverse reflection of the living one, where already the lunation takes place in a sinister direction, that is, opposed to that of the daily journey of the sun. And it is in the same way that, on the great mixing-bowls mentioned above, the cohorts of human and animal figures proceed from left to right. Is not the moon, indeed, like Medusa, credited in many European legends with the power of turning living creatures to stone? And, on the lid of the Vix vessel, is not the Gorgon the associate or protectress of a figure who might be the moon goddess Artemis?

Moreover, the mixing-bowl seems to have had, at least among the Scythians, ceremonial and funerary functions that fit in with this: the nomads authorized to take part in the royal libations were those who had scalped enemies and could produce the heads as evidence. Then, according to Herodotus, the heroes poured themselves great drafts proportionate to their trophies, and drank them at one go—Russian fashion, we might add! Impressive receptacles were therefore needed for mixing

223

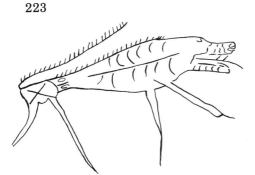

224

water with a strong, full-bodied wine that was usually flavored with resin and aromatic plants. From all this, which is confirmed for us by the ancient texts, it results that the Gorgons were indeed mythical monsters invoked by the Greeks in the case of any good or evil fortune that was not attributable to the traditional gods. But these animal creatures often seem like a late importation from abroad. If one is to believe their stories, in which the Amazons engaged in conflict against the Gorgons in far-off lands of which the narrators knew little, these mythical creatures (of which the former, as we have seen, suggest the Sarmatian girl warriors) were perhaps simply barbarian women who had learned everything, including the handling of weapons, from the horsemen of the Steppes.

225

The Function of the Nomad Bestiary

Were the sphinxes with women's heads and breasts, feline bodies, and raptor wings really, at least at the beginning, unreal creatures giving to Oriental and Eurasian mythology a coloring of fantasy? This problem is in fact that of all the strange aggregates of animal and human forms that are found in the indigenous art of the Steppes and in barbarian art in general. Among the monsters frequently de- 358 picted, we see the eagle with long ears and with its head bearing an enormous toothed crest which, 78 starting at the top of the head, runs a long way down the neck—or again the winged tiger which, in the 366 Altai, is simply a local variant of the classic griffin of the Iranian plateaux. In this case the Siberian 340 feline replaces the lion, whose biotope is more southerly. And the Scythian prototype, keeping the wings but abandoning the feet of the bird of prey, exchanges the poisonous tail of the scorpion for the horns of an antelope. These ornaments and weapons on the forehead terminate, in such cases, either 294 in balls or in volutes. They resemble those of similar monsters on reliefs and enameled bricks decorating the palace of Artaxerxes II.

This sovereign, as is well known, was the one who subdued all the Greek cities of Asia and who adorned the walls of his palace with scenes showing the victorious combats of the royal hero with beasts and monsters that were worthy antagonists. A Greco-Scythian calathos, found in a burial at Great Blisnitza, also represents young nomads engaged in an unequal combat; one of them has been laid low by a griffin, a second is striking a griffin with his sword, and a third, coming to his companion's assistance, is brandishing an ax against the beast. The fight does indeed seem a hard one, its result uncertain.

And in the battle scenes of the art of the Steppes in which they feature, the griffins are always 229 conquerors and dominant. The swift stallion, stag, and ibex are losers in the fight, just as in their 347

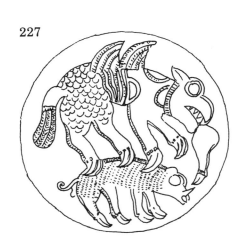

227

Scythian representations the horse, ibex, or hare, though excellent runners, succumb to the lightning attack of the tiger or the eagle. Thus, besides its strength, the griffin in Eurasian art seems to possess. extreme mobility, and a notable sign of this is its antelope horns. In this it is like those leaping warriors with gazelle heads that are to be found in the African wall paintings. In the same way a successful footballer from the Cape is called a "Springbok"—a vigorous kind of chamois whose name is appropriate in view of its speed and agility and of the butting competitions in which it indulges, playfully when young and seriously when fully grown.

228

Scythian art, like Paleolithic animal art, is far from including all the animals, or even all the edible ones. The difference between those used for food and the ones in the depicted bestiary is striking. It excludes any hypothesis to the effect that the motive of these representations if magic designed to increase the fertility of the quarry, for their subjects seem to have been essentially chosen from animals exhibiting some particular trait of character or behavior. And the ethnographic rule is that, when in fact the artist is guided by alimentary preoccupations, the beasts are then represented as though transparent, with their coveted internal organs showing, because then the animals are conceived more with the belly than with the eye or the spirit.

Among the carnivores, the Eurasian artists singled out principally the tiger and the wolf; among the ungulates, the elk, the stag, the wild sheep and the ibex; among the birds, the eagle and the rooster; and finally, in the order of the fishes, the carnivorous eelpout. On the other hand, they far less often depicted saiga, hare (whereas Herodotus tells us of the pleasure they took in hunting the hare), swan, or goose. A similar preferential treatment applied to the species represented by Paleolithic man: in the decoration of his walls and equipment, the horse, bison, mammoth, deer, and ibex are more conspicuous than the reindeer, though this was the basis of his food and of his raw materials. Nor were animals of the horse tribe, which supplied milk and hair or were used as mounts and as draft beasts, more favored by the Scythian craftsmen.

229

230

231

232

In representing apparently supernatural creatures, stress was laid above all on those of their qualities which seemed to ennoble their owner, human or animal: strength, impetuosity, speed, keen-ness of sight and hearing, flexibility, and agility. So the tiger is represented roaring, his jaws open and displaying threatening fangs, like the wolf. The feline's back is shown so supple that it can flow, twist, and almost coil in the close fighting in which it keeps the mastery. The stag and ibex rush along or leap impetuously, like the leaping animals of the horse and deer tribes on the Paleolithic ceilings. In the bird of prey, the hooked beak and the eye are exaggerated so as to stress the essential function. In the griffin, the ears are as long as those of the antelope watching for the slightest alert. 228 366 63 48 259

Being constantly engaged in hunting wild beasts, not only to feed on them and to protect the herds from them, but also for the sake of sporting exercise to develop warlike aptitude and force of character, the barbarians were well placed to observe those animals which possessed specific qualities and defects that could be used to illustrate the human ones. As Marcel Cohen has stressed, technical language is the essential source of new nominations. As a hunter and herdsman, Paleolithic, Altaic, or Persian man used a bestiary and a hunting terminology for the concepts he needed to express, both on the verbal plane and on the graphic. And without there necessarily being any ethnic filiations, there are resemblances between the themes of monsters, and between the ideographic aggregates that crop up in regions far distant from one another; and these, even if fortuitous, arise nonetheless simply from the fact of the common laws of human language, whether of words or of forms.

Such is the case with the wolf with ram's horns, which is one of the animal composites, formed of disparate realist elements, that are represented in the Siberian art of the Tashtyk. In that Siberian en-vironment the wild predator is frequently the wolf, but in more southerly latitudes he would be feline, like the leonine ram-headed griffin from Arslan Tash—an Assyrian site. One thinks also of the ram-headed serpent that accompanied gods and war leaders in the art of Gaul. In this last case, the animal was not just any species of snake, but definitely a long adder, which surpasses the common viper in combativeness and aggressiveness. Nonetheless, the strange monstrous forepart is that of a ram with its characteristic hocks, as though the image of a warlike sovereign had to unite the qualities of differ-ent animals and to include the outward signs of identity which well-developed horns gave to the leaders of animal tribes. Thus, whether royal or divine, the impetuous bull and ferocious boar of Celtic sculpture were given three horns, the better to mark their superiority. In Egyptian art, however, the princely bull overthrowing a human enemy seems to have been thought sufficient, with its brutally explicit allegory, to convey and locate a supremacy of this kind, just as in the Rhineland there are several works from Gaul showing bulls overthrowing a man, which can leave no doubt as to the identity of the victor. 287

For, in a society where the relations between human groups were often limited to those of force, the exaltation of the combative qualities was conveyed in verbal images and ideographic aggregates that illustrate and define them in a more or less complex manner. There therefore seems to be no a priori reason for separating the neighboring Scythian images that represent fights between animals and those opposing real animals to fantastic creatures, with forces increased tenfold by the physical means with which they are armed. With the feline tearing an elk, in an appliqué on a saddle found at Pazyryk, it is the same as with the image of another elk being carried off by a fabulous eagle, or that of a winged tiger pouncing on an ibex. Sometimes indeed the fight is depicted in an entirely conventional manner: the head of a deer or wild sheep is held in the jaws of a wolf or has been seized by an eelpout, or the stag's head is inserted, even more strangely, into the beak of a monstrous griffin. 72 284

As Griaznov, one of the chief excavators of the Scythian barrows, has written: "All these images 358 and many others must have represented symbolically the strong dominating the weak." That said, there remains the problem whether these were fabulous fights forming an integral part of Eurasian mythology, or fight themes serving as decorative and ideological leitmotivs in a hunting and warlike society. The problem is relevant to the whole of the Middle East. The fantastic animals appear, or rather reappear, after the Bronze Age, but in the arts of Central and western Asia. From 3000 B.C. they were already dominant in the visual arts of Mesopotamia. In the second millennium B.C. lions with threatening maws protect Hittite citadels, temples, and palaces. Other animals do the same for the Assyrian monuments. On the walls of the palace of Persepolis, winged lions at grips with bulls are a reminder that force is a state virtue.

The prehistoric barbarian art of Europe and Asia has, therefore, as a common characteristic, an abundant use of wild animals. And that of the Celts does not escape from the rule, indeed it allows of useful comparisons. The island literature of Celtic inspiration alludes to such exalting creatures, thus described by the Lebor Gabala:

I am the bull with the seven fights
I am the vulture on the rock
I am the boar of hardihood
I am the salmon in the sea.

233

The half-poetic, half-realist description, designed to outline the high combative qualities of the depicted person more clearly than any more abstract terms could (and indeed there were perhaps none of these in that language), leads naturally to what might seem a fantastic transcription into plastic terms: lawyer or economist is, for instance, among other criteria, to be rated higher, being more of an asset in the context of a modern state.

The art of the Scythians and of their allies or neighbors, by virtue of its martial themes, its pictorial or plastic exaltation of the various animals laying low the vanquished, and the preeminence it accords in general to the predatory carnivore, implies that to earn one's living by labor was an activity less honorable than rapine and was just about good enough for women and slaves. In the pastoral and nomad economy that is particularly characteristic of prehistory, prosperity consists first in owning cattle and land, and then, as soon as a man has become a titled proprietor of these, in owning enough

234

it would be that of a monster with a boar's body ending, at one extremity, in a salmon's tail and, at the other, in the head of a bird of prey completed by a bull's horns. The art of Gaul, like that of the Steppes and like others still nearer to prehistory, is rich in such supernatural creatures which have, however, nothing about them that allows us—in the absence of any evidence of rites held in their honor—to confer on them any divine attribution. At most, in the fight scenes, they appear as Herculean protagonists or as the symbols of their strength.

235

The legendary hero of the Celts, like the Greco-Latin one, has his homologue or predecessor in Gilgamesh, a sturdy hero, worthy of the nomads and warriors of the Persian plateaux, who fights the

270 great wild beasts and protects the herds. In the art of primitive Iran, the theme is often suggested
273 through a hero shown as only a torso, then as only a head, and finally as having no human feature. Among the neighboring Scythians, as in Luristan, no place is reserved for him even in the scenes of animal fights—at least not openly, as a fighting biped. At most, among the known evidence, there is a Sarmatian motif illustrating a joust between two autochthons—a joust which has been described as ritual, but in which neither protagonist stands out. True, the Turco-Mongolian epic poetry sings the

236

exploits of a hunter at grips with legendary monsters, celebrates his war-horse and his single combats with other great fighters, the fraternization between them, and then the treacherous assassination of the paladin, followed by his resurrection; but it would be difficult to establish at what point the real serves as a springboard for fable and for myths, or to be sure that the early barbarians regaled themselves with recitals of heroic exploits whose heroes were already deified.

In this context, the legend of the Greek Hercules is worth attention. It tells us that the god had three sons: one of them, Scythes, evidently the eponymous prince of the barbarians inhabiting the northern shores of the Black Sea, became the king of that land and the worthy successor of his divine father, because he was the only other person who could string the national bow and wear correctly the baldrick to which the weapons were attached. To anyone who knows how difficult it was to bend the short, curved Eurasian bow, the test was certainly worthy of a young man so highly born.

This example shows once again how mythology reflects the technical competence of believers—who in this case were first and foremost archers—and how rites are a means of discovering the strength of character or expertise of the future adult. In fact, the rites in this case reveal the stiff tests for social admittance to a certain age category, quite as much as they convey their later "religious" implications—in the modern sense of the adjective, denoting a well-defined and differentiated ideological superstructure. Thus, in the present case, the fable content is at most contemporary with the economico-political way of life of the protohistoric tribes of western Eurasia. Imbuing it with religious meaning nevertheless brings about an alienation of its purpose that works against the original aim; for the result is to put a brake on the progress of the very society which formulated its rules to regulate rank and eliminate the unfit. In our own time a party leader can obviously no longer be chosen by reference to his skill in drawing the bow or in riding in the barbarian style: his training as a people to exploit or guard them. But possession and fortune are not synonymous with honesty; and while the ancient god Mercury appears, from his youth, as god both of wealth and of herds, Sophocles does not hesitate to describe him as a "stealer of oxen." Similarly Ossetian epic literature includes among other heroic exploits the seizing of cattle belonging to neighbors! And it was no doubt very aptly that Caesar described the chief god of Gaul as pecuniary, for the Latin word *pecus* denotes a herd. The same would apply to Volos, the equivalent god of fortune among the ancient Russians, since his appelation *skotskij bog* signifies god of cattle, of flocks and herds, and, by extension, god of riches, god of abundance.

Moreover, wars increase the military power of the supreme leader and that of his subordinates. Virile dominance, when men's fortune depends on the fortune of arms, becomes established and leads to a juridical state of affairs that has been analyzed by Engels: the introduction of patriarchal law follows the development of masculine power in nomad societies of military democracy; "Heredity, at first tolerated, then claimed, and finally usurped," is thus clearly apparent in the action of Hercules—the king, Scythes, being consecrated because of his divine descent, and as an additional justification, his inheritance of Herculean capacities.

On the other hand, the Paleolithic bestiary does not give primacy to martial individualities. Hunting is certainly a strenuous activity, but it furnishes no motive for representing scenes of fighting designed to exalt strength as a civic virtue. Even if, in cave art, certain oppositions—sometimes latent, as in the gallery of paintings in the Lascaux cave, or really tumultuous, as on the painted ceiling of Altamira—are evidence of social conflicts, the antagonistic groups (in each of which rank is indicated by outstanding animal personalities being depicted on a larger scale than the other) have sufficient members to convey a broad community of varied age classes, which also implies secular or sacred activities that are not very specialized, within the framework of an organization more collective than that of the royal Scythians was destined to be. In them well-being does not seem yet to depend on the plunder, rapine, bloody expeditions, and warlike virtues that are the necessary accompaniment of the age of archery and the military profession.

And yet, how are we to explain the allegory of the stag, that timid and hunted beast which, paradoxically, is as common in Paleolithic art as in protohistoric—in the form of old symbolic antlered beasts, as much prized by the stealthy hunters as by the turbulent herdsmen and warriors of the Steppes, whether Mongols, Celts, or Eurasians? In spite of his seated and essentially anthropomorphic pose, the Gallic god with the stag's antlers reminds us of the fine beast of Scythian art, whose depicted attitude, though more natural in its animality, is nonetheless one of great nobility. It shows the animal kneeling, as regards his front legs, and at the same time seated as regards the hind legs and hindquarters. The muzzle is often stretched forward, slightly raised, and the gaze straight ahead. The ears, flattened far back, indicate that the animal, though resting, is in a combative mood. In rare cases the head is turned toward the rear, in an attitude of repose that is characteristic of the animal. Whether he belongs to Gaul or to Scythia, each of these subjects—each personage one might say—certainly appears well "settled in his position."

And this ideogram of the majestic stag was treated again and again by the barbarians, the examples being so numerous and varied that only the most famous ones can be reproduced or mentioned. Clearly it is the typical motif of the bestiary preferred by the nomads of the Steppes. Some examples, indeed, convey subtle connections between man and the animal, symbolic relationships that were already explicit in the antlered monsters of the Paleolithic caves. The felt hanging from Barrow 5 at Pazyryk is even decorated with two confronting creatures that combine morphological characteristics from several animals: birds, felines, deer. Two fighting creatures have human heads bearing antlers, and one of them has mustaches; one has the body of a lion, the other that of a bird—with the powerful wings, feathered tails, and well-sharpened talons or claws that best fit them for striking, gripping, and tearing. If our own phraseology had its equivalents, direct and figurative, in the language of the Scythians, one would say that a "fighting cock" was confronting an adversary "brave as a lion."

A plaque of repoussé gold belonging to the Ziwiye treasure is equally representative of this imagist style, though the theme is a more peaceful one. Forming a leitmotiv whose repetitions are linked by embracing signs, lion heads (with pronounced cheeks) delimit between them free spaces containing figures of venerable stags or ibex with their characteristic frontal ornaments and in the pose that was traditional in Scythian art—the animal is lying down, seen from the side, with its front feet folded under the hind ones. The interlacing motifs are Urartian, but the animals show striking Scythian features. It has been suggested that this treasure found in Iranian Kurdistan belonged to a Scythian war leader and therefore contained works by contemporary artists from various neighboring ethnic groups, Assyrian, Median, and Urartian, with their preferred subjects, their specific bestiaries, purposely brought together on a single piece. In that world of conflicts, where the ups and downs of war were frequent, the native goldsmith bowed to the internationalization of the market, using several dictionaries of motifs in order to have the best chance of disposing of his work, whoever it might be who ordered it.

The lion, for instance, is a traditional symbol in the southern Transcaucasian regions because, being found there, it could be observed and, as king of beasts, was a natural choice for the image of sovereign power. It is against that feline that, on the walls of Persepolis, the royal hero measures his strength and skill. The present-day coats of arms of Iran still carry a lion brandishing a saber to defend

237

his crown and his realm. In the barbarian heraldry of the Scythians, however, the feline yields pride of place to the king of the forest, if not to the king of the mountains. Seeing that, on the Ziwiye plaque, these three animals—the lion, the full-grown stag, and the ibex (which may also be thought to symbolize specific age groups)—are shown together and with similar prominence, the implication of their several biotopes may also have been a sufficiently explicit way of conveying neighboring ethnic and geographic groups, more or less equal or associated.

239
256

The Example of the Stag

The ibex-stag correspondence or close affinity occurs in other connections: for example, the custom of tattooing the body, as we have seen, existed among the Scythians and, no doubt, among the men of Luristan. This distinctive practice, clearly attested in the case of the nobler dead in the virile society of the Steppes, seems to be confirmed by a bronze statue dating from the seventh century B.C., which shows a bearded man, a Lur of mature age, wearing a short loincloth and with his chest bare: on his back there is a design of a male ibex, old and experienced, to judge by its horns. Also, near Issyk, in Kazakhstan, a man of the sixth or fifth century B.C. had been taken to his last resting place with clothes decorated with gold plaquettes, each having on it the figure of an ibex. The characteristic animal motif of Scythian art is of the same order: a stag with branching antlers that indicate age and express his patriarchal function.

It is not, however, certain that the Ziwiye gold plaque is therefore an equivalent of the Rosetta stone. The symbolic affinities of the stag and the ibex—through that common denominator, the resting but vigilant male—cannot conjure away the fundamental differences between them: the former ranges the Steppes and forest, the second climbs the mountains; the one therefore, may symbolize the nomad of the great plains, the other the alert mountain dweller, owner or exploiter of alpine pastures. With regard to the ibex, one remembers the mention in Herodotus of certain neighbors of the Scythians and Issedonians, whom he describes as "goat-footed" men inhabiting a region of high mountains. This is probably a transcribed metaphor, more or less well understood by the Greek historian. In any case, one glimpses from this angle, if not the certainty, at least the possibility of a vassaldom or subordination of these two pacific beasts, perhaps dominated by the king of the jungle—that is to say, by the king of a human society that likewise practiced the brute law of the jungle. But the plaque may, by the lion, be reflecting the idea of a peaceful sovereignty: this would be borne out by noble attitudes of the stag and ibex—the same, indeed, as those of many animal figures, of Scythian and Urartian style, that decorate that sheet of gold from an ax handle from one of the Kelermes kurgans.

Moreover, these two examples provide food for thought about the determinant value generally accorded, in the bestiary of the Steppes, to the stag's antlers as an indication of the symbolic importance of the one who bears them. For stag's antlers are represented ad infinitum in the art of the Eurasian nomads, especially in the eastern part of the great continental plain. The tombs in Hunan have yielded many small, wooden figures representing men or animals, all bearing these frontal ornaments; and this is a southern province which the Chinese chroniclers also considered as "barbarian." These chroniclers even mention mythical creatures with animal bodies and human heads

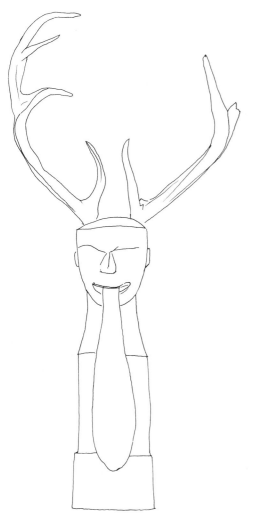

238

crowned with antlers. One thinks of the Pihsieh, that fantastic beast resembling a stag and believed, in southern China, to ward off the evil eye. Lastly, until quite recently, the Siberian shamans used antlers for similar purposes in their religious ceremonies.

It has been said that the allegory of the stag could be explained exclusively by themes of resurrection, since the male loses its antlers every year and grows them again: it is therefore the best possible symbol for the rebirth of the dead. But the association of lion, stag, and ibex on the Urartian plaque weakens this explanation, since neither the ibex nor the lion carries seasonal ornaments. In the pose given him by the Eurasian artist, the stag seems to have a virility in which sexual appetite is beginning to give place to a noble and reassuring calm, similar to that of the Celtic Cernunnos, whose fortune is settled and who radiates the same impression of plenitude.

And this function of director, of leader, can no doubt easily drift, in course of time, into that of *psychopompos* (the Greek word for "guide of souls"), in which guise the stag still appears in the medieval Christian bestiary, where the animal is the patron of catechumens aspiring to the initiation of baptism. On a Hittite ensign an old stag is even to be seen apparently directing and herding two bulls or bullocks, whose scale the artist has reduced in order to show their subordination.

While mythology and protohistoric art thus offer considerable food for thought in their many examples of stags whose antlers attest advanced age, the same is true of the Paleolithic ones, such as
278 those in the paintings of the Lascaux cave. Here they are grouped as though in a class united by age under the direction of a huge bovine creature. No less indicative of age are the antlers of the bearded
245 monster, half man, half beast, painted in the Trois Fréres cave. The same applies to those of a certain
282 Hittite statue of the ungulate, and to those in a famous and clumsy Paleolithic engraving, crowning a
246 bearded individual whose venerable baldness also attests his maturity.

The male and patriarchal function of the stag is equally evident in the religious art of Gaul: Cernunnos—the god whose head is adorned with a luxuriant pair of antlers and who is shown carrying in his hand, or wearing on his arms, around his neck, or on his antlers, the Celtic torque, that sign of royalty or of identity in tombs—is likewise generally represented as bearded, or even bald.

242 Whether in the Val Camonica, in Cisalpine Gaul, or on a stele from Reims, the god is accompanied by a young and virile adviser, or by divine sons, whom the Roman conquest immortalized as those handsome youths called Mercury and Apollo. Whether by being reduced in scale or by being turned toward Cernunnos, the young men seem to recognize in him a superior authority and to be subordinate to him, as vassals and children would be to the sovereign father. On the great silver caldron found in Gundestrup (Jutland), which has been held to be influenced by Scythian art in spite of its Celtic technique, this prince may perhaps be commanding and directing the animals that are approaching him. As in other representations from Gaul, the god is shown seated as a king in majesty, with his legs crossed in the Buddhist and oriental way. On the relief in question he appears as the assured man and leader; as a sign of his economic power, he is holding a bag from which coins and other signs of abundance are streaming.

In the Tuva, as mentioned above, there are also funerary stelae engraved with stags: these clearly refer to the dead, to the famous warriors buried close by. Chenova even considers the animal as the tribal totem of the Sacians, the word *sag* meaning "stag" in modern Ossetic—and indeed an old Ossetian story makes a young hero say that his father was still "as vigorous as a stag." (See Dumézil, *Le Livre des héros.* Causasus series. Paris N.R.F., p. 77)—and the field where these stelae are to be found extends from the Altai through southern Mongolia into Transbaikalia,—that is, throughout the regions of Central Asia which were dominated by those peoples, at least as a thin ruling class.

239

240

241

What, then, is the origin of this important role assigned by symbolism to the stag? In the herd of deer, it is not the stag who leads: the troop is organized matriarchally under the direction of a sterile hind. The male, apparently, is there only for reproduction: he trails behind the group, often accompanied by a young subadult male, as we see in the rock paintings of eastern Spain; and at the slightest threat the hinds, old or young, whether followed by fawns or not, abandon them. But in this solitude the fraternity that unites the two animals—the old one and his "page" (or brocket)—sees to it that the younger one, nervous and always on the watch, warns the old stag, who then arranges his flight in such a way as to draw the hunter after him and let his young sentry escape. In this respect the old stag is an excellent guide, a wise protector drawing the dangers upon himself and away from those under his protection—first of all, perhaps, the horde of females and fawns, and certainly his young attendant. The ibex also has the same altruistic customs.

In the classical Scythian version the artist treats the stag as an experienced male at the peak of his glory, equipped with his antlers at the season of mating, of which he is still capable, and so, in spite of his relative placidity, ready to fight with ardor to hold his own both against pretenders, against those who would contest his title as leader, and against dangerous predators. But the animal is also depicted in repose, with his muzzle raised in the contentment of his dignity and his experience, with his antlers resting on his back, and still ready to bell with his full force. Is he already somewhat solitary? Does he represent the old guard of the veterans, the class of the elders? There is really no means of knowing precisely, perhaps not even approximately, what age category he represents; one hesitates between the individual at the top rung of the social ladder and the venerable patriarch, worthy to represent divine justice by dispensing the human sort,—that is to say, having more or less conferred a sacred quality on the latter in exchange for some gerontocratic advantage. For more than one reason this animal, which refuses any taming, was bound to attract the Eurasian warriors and hunters for its symbolic qualities—and priests and pontiffs, too, insofar as they wished to spread a belief that the knowledge of the elders became transformed into an occult power, capable of propitiating the gods.

There must also have been a need for an economic basis by which the elders, through their experience, would be useful to the society in which they lived and would not be merely mouths to feed. The ancient authors have, for example, recorded that among the barbarian Issedonians of Central Asia the useless old men were put to death. The importance given to the old stag as a symbol does therefore make it possible, in the case of a given culture, to measure the consideration or contempt in which aged persons were held—and so to judge its degree of civilization.

However, even when the traditional Scythian motif at Kul Oba is a stag decorated with other animals, one can have no clear certainty (any more than with the Cernunnos on the Gundestrup 250 caldron, toward whom griffins and aggressive males are also converging) that the stag has been depicted as sovereign over inferior categories, or that these additional beasts are designed to complete the symbol of supremacy, to which the allegory of an old and majestic stag was not judged sufficient. 257 True, the translation veers about themes that are close together; but in this case the picto-ideographic language shows its fundamental imperfections as a means to any exact version of the original meaning.

The fact remains that, with the crouching animal from Kul Oba a symbolic range seems to appear that groups together the griffin, the hare, and the lion, as if to show that the stag possesses the attributes of each,—speed, agility, and feline suppleness. And close under his chest a dog, that faithful companion of man, but also pursuer of deer, singularly reinforces the allegory and humanization of 103 the crouching beast. It does seem that, if the dog had been there only to reinforce the dynamic qualities of the stag, he would have been part of that range which includes the other animals, and would have been standing on the defensive; but the dog, like his enormous protector, is lying down, at rest. He gives the impression of being there like the anxious attendant, as an associated and protected subadult, having escaped from the sad fate which no doubt awaits the hare hemmed in by the two carnivores.

Thus in Scythian art the presence of the stag never conveys any limiting religious motivation, open, intrinsic, or implicit. Since the evidence of ancient writers makes no mention of any mythical bestiary among the Eurasians of their time, everything incites us to see a symbolic, generally secular, significance in the animal figures, even when the images are at their strangest. But the hypothesis calls for many confirmations.

What, for example, can be the significance of a famous carved wooden head which its Mongolian
238 craftsman crowned with antlers, while he depicted, hanging from its mouth, an enormous tongue, disproportionate not only to the human being but to the animal?

242

Certainly other lingual subjects exist that are similar, if not in their meaning, at least in their singularity. Lucian notes that a certain autochthonous representation of the Gallic god Ogmios has greatly perplexed him: the god is shown as an old man drawing toward himself a multitude of small-scale individuals caught by the ears with thin gold and amber chains of delicate workmanship. The captives seem to be not at all anxious to escape: "They are following their guide with joy, they are praising him, they are eager to reach him," so that, instead of pulling on their chains, they are letting these fall loose. "It looks as if they would hate to regain their liberty . . . . The oddest thing about this painting is that the artist, not knowing where to attach the ends of the chains . . . . has had the idea of piercing the tip of the tongue and having all these men, his followers, drawn to him by it." Thus the clear symbol of eloquence—by which the orator "enchains" his hearers and "captivates them" in the metaphorical sense—has completely escaped that cultivated Greek, Lucian, although the subject was one appropriate to barbarian iconography—in which a highly secular figurative expressionism was clearly conveying the idea of high oratorical competence (which in itself had, indeed, nothing specifically divine about it).

In the light of such an example, the strange anthropomorphic creature with antlers and with his tongue hanging out, mentioned earlier, becomes less monstrous, less necessarily conditioned by myths. Besides, it is well known that the stag, when exhausted, lets its tongue hang out: Paleolithic art has sometimes depicted it in this way, tense with effort—and with a meaning that remains to be deciphered.

Moreover, the secular or religious symbolism of an animal becomes multivalent through the varied, though characteristic, traits that define it in its attitudes, customs, and specific qualities or defects. This has happened, for instance, in the case of the bear, whose image may equally well illustrate greed, lust, or the solitary life. The stag is quite as rich in possibilities and meanings.

265
266 Certainly it is a priori difficult to explain, for example, the function of certain antlered hoods made for horses that were sacrificed beside their wealthy masters in the Altaic kurgans. For, these curious leather objects, adorned with colored motifs, pieces of fur, and gilded roundels or crescents, were (as we have seen) surmounted with a pair of stag's antlers, also gilded. Several excavations have yielded manes of horses treated in the same way. There is one with false ears, between which, fixed on
257 a pad, there rose a leather ibex head: on the neck of the ibex was perched a bird of white felt, also covered with leather, with gilded wings half spread, and a plumed tail, as if to suggest that this whole
239 bestiary was making eagerly toward something—material, allegorical, or spiritual.

240 This brings us back again to the uncertain identity between stag and ibex, and one cannot be sure

243

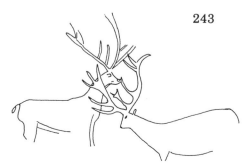

244

if the symbolism of leader and protector of the living, or of guide of souls, remains valid also for those masks associated with funerary practices. Rudenko, one of the leading specialists in Scythian art, considers that this way of adorning horses originated in Western Asia and is likely to have become fashionable at the beginning of the first millennium B.C., so that it found its way onto Assyrian bas-reliefs. Rudenko is also convinced that the hoods were not of exclusively mortuary use, in view of the signs of wear which some of them show.

Other points may perhaps be useful. The animal heads (stag, ibex, goat) adorning these hoods are those of dominant individuals, of specific leaders of herds, just as in herds of wild horses the stallion is the leader. All animal societies, whether of the patriarchal type (horses) or matriarchal (cattle), have their recognized leaders. When the shepherds in the Alps crown the "queen of the cows" with distinctive ornaments at the end of a dairy competition, they are indicating in the eyes of all, human beings and animals, who is the leader of the herd. Who can tell whether the Eurasian herdsmen and horsemen did not have customs of this type, whether in the trappings of their horses they were not confirming that hierarchy which animal society itself had made for itself—as indeed the Eskimos do, with the packs of dogs that draw their sleighs?

However that may be, it has been pointed out that in the Scythian burials not all the horses wore hoods. It seems to follow that these rich trappings were reserved for those horses which led the funeral procession, being also perhaps the leaders of their companions. If so, the masks equipped with antlers would simply indicate the distinction of their wearers, or rather that of the dead man; the cult of the stag could thus be relegated to the collection of false religious explanations.

So this survey across the ages leads us back to the art of the Steppes. It is indeed natural that, in the same latitudes and in similar biotopes, societies whose forces and types of production are of the same order should use verbal or visual modes of expression that carve out reality in a similar manner. By concentrating on the pursuit of artistic affiliations from the Breton peninsula to that of Kamchatka, people sometimes forget the essential—which is that, independently of ethnic groups, the warrior, hunter, and herdsman peoples all used for a time the same animals, not only to supply them with food, furs, tools, and transport, but also for denominative purposes remote from the mere interests of hunting. It is, therefore, hardly surprising that the canonical stags with their venerable antlers, present in the art of the Lascaux hunters as well as in that of the herdsmen or warriors of the Altai, seem to have a family resemblance, even though there be none between their creators. To claim a literal, so to speak, word-for-word interpretation of the animals depicted—in short, to try to consider their inherent meaning to the exclusion of the depicted image—is to beg the question; it is unjustified and leads to self-deception.

Some writers, while admitting that the stag image has a symbolic value, but on the ground that it is found disseminated over the vast expanse of the Steppes, have deduced that it had a function as a clan emblem and totem: it would thus have become proper to vast Sacian and Scythian kingdoms as the result of territorial extensions—the independent Sarmatians alone having rejected the symbol. The sign being such an ancient one, this type of hypothesis would, if taken to the extreme, lead us to push the ethnic group represented by the sign as far back as the Paleolithic age—which few will maintain. Still, it remains tenable that, having become a royal emblem—and this hypothesis seems to find confirmation in the case of the crown of the Parthian kings, decorated with several figures of the stag—in consequence of a transfer of power from age categories to an aristocracy and to a leader, the stag may, in its new allegory, have in fact corresponded to certain empires. However, their line of demarcation is often very hard to trace, given the international distribution, simplicity, and commonness of the stag sign.

On the other hand the representations of animals, of deer in particular, cannot have been either literal or emblematic depictions of local deities: the pantheon of the Scythians is known to us through the writers of antiquity, and they never mention zoomorphic gods. Also, barbarian art always represented the Great Goddess with human features, and the Greek and Roman authors tried to assimilate the native gods to their own—which again confirms their anthropomorphic nature. Since cynegetic magic has also been rejected, we are forced to turn again to what can be ascertained about Scythian society.

Because this included age classes with specific activities, and because ethnography teaches us that societies of identical type, in Africa for instance, use animals to symbolize human groups, whether they be tribes, clans, or age categories, a possible common factor comes to mind. Among the classes of Eurasian societies, did not certain associations have the stag as their sign? If so, this symbolic community across vast expanses would be fortuitous and would not necessitate the hypothesis of a single kingdom. Or, at least, if the social organization modified itself at the expense of the communal one (which still persisted in its outward customs), the later attribution of supreme authority to a single powerful man and wealthy hero, who in the course of time became a potentate, was joined with the adoption of a laudative zoomorphic terminology which it was useful to retain for the new royal beneficiary. Parallel to this, the divorce between the metaphorical nomenclature and the social change which had come about was bound to contribute toward making the original image less real and more abstract—toward making it, if only by the fossilization produced by hereditary kingship, a concept more and more detached from life, idealizing it until it could nourish the most varied mystifications. This dialectical phenomenon would have no need to be explained by invoking exclusive ethnic affiliations—still less, vast empires.

245

So the problems raised by the stag in Eurasian symbolism bring us back once more to the gnoseological sources of religion. Detached from all reality, taking on an independent existence that is separated from its original metaphorical purpose, the concept—in this case, that of the stag as an allegory of a man—becomes an isolated, fabulous being. Let us say, paraphrasing Lenin, that "it seems strange, monstrous (or more exactly, infantile), absurd . . . . through an act which includes the possibility of transformation (imperceptible, and of which the man is unconscious) of the abstract concept, or idea, into an imaginative fantasy (in the last analysis—God)." Such is, on the symbolic plane, one of the processes explanatory of the mysticism which the old stag brought with him, though the traces and prolegomena of it are not necessarily apparent in its earliest prehistoric figurations—or at least they have never been demonstrated, in spite of their being latent as soon as language makes its appearance along with the possibilities of idealizing thought which it expresses and allows.

People do nonetheless persist in seeing in bestiaries of prehistoric or protohistoric art traces of totemic beliefs. Even one of the Soviet specialists postulates that the animals of Scythian art had formerly been considered as totems, ancestors, and patrons of a clan.

But recent ethnological researches have led also to a laicizing of totemism; they have shown that the place reserved for animals, vegetables, or even common objects was initially justified by the requirements of symbolizing and clarifying, and that it was sometimes only much later that ritual and religious attitudes grafted themselves on, and then not systematically.

Evans-Pritchard, who has converted Lévi-Strauss to his thesis, sees in the link between human groups and animal species chiefly a relationship of a metaphorical kind—that is to say, parallel to that which we believe we have found in the art of the Steppes, whether prehistoric or protohistoric. Lévi-

Strauss adds: "By means of a special nomenclature, made up of animal and vegetable terms (and this is its one distinctive characteristic), the supposed totemism is merely expressing in its own way—we nowadays would say, by means of a particular code—correlations and oppositions . . . . The animals of totemism cease to be merely or mainly creatures that are feared, admired, or coveted: their perceptible reality allows to be seen through it notions and relations which are conceived by speculative thought on the basis of observed data . . . . As the conclusions of Radcliffe-Brown show, his analysis of the Australian facts leads him beyond any simple ethnographic generalization: to the laws of language and even of thought."

An etymologist has written that "metaphor, in fact, constitutes one of the constant methods of so-called popular denomination," and he points to such facts as that, to a modern man, the sea may be covered with white horses, his workshops may contain dovetails, and his garden may abound in snapdragons and larkspurs. Indeed, a study of the country names of plants makes it clear that one of the most fruitful and constantly used ways of classifying them has been to compare some part of them—leaf, flower, ear, root—to the similar part of an animal. Hundreds of plant names have thus 248 been formed upon zoomorphic models, borrowing from the bear, from cattle, from birds, or from deer their tails, feet, ears, or hooves, in order to designate expressively the constituent elements of the plants. One can feel here traces of an archaic technical vocabulary that belonged to men who were beginners in agriculture, but which had already been created by the hunters and herdsmen they formerly were. This previously acquired terminology takes nothing away from the conventionality of the new verbal signs, for the conceptual names used by the farmer and artisan for their plants and tools were only made easier to assimilate and remember by their known and evocative roots.

But the result is valid as regards the illustration of human characteristics, economic classes and age categories: as in *Reynard the Fox,* a bestiary allows of defining things more easily. If, then, in 55 popular fables and speech, the fox, the wolverine (or glutton), and the hare describe the human being 57 who is crafty, greedy, and cowardly, and since in Scythian art the eagle, lion, and stag are at least either the earthly kings of human or animal societies or the leaders of their age or sex groups, divine qualities can also be expressed by means of animals, and, in the same way as the profane ones, by evocative outlines or ideograms.

Thus in ancient Egypt there was no word for "omnipotence": the formidable god Amon is therefore described simultaneously as the "savage-looking lion," the "rampant bull," and as the "crocodile that flies and carries off its attacker."

Reciprocally, the existence of a religion requires some other demonstration than a random presumption based on considering certain archaeological finds as strange and irrational when, often, our ignorance is all that they show. For example, just as a number of half-human, half-animal subjects in European or African prehistoric art are put down, without proof, as signifying divine beings or as representing sorcerers disguised or masked as animals, in exactly the same way Eurasian art receives its 245 own quota of such inventions. Thus the "sorcerer" of the Trois Frères cave in southwest France would 277 be simply the colleague of the one engraved near Lake Ladoga—or even, long before those of the Siberian nomads, in the Okunev culture—that is, some four thousand years before our time: here we find, for instance, a wolf with gaping maw, bird's feet, and a mane along its back and neck; or, again, a man with a wolf's head surmounted by horns, and another with an eagle's head and an animal's tail. 223 That these may have had a sacred significance is by no means excluded, but it would not be proved otherwise than by begging the question, and it would have to be borne in mind that the simplest concrete signs generally have accepted meaning of their own and a figurative sense. This includes the animals.

It is therefore no paradox to extend the classification of animals to that of gods, since in fact it helps to define them better, instead of letting them be distorted simply by failure to understand a foreign language that is called barbarian. Modern knowledge of the general laws of thought and of oral, plastic, or pictorial means of expression demolishes the mythical monsters or explains their late appearances. It transforms the supposed masked sorcerers, which often encumber the prehistoric art of every continent, not even into anodyne members of a group disguised as animals, but into simple ideographic aggregates, precursors of writing and not necessarily having a mystical significance. This does not mean that certain religious concepts are excluded.

On the contrary, barbarian art gains from this its letters of credence as a rational mode of expression, and is at least vindicated against those who, though in good faith, think it their duty to mystify it.

246

246

147

248

249

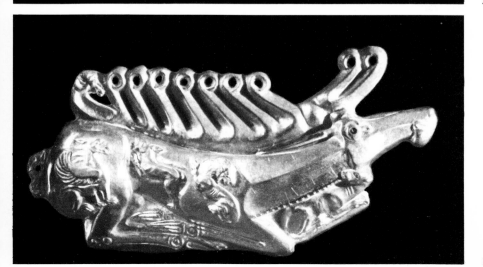

250

251

252

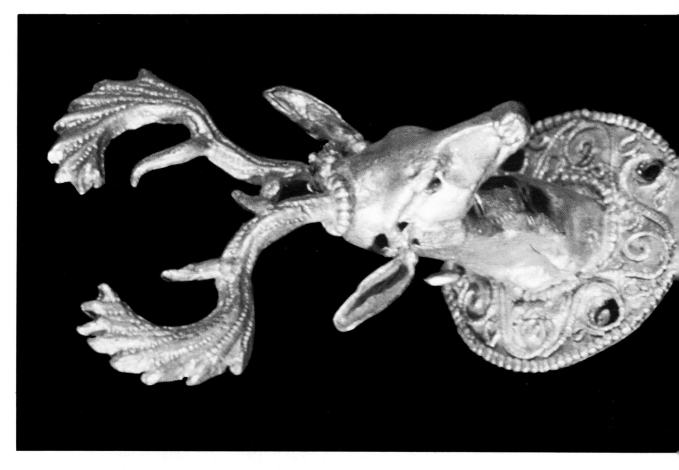

253

254

257

256

258

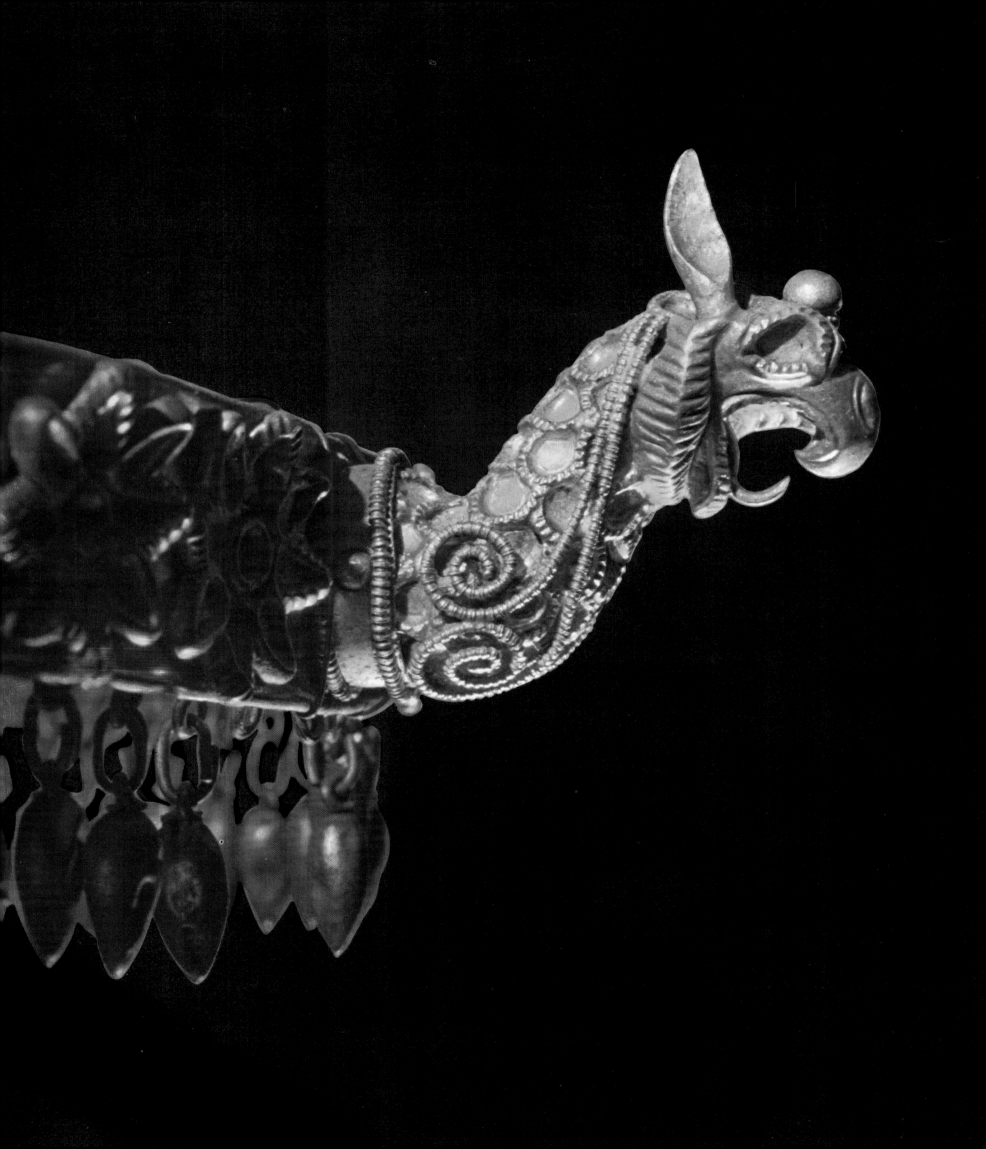

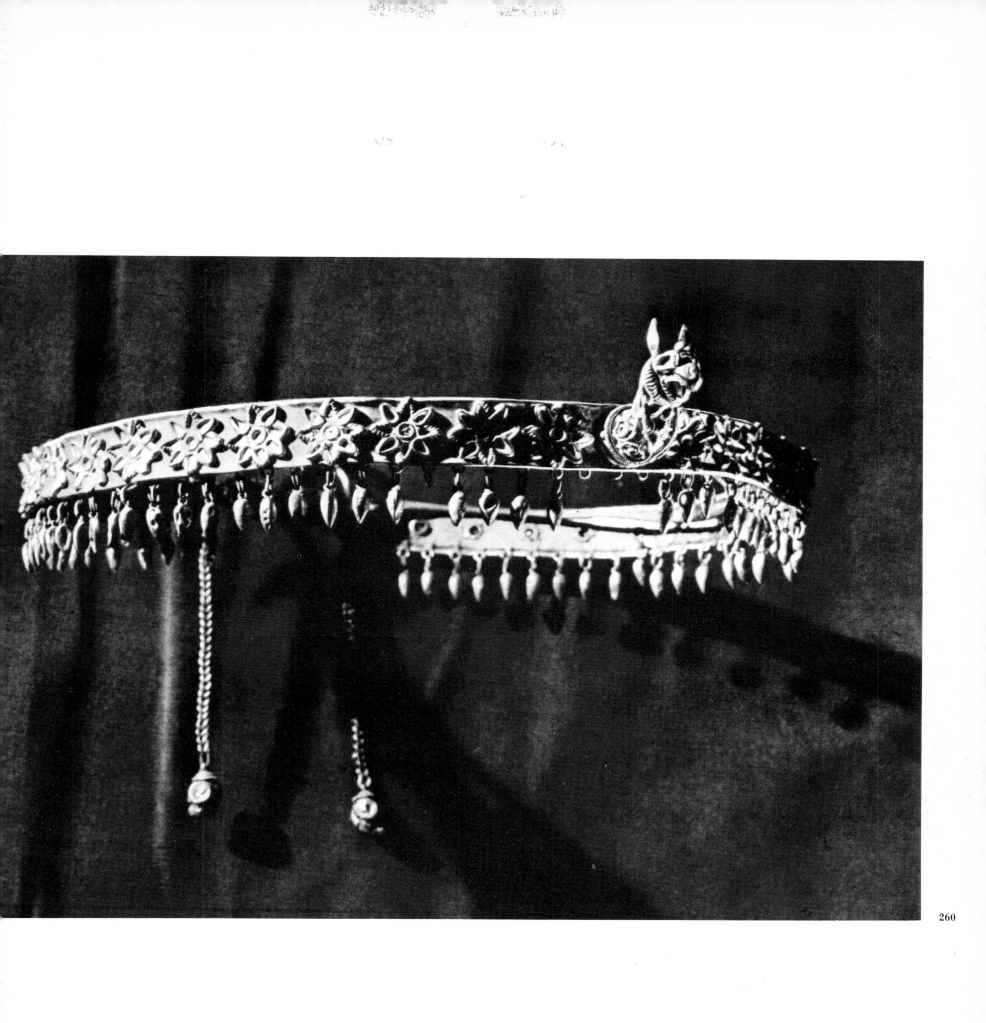

261

262

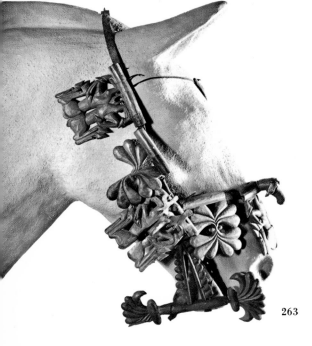

263

264

265

266

267

268

269

270

271

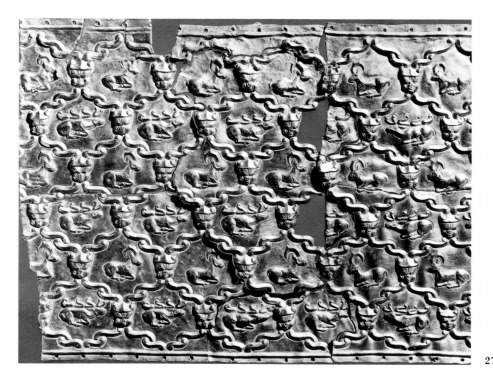

27

273

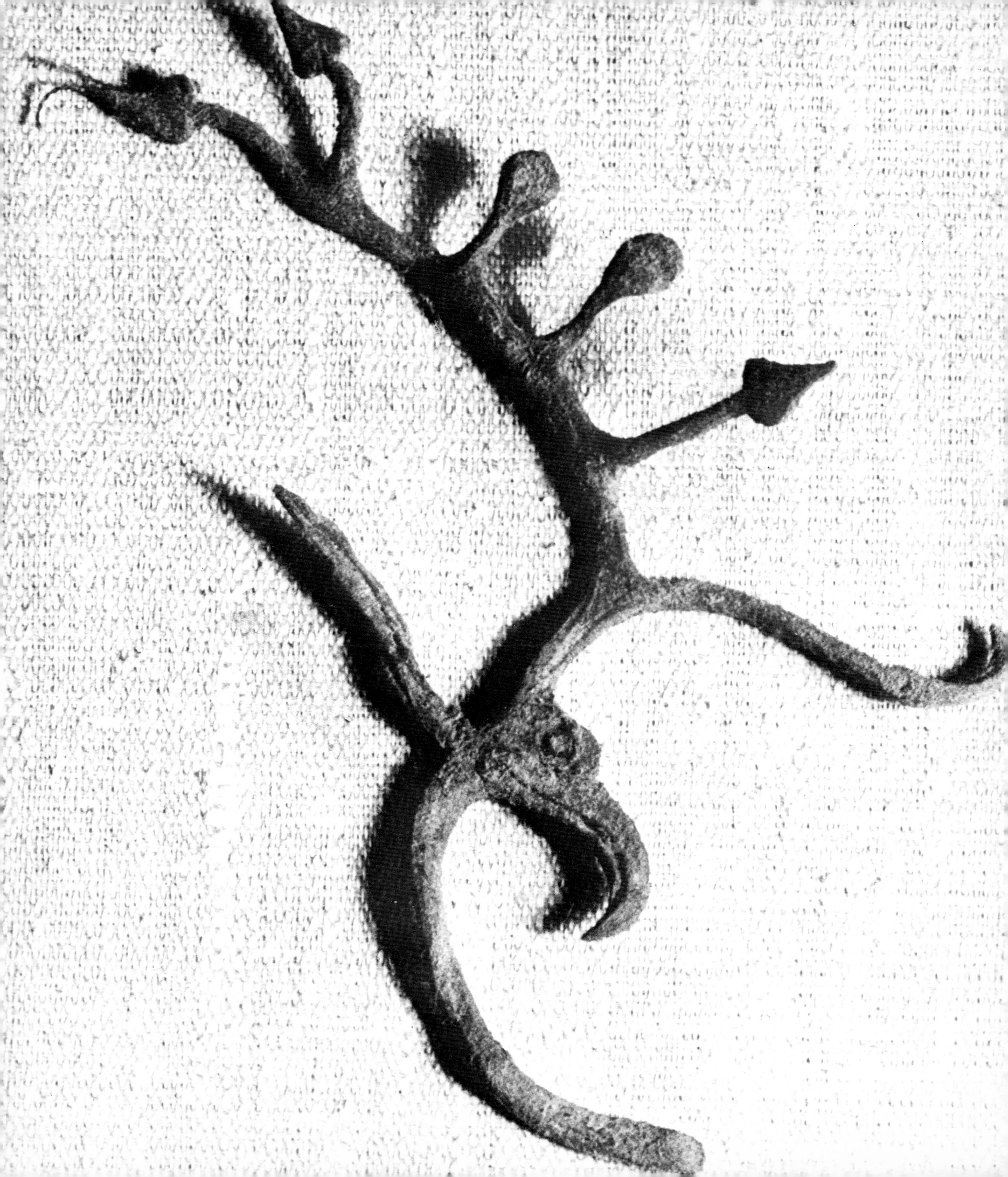

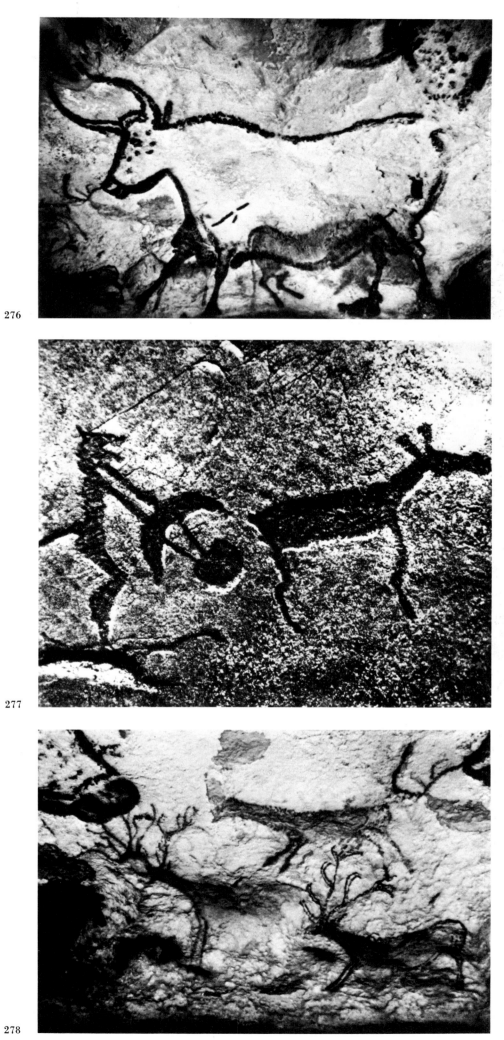

276

277

278

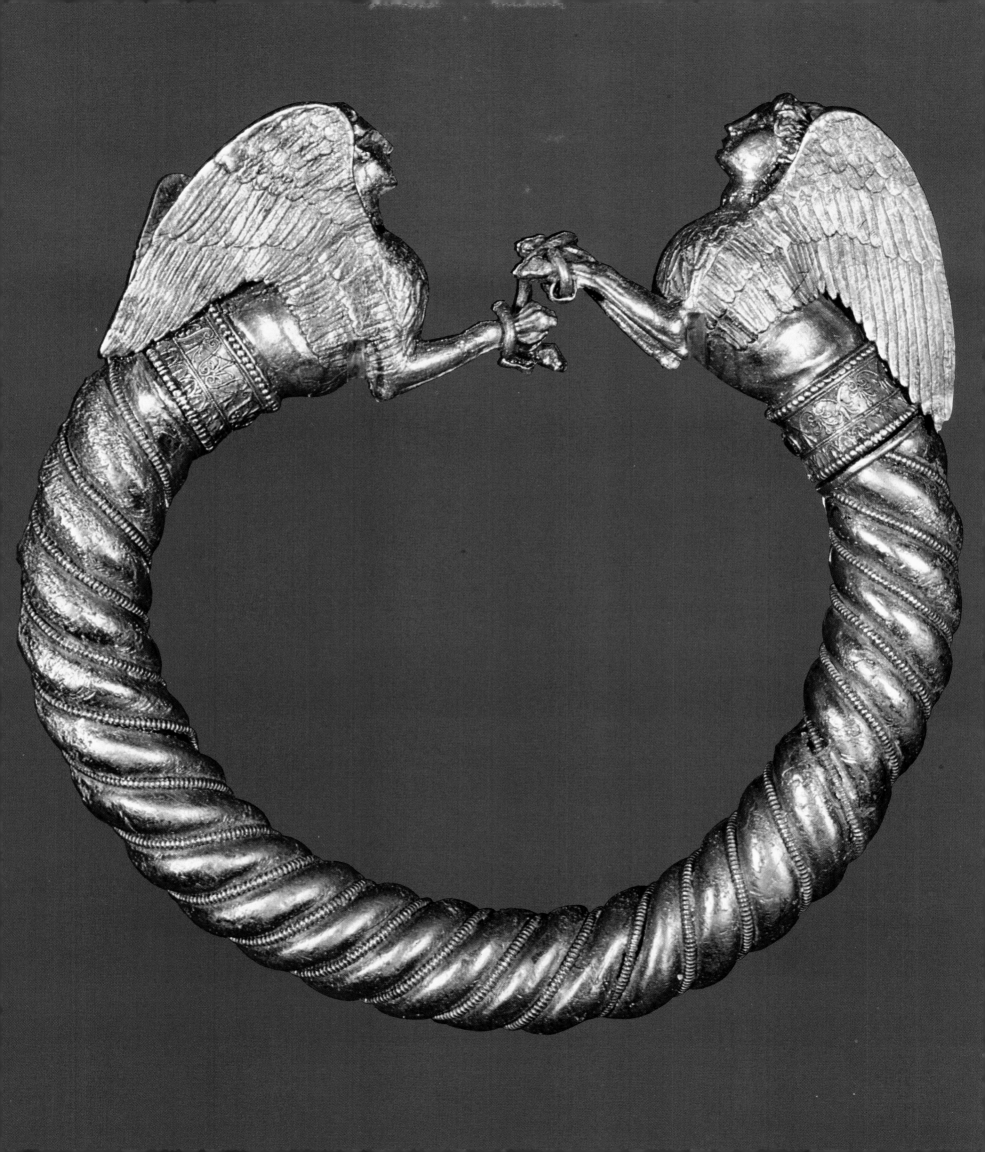

284

283

285

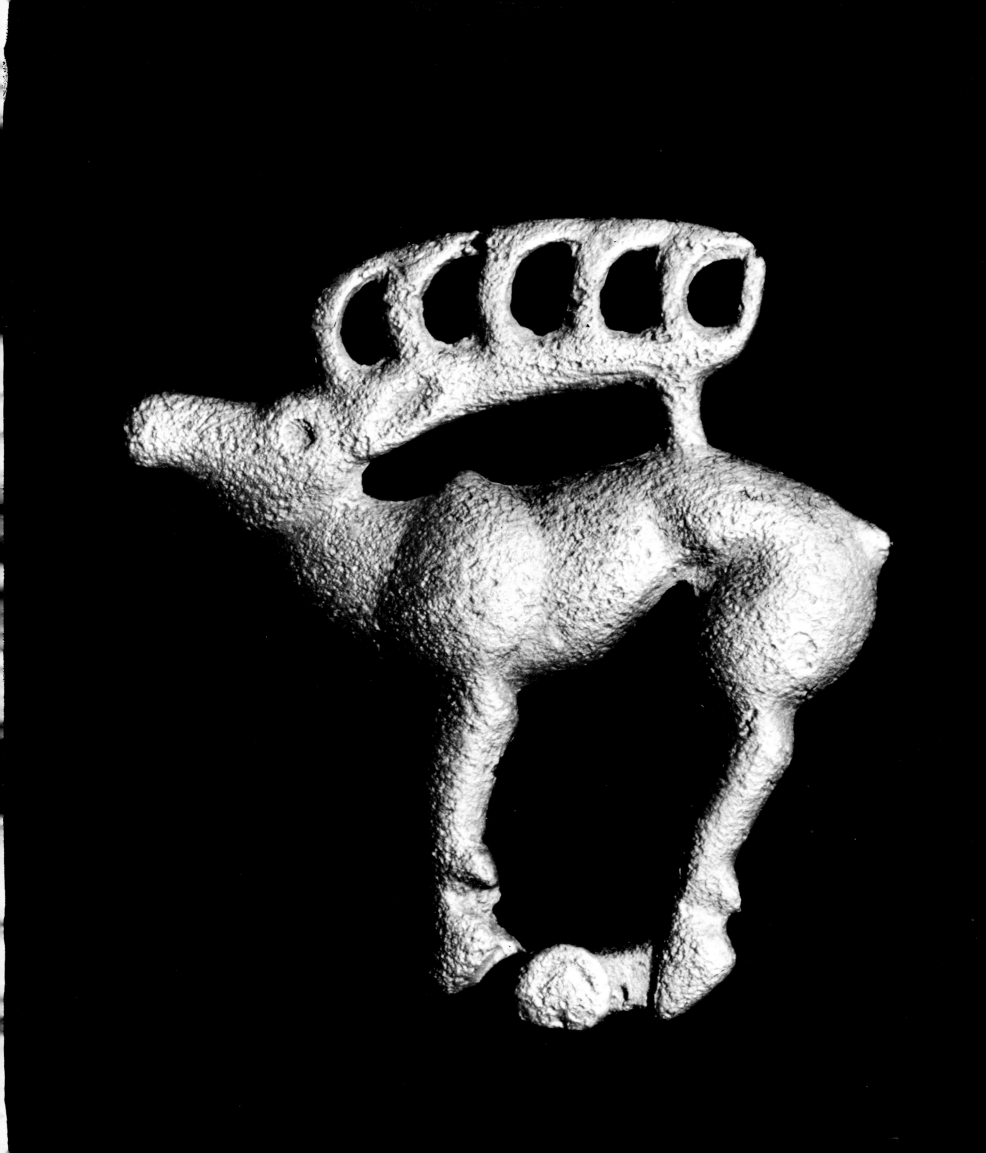

287

288

289

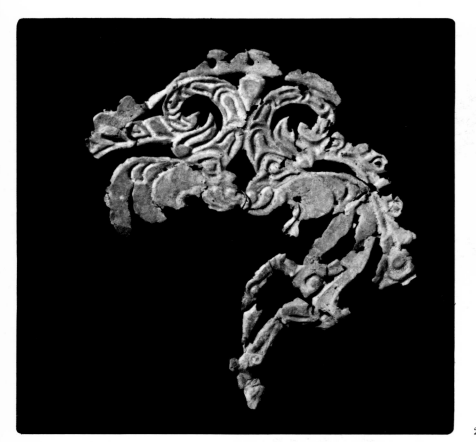

294

292

293

THE ARTIST IN BARBARIAN SOCIETY

The Barbarian Period

Engels, in his celebrated book on the origin of the family, of property, and of the state, wrote that "the characteristic factor of the period of barbarianism is the domestication and breeding of animals, as well as the cultivation of plants . . . . " And "the ancient world possessed almost all the animals capable of domestication and all kinds of cereals suitable for cultivation . . . . "

The earlier stage of barbarianism is marked especially by the invention of pottery, an art which
352 necessitates some degree of sedentary life: as Franck Bourdier notes, not without humor, "the stockpot
353 has become the symbol of a mentality which is not that of a hunter." This stage of incipient stability, indeed, follows the last stage of savage life, which is marked by the appearance of the bow and arrow: these "already form a highly complex instrument, whose invention presupposes prolonged and repeated experiment and increasingly sharpened mental faculties—therefore also the knowledge of
312 many other inventions at the same time . . . . The bow and arrow were, to the savage state, what the
318 iron sword is to the barbarian age and the firearm to civilization: the decisive weapon . . . . " Engels concludes with brio. (And on the plane of art, ideographic sculpture has no complexes about using modern weapons: an artist of Dahomey, for instance, depicts a carabineer with an animal's head in order to recall the creation, by King Glélé, of the corps known as "raging antelopes," equipped with European guns.)

In accordance with the knowledge of prehistory available in his time, Marx's friend suggests that the barbarian period in the Eurasian continent began in particular with the domestication of animals, and that the cultivation of the cereals and other foodstuffs for them followed immediately upon this.
47 The hypothesis is not impossible as regards the breeding of sheep, which are native to plains and steppes—indeed also as regards the horse. At certain sites where there is evidence of these animals
57 there is still no pottery. On the other hand, cattle and pigs, whose wild ancestors are forest dwellers,
327 seem rather to be bound up with a proto-agricultural economy in cultivated clearings forming part of
356 a wooded belt, where the animals, in enclosures on the frontier between the cultivable lands and the thickets, were therefore more easily bred.

In the last resort, the questions and answers regarding this problem will depend, for their clarification, on the development of the archaeological excavations, with all the variants to which the zigzag path of human progress has accustomed us, with its tendency to jostle the excessively simple traditional nomenclatures.

Be it said in passing, the terminology used by the first prehistorians and retained by those of the present day—that of "Paleolithic," "Mesolithic," "Neolithic," "Chalcolithic," etc.—merely defines the ancient societies in terms of one aspect of the means of production, namely the nature of the materials used, leaving aside the experience gained and, above all, the relationships between men harnessed to their tasks, with clearly determined tools.

The Marxian classification, on the other hand, has the merit of reestablishing each factor in its place and in its intrinsic relationships. For example, the barbarian period also corresponds to the "first great social division of labor," with its repercussions on the status of women and of prisoners of war, who were transformed into slaves and were therefore coveted and sought after.

The middle barbarian period then begins with the domestication of cattle, the formation of considerable herds leading to a pastoral life on the plateaux and the great grassy plains, where the herdsmen moved about according to the seasons.

295

The last stage is established with the smelting of minerals, as also with the "invention of alphabetic writing and its use for literary notation." This period, Engels adds, is that of "increased production of natural products thanks to human activity," civilization being the stage "at which man learns the supplementary elaboration of natural products, the period of industry properly so called, and of art."

The barbarian age, therefore, is the first age of superfluous products, ranging from transported provisions to their appropriation by weapons and bloodshed. It extends roughly from the Mesolithic periods to the age of metals as defined by the archaeologists.

Engles traced this web of development in the years 1884-91. But it was four years later that Riviere reached the stage of demonstrating the genuineness of Paleolithic mural art in the La Mouthe caves at Les Eyzies: the few earlier discoveries, which began in 1847, had been considered as fakes, more or less created by the theologians, or as undatable. Marx had died in 1881—too early, therefore, to witness this important reopening of the question of the origins of art or to have read, for instance, Cartailhac's book, *La France préhistorique*, with its Chapter IV entitled: *"Premières Manifestations artistiques de nos ancêtres"* (First Artistic Manifestations of Our Ancestors). It is true that, ever since Peter the Great, Scythian objects had been officially protected and collected in Russia; but regarding them, as well as "Celtic antiquities," and the Paleolithic works of art of western Europe, atheists and materialists were practically in agreement in holding that primitive man practiced art for art's sake, decoration for the pleasure of the eyes. This orthodox position, which seemed to attest the lofty, ideal, and so to speak eternal spirituality of man, suited those who wanted to believe his descent from animals impossible—a belief which paleontology was already undermining, and which could only render suspect discoveries from which such arguments were drawn.

The reason why, for almost half a century, Marx and Engels seem to have ignored the art— not the tools—of prehistory (though they remained prudent, that is to say, refrained from pronouncing on the subject) is that ethnography also was not sufficiently developed to yield a knowledge of the arts of savage peoples, which might have succeeded in hypothecating suspicion. Even today, indeed, it is not always known for certain whether some of the more backward peoples contemporary with us have really remained at an earlier stage of civilization or have relapsed into it, at least on the economic plane—that is to say, while having retained a cultural and religious heritage that cannot be described as primitive and used for comparison.

Thus Marx and Engels, silent as regards the art of "savage peoples," deal only with that belonging to class societies. In this exclusively protohistoric framework the work of art, according to the two philosophers, was essentially dependent on the division of labor. For example, to enable men as eminent as Mozart or Raphael to exercise their craft, there had to be a demand for their productions, and this "in turn depends on the division of labor and on the conditions of education that result from it," and "the exclusive concentration of artistic talent in certain individuals and the stifling of it among the masses" derive from this specialization of labor, which makes the artist a specialist in his own field. "The foundation of art and that of science were only possible thanks to an intensified division of labor, which had necessarily to have as its basis the main division of labor between the masses providing mere manual labor and the privileged few engaged in the direction of labor, in commerce, in affairs of state, and, later, in artistic and scientific activities."

Now "the simplest, most natural form of this division of labor was, precisely, slavery." And nomadic art is an example that illustrates this observation. The general perfection of its motifs fits in with a society which in fact included both artists and slaves proper, whereas the Paleolithic works of

296

art, which are very uneven in accomplishment, bear witness rather to a relative absence of specialization—that is to say, to a much more communal organization.

296
299 As regards Altaic art, indeed, Griaznov has laid stress on the amazingly fine quality of the works which served to adorn harness and headdresses—and the same time the extreme crassness with which they were jumbled together, possibly by their owners. It seems, for instance, that while the artists had put all their knowledge and skill into their products, those for whom they were made revealed their ignorance by grouping those splendid ornaments quite incongruously on the bridles and straps. It is likely that the masterpieces of the Siberian nomads are already the work of people who were detached from the mass of warriors, while retaining their rights as free citizens—as in the case of the blacksmiths in Viking society.

297

Here a discovery at Karmir-Blur may be significant: in that Urartian fortress, just before a Scythian troop took it by storm, a man had the time to begin carving griffins' heads on an antler; his workshop was clearly an improvised one, soon abandoned for more vital tasks. The legend of the blacksmith-king, in Central Asia, no doubt also fits in with this old division of labor, in which the workman and the craftsman were still the equals of their warrior compatriots. It perhaps explains why Genghis Khan was not only considered as the son of a deer and a wolf, but was also called Temujin, which means "blacksmith": the conqueror of the Steppes may in this way have been associated with a past, grown distant and mythical, in which the art of working metal was born. And a few centuries later than the siege mentioned above, the more and more intensive division of labor caused the Scythian nomads to rely entirely, for their social and hierarchical ornaments, on foreign specialists and craftsmen who frequented the cosmopolitan centers of exchange that had been set up on the edge of the Steppes. In the neighborhood of the royal kurgans of the Dnieper a whole district
379 occupied by blacksmiths has come to light, and the numerous amphorae found there show that these craftsmen consumed Greek wine in abundance, and of good quality.

But how was this clear-cut division of tasks arrived at?

The advanced tribes of the Steppes in the Bronze Age, already accustomed to moving their animals from winter pastures to summer ones, were no doubt ripe for the nomadic life as soon as they became used to riding on horseback and to using the wheel for their wagons. Their definitely pastoral way of life had itself been preceded by an earlier, more agricultural stage in which, gradually, man moved from being a mere predator to being a producer, with the slow but sure improvement of productive techniques and relationships which that presupposes.

One of the more likely hypotheses, as we have seen, is that cattle-breeding derives from agriculture, because the captured wild animals could be fed on the cereals which man had learned to cultivate as early as the seventh millennium B.C. in western Asia. In other words, the nomadic life presupposes a Neolithic society in which domestic animals, at least of the bovine kind, were raised with the help of agricultural techniques. Indeed, signs of the breeding and protection of sheep—which were valued, early on, for the ewes' milk—make their appearance around 9000 B.C. in northern Iraq, that is to say, even before the definitive cultivation of cereals. These small animals were no doubt easier to cope with than the dangerous aurochs, and also easier to feed. In mountain environments goats, sheep, or llamas move seasonally according to the vegetation at various heights, and so does the semisedentary farmer. This parallelism has allowed man to tend the smaller kinds of livestock with ease and to domesticate them completely as farming techniques progressed. In any case, the taming of wild animals would make it possible to gather large herds at the edge of the cultivated lands, and later to make use of the pastures of the Steppes. But it was necessary for nomadism to become more productive than at this uncertain stage—that is to say, to become an extremely

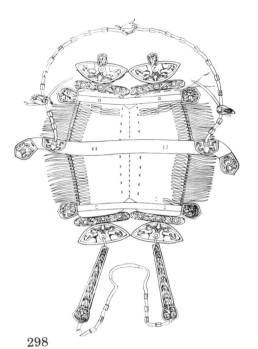

298

specialized mode of life in which men could effectively use very wide expanses where it was not possible for simple pastoral and agricultural communities to settle. A range of animals suitable for grazing in each place (high grass for the horses, short for the sheep and goats), together with vast regions supplying forage in the springtime and early summer, and narrower pastures in which to spend the winter, made the itinerant life possible, along with the appropriate means of transport—vehicles and mounts.

It is certain that the horse had been used as a draft animal as early as the Tripolye culture, in which a mixed agriculture of Neolithic type was practiced: clay models of sledges prove this. And above all, in a tumulus at Storozhevaya Mogila, near Dniepropetrovsk, the vestiges of a wooden wagon with two disk wheels show that the wheel was already known on the Pontic steppe before the 334 third millennium. Similarly at Budakalasz, in Hungary, a tomb contained a model of a four-wheeled 333 wagon, while at Mingechaur, in Azerbaijan, clay models of covered wagons form an archaeological 300 30 find that has been dated at 1800 B.C. This dating gains probability from the fact that in Mesopotamia, around 3000 B.C., the Sumerians had also converted the wagon into a heavy, solid-wheeled chariot of war drawn by onagers. The appearance of the wheel is at present put at about 3650 B.C. in Lower Mesopotamia, and at about 3700 in Transcaucasia, where Soviet archaeologists have discovered as many as twenty-three vehicles.

The wild ass was soon replaced as a means of traction by the more docile and speedy horse. The Hurrians of northern Syria, under the direction of their Indo-European leaders, seem to have harnessed the horse to a lighter, military chariot, whose wheels were perforated and spoked. This engine of war than became an important factor in victory, and it makes its appearance not only in the Near 332 East, and then in Europe, but also in China, where it is to be found as early as the twelfth century B.C.

But fighting with horse-drawn chariots presupposes a well-kept stable and, strictly speaking, battlefields prepared and chosen in advance—in short, types of warfare in which empires and civilizations at the same stage of development confronted one another. Certainly the use of wheeled vehicles is attested by finds of wagons or of their models throughout the Eurasian world from the Bronze Age onward; but these are often types for funerary or ceremonial use—that is to say, for traveling over country by chosen and traditional routes. The famous wooden wagon from Barrow 5 at Pazyryk, which still has 330 its front shaft rigid, proves by this its limited use. The vehicle found at Lchashen (Armenia) had necessitated the cutting of ten thousand different mortises, a fact that implies an abundance of wood and of metal tools.

On the other hand, for drawing vehicles across rough country, the ox had many advantages over the horse: the ox is more surefooted, and this is important when roads are bad. Moreover, the manner of harnessing that was in general use until the Middle Ages was better adapted to the physique of oxen than of horses, for the collar transmitting the pulling power bore too heavily on the windpipe of the horse and so limited the strength he could exert. Lastly, the upkeep of the horse is more expensive: he requires grooming, attention, and, in winter, three times as much food as an ox.

In these conditions the horse-drawn wagon is evidently a luxury of speed, reserved for warfare or for funerals—that is to say, for activities where its tactical or prestige advantages are decisive. For, to transport such heavy loads as the movable dwelling which the covered wagon sheltered, the only rational and economic mode of traction was the ox. The Scythians, according to Herodotus, used these reliable animals to draw their family caravans. (The nomads of the Altai seem to have made more use of tents, yurts, and huts which could be dismantled and which were made of wood, bark, and felt.)

The fact is confirmed by the discovery, in the Altai barrows, of rudimentary yokes, and of vestiges of small, primitive carts with log wheels.

It is, however, difficult to be sure at present whether the nomads domesticated the horse before the ox, simply in order to have mares' milk, and whether riding was originally secondary to the use of these animals as a means of subsistence. Evidence that horses were ridden appears at the end of the second millennium B.C. Thus, at Tell Halaf, a Hurrian relief dating from the fifteenth or fourteenth century shows a warrior on horseback. A thirteenth-century seal depicts a mounted archer. It seems, then, that equitation became current in the Near East after the fourteenth century B.C., and that with these riders came the first of the marauders who took advantage of their mobility to plunder the livestock of the herdsmen. The latter no doubt then reacted by adopting the same means of defence or attack and, with the help of the ecological context, the military impetus brought about the orientation of the people of the Steppes toward a half-pastoral, half-military nomadism, with an increasingly marked tendency toward the highly profitable military supremacy given them by their new means of locomotion. And yet who knows whether the catalyst of these revolutionary changes was not the greater ease with which the predecessors of the cowboy were now able to tend herds of sheep and cattle? On the steppes of eastern Europe and Kazakhstan, bit bars—evidence of the first attempts at mounting the horse—appear as early as the fifteenth and fourteenth centuries B.C.

In any case, the nomad riders—who became idealized as centaurs in the classical Greek mythology—were now in the saddle almost every day and all day and Greek iconography depicts them as seizing everything falling into their hands, including desirable women. The nomads, with their hit-and-run cavalry, became a scourge to the sedentary populations, and subdued them: in summer they undertook long-distance expeditions, right into the heart of the forest regions or of the empires of the Middle East; in winter they crossed the frozen rivers to threaten the settled villages. Ovid, in his *Tristia,* says "very rare is the man who dares to cultivate the countryside, and this poor man labors with one hand, in the other holds a weapon." In the fourth and third centuries B.C., agricultural China, to defend itself against the mounted hordes, built the Great Wall, 1,500 miles long. The same was done in the Ukraine, where, stretching for tens and hundreds of miles the powerful fortifications known as "serpentiform walls," or "Trajan's Ramparts" were raised.

The many peoples of the Steppes, who at first had each had a certain originality in their economy and so in their culture, acquired more unity along with nomadism and its formative virtues, because a life of constant movement, fights, and raids did to some extent facilitate the diffusion of luxury objects, know-how, and inventions: the fruitfulness of peace is only reality at a stage of civilization when war is no longer inevitable, and this was not then the case.

Art, with no chance of emerging in the form of monumental works, and able to assert itself only in objects fabricated in makeshift workshops, became concentrated from then on in the so-called minor sector—the adjective being a chauvinist one used by the established feudal and imperialist societies to exalt their own art, though this was equally a reflection of their own civilization. And so barbarian art distinguishes itself in objects typical of nomadic life: gourds, furniture that can be dismantled, harness for horses, etc. And its masterworks are often made up of assemblages of small elements, which could be made as and when the nomads' peregrinations allowed. At the peak of nomadism, indeed, art was more and more a preserve of foreigners, because the barbarian par excellence had become a man who was exclusively occupied in wars and plundering. In consequence, in spite of the native traditions of the nomads and the taste they had for animal forms treated in their way, the workmanship and style of many art objects betray at this stage Persian, Chinese, or Greek

299

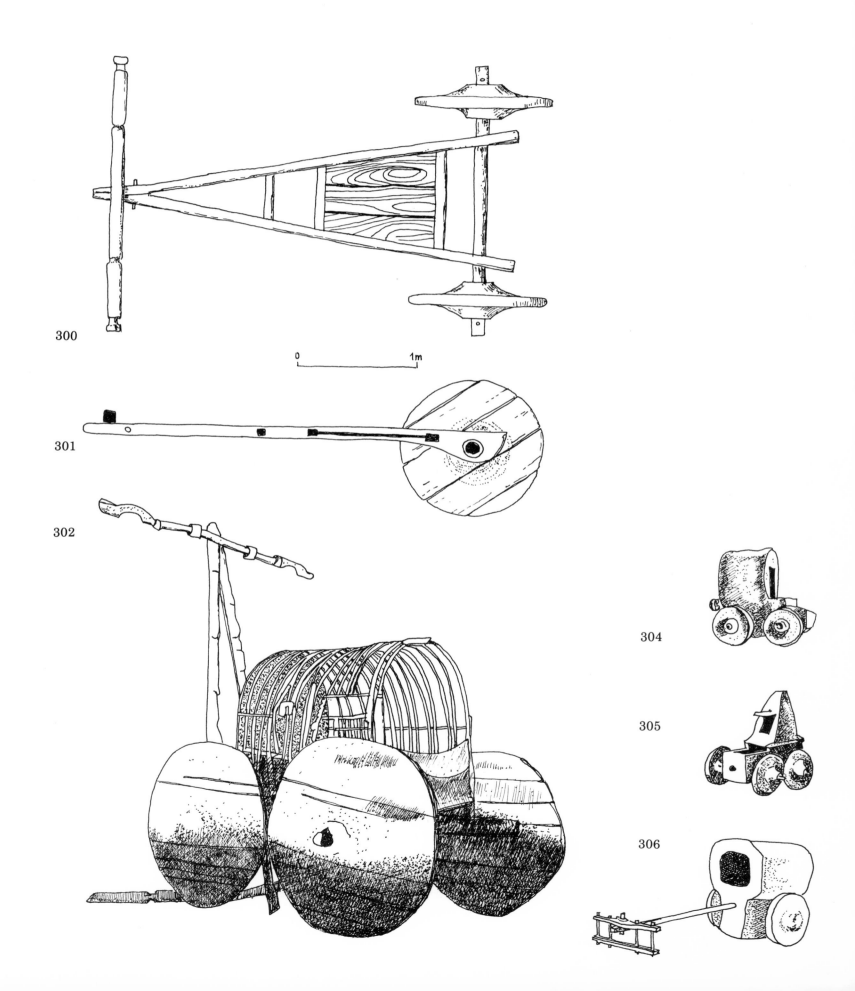

300

0   1m

301

302

304

305

306

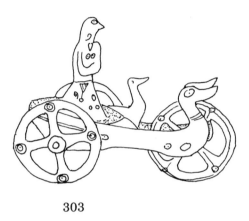

303

347 influences—to mention only the most important. Influences from Central Asia, Afghanistan, and the Greco-Bactrian kingdom are also in evidence.

Lastly, nomadic art further confirms the development of the relationships involved in production and the cultivation of virile and fighting qualities. Woman is by no means a common subject, and this, as Griaznov has rightly pointed out, fits in with the same state of dependence that has been noted in the Siberian burials; gradually, in spite of the sinuous paths taken by progress, this was paid for, in the case we are considering, by a development clearly shown in the tombs of the cultures that are superimposed in the sites on the Steppes—namely, an increasing subjection of woman, which leads to her being sacrificed along with her master, as his companion in his last resting place.

War being thus the factor of power, the Scythians and related nomads were in turn dominated by the Sarmatians who, by using the stirrup, were able to have a better seat on their mount and so could guide it in a close-ranked attacking formation equivalent to a phalanx of cavalry. Then the Hiong-Nu and the Huns completed the armament of the nomad horseman, by equipping him with an extremely powerful curved bow, resulting in a new supremacy.

The progression of these various hordes, driving other peoples before them, precipitated the fall of the Roman Empire. The advance of the Huns into Europe marks the second era of the nomad horsemen, dominated by the men of the Altai and the Mongols. This brings us to the beginnings of the Middle Ages. The bestiary of the Steppes would remain as barbarian as ever, if not more so, to the Christian of agricultural and sedentary lands. And since the ancient authors, Greek or Latin, had already admitted without skepticism the existence of monsters (griffins, sphinxes, sirens, etc.) the Catholic believer—as he saw these barbarians with their languages worthy of the Tower of Babel flooding into his country, and subjected as he was to scholasticism, and convinced that there was nothing that God or the Devil had not been able to create—had no reason to doubt the existence of zoological anomalies, as reported by fables that were more and more obscure. And so the bestiary of the Steppes would end up in the illuminations of Christian manuscripts, and in those hellish monsters which animate tympana and capitals in the medieval cathedrals or grimace as their gargoyles.

But these hordes were no less structured than were the sedentary societies on which they fell. Herodotus noted, in the legendary past of the Sauromatians, that they were supposed to be descended from a class of Scythian ephebes, just as we now know that the Parni did not form a separate people, but were only a class of young Parthians. It has also been pointed out that the length of time spent by Scythians in Near Eastern lands, as reported by the Greek chronicler, is about the same as the period during which a warrior served under the standards of his people.

As regards the neighbors and cousins of the Eurasians, indeed, another example is supplied by Xenophon: the free Persians, who already formed a dominant class, were also divided into age categories. At sixteen and seventeen years of age, the adolescents moved up into the class of the ephebes and were placed under the direction of a personal leader, who was carefully chosen and allowed to conduct vanguard operations in his own way. At twenty-six the young men were admitted into the class of married men, and constituted the bulk of the army. At fifty-two they attained the category of elders, to whom was reserved—since they were supposed to have acquired wisdom and experience—the function of councillors and judges. The same applied to the king, at least at the beginning: he too had to resign his military prerogatives and functions. There is also evidence that a similar social division extended to the Greeks—notably the Spartans.

While communal organization survived in spite of the coming into being of castes, a social structure based on sex or age groups derived efficiency not only from a physical and psychic adaptation to specific elementary tasks, but also from the group's defensive potentialities. Nomadic life, in its military or hunting aspects, adopts or maintains an indispensable discipline in action, and this generally goes with an extremely strict organization as regards the movements of the community from place to place. At the slightest alert, human societies—like those of the monkeys or of the larger herbivores—find it is in their interest to form cohorts in which each individual has his place in accordance with his age, rank, and capabilities.

At the stage of military democracy it seems reasonable to imagine—making use of comparative ethnography—that the nomads were divided into tribes, phratries, and clans, each of which may have had its own animal emblem, drawn from a zoological classification whose purpose was to specify the human one in an imagist—that is to say, mnemonic—way. Apart from the example of Attica, such an organization is known to have existed among the nomadic Huns: they were divided into six eastern and six western *gentes*. Similarly the ancestors of the Uighurs had twelve clans, and the western Turks of the seventh century were grouped into five "Doulou" and five "Nouchibi" tribes.

The archaeological finds also help us to form a precise idea of the appearance, maintenance, and disappearance of various types of social relationship. The burials reveal the more or less eminent status of the dead, the family or communal organization to which they belonged, the degree of equality or inequality between the sexes and age categories, the presence or absence of slaves, and even marks of ownership on certain objects—or else the lack of respect for such ownership as shown by the evidence of robbery, not long after the burial, for instance in the Scythian and Altaic barrows.

The age of nomadic military democracy marks definitively the transition to private ownership of the herds and of the human cattle assigned to look after them, namely the slaves. The descriptive marks of *gens,* tribe, clan, or age category, which besides dress or hairstyle made it possible to place the individual, acquire an ostentatious luxury designed to reinforce the prestige and social standing of their possessor.

In consequence, a smith's qualifications and specialization become the indispensable condition for his work to be properly completed and to find a market. His skill in the mastery of a single material

³⁴⁹ leads at the same time to classicism and purism in his art. And, as Marx noted, although gold and silver are of no value to the manufacturer of common tools of production, these metals nonetheless "have not merely the negative character of superfluous things, meaning things one can do without: ³⁵⁰ their aesthetic qualities make them the natural materials for luxury, adornment, sumptuousness, the requirements of days of festival—in a word the positive form of the superfluous and of wealth . . . . since silver reflects all the rays of light in their original mixture, and gold reflects only the red, the highest power of color. So barbarian art needed the precious metals for the use of the men of power in ³³⁵ its world, since the aesthetic qualities of gold and silver and their suitability for fine workmanship ³³⁸ combine to render the finished products more perfect and more costly. The goldsmith's and silversmith's is the barbarian art par excellence; filigree and gold-and silver-plating were the manifest proof of the value attached to those metals for ornament and luxury, making them as precious as the ambers and stones set in them. Art then concentrated on objects that were small but robust, costly, and in any case easy to wear, transport, or loot.

On the shores of the Black Sea the workshops of various artists—sometimes Iranian, but chiefly ³⁶⁴ Greek—created at that time the celebrated objects of Greco-Scythian art, the gold cups of Kul Oba, ³⁴⁶ the comb from Solokha, the vases from Chertomlyk and Voronezh, etc. The new style, less ornamen³⁴⁷ tal and exuberant, but more realistic and meticulous (though not exempt from a formalism of its own), shows that from now on the aim was to get the maximum effect from a single material. It is a hybrid and Hellenizing art, and is characterized by the importation into Scythia, in the fourth century, of a delicate kind of jewelry, of which the famous earrings with gold pendants found at Theodosia are the typical example. And in the Scythian tomb at Kul Oba the native leader who was buried there had a sword with a gold-plated sheath depicting the symbolic animal fights dear to nomads—a lion and a griffin tearing a stag to pieces, and a leopard attacking a deer; but the top of the sheath was adorned with a lion mask that has above it an inscription in Greek letters, ΠΟΡΝΑΧΟ. This may have been the owner's name or—already—the craftsman's signature, unless indeed the word has to do with the object's function or decoration.

Scythian art, tied as it was to a nomadic and warlike economy that both used and repudiated a commerce reserved for foreigners, now moved toward this luxurious and decorative type of work. The barbarians, not having any accounts and commercial reports to transcribe, did not need to possess or create a precise code, such as for instance an elementary picto-ideographic one—still less a syllabic writing of their own, which would indeed have had to compete with the ones in use among their more advanced neighbors. Toward the fourth and third centuries B.C. the Scythian art of the Black Sea region thus tends naturally toward a graphic schematization of its forms, which makes them more of a linear ornamentation than a pictoscript.

For, the fewer realistic features this art has (while not emerging into writing), the more elements ³⁷⁶ of Greek origin it accumulates: these stifle it and make it degenerate into a local version of Hellenistic ³⁷⁸ art. In contrast, the animal style continues to flourish in Siberia, keeping its lyricism, persisting and perfecting itself in neighboring directions, in the hands of the Sarmatians and the Huns, who would then take over from the Scythians. Thanks to the great invasions, barbarian art would set its own ⁸⁸ mark on Western medieval art, spreading into those peninsulas of the Eurasian world, France, Spain, and Italy, where the toponymic trace of these ethnic contributions would survive in place-names like the French Sermaize (Sarmaticum).

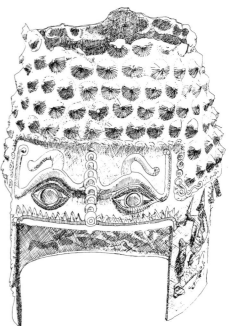

307

Conclusion

Barbarian art—a product of man, a mode of expression and materialization for his thinking, a reflection of his problems and states of knowledge—has shown us, by means of the Eurasian example, that it was essentially like man himself: that is to say, it was at every instant the same as or similar to its fellows, and yet different, irreversible in the evolution of its form and content.

Besides, graphic and plastic art is always a material activity, partly because it is sensory, cerebral, and manual, partly because of the tools and materials used for it, characteristic as these are of a given stage of civilization which, moreover, implies that the artist is specialized or is anonymous. The product is therefore at every point the fruit and witness of its time. "It creates a public sensitive to art and capable of enjoying beauty" (K. Marx, *Contribution to the Critique of Political Education*).

As a historical phenomenon bound up with the millennia-long education of the senses, art makes its appearance as soon as men not only have something to say to each other in the present, but intend also to express a message that must defy age and space. And yet the nature and content of the work produced change inevitably in accordance with experience and development, because the signifier, being less strictly abstract than mathematics, necessarily follows technical developments—not only those of writing, but also those which directly condition ways of life and affect it at least by ricochet.

So barbarian art evolves, like other arts, dialectically, since it reflects the phenomena, problems, and human relationships of a definite society, their mutual realtions and conditionings as well as their appearance and disappearance. For this code, though remaining to some extent necessarily the same, if only in order to render the new realities comprehensible by means of habitual and conventional signs, is nonetheless in the long run influenced by these realities; that is to say, it follows—not with absolute synchronism, but with greater or less delay—the structural changes of society, of its productive forces and their intrinsic relationships. What is involved, therefore, is not so much the conventional aspect of the form of expression as this form itself, which has to be renewed because, in this way, in a context now modified, it seems more efficacious, universal, and mnemonic than the one that has become anachronistic.

As a mode of expression that is closely attached to the communicated message by reason of an extremely close interlocking of form and content, art therefore distinguishes itself as fundamentally from language as from any exclusive ideological superstructure. Its nature as a sign-image produces its originality. Thus the nomad chieftain who wears an intricately worked gold buckle on his belt will have no need to say: "I am rich and powerful"—the ornament, by its workmanship and material, will speak more convincingly than words, the work itself having even become eminently salable.

The course of art therefore enables us the better to understand human nature and, by our various means of communication, to advance its ways of acting on itself and against the nature external to it. The present inhabitants of the Steppes or of Eurasia, reflecting on the why and wherefore of their verbal or plastic signs, have thus no feeling of having been either more or less barbarian than the other peoples of the earth. It is, for example, not profitless to study how each people uses animal metaphors in its national language, and how frequently it employs beasts for its emblems. And it is by no means fruitless, in order to avoid an alienating idealization of them, to recognize the practical sense of origin of our conventional social customs and gestures, the time-honored rules of the ancient arts, of which the present-day ones are the heirs—and this even in the elements they may reject, because of that liberation which the invention of writing brought. The limiting taboos and canons of religion and sacred art have then little chance of making their appearance.

A book devoted to popular traditions would be insufficient to illustrate even the formal, decorative, and folklore traces bequeathed by the Scythian nomads to—most of all—the various symbolic codes belonging to the populations of the USSR and neighboring countries. The same might be said of the civilizations that preceded them or were their neighbors and successors.

By moving constantly further back toward the sources of humanity and by exercising real detective tenacity and skill, the archaeologist, art historian, and ethnologist, who often use the most modern and scientific means and methods, are helping to dissect man's past, the better to analyze the present and to build the future—not only in the field of their own investigations, but also to the advantage of the other sciences, techniques, and disciplines: they are developing these by setting them new problems, sometimes even supplying them with fresh data.

And so these objects of an extremely localized art, drawn from the frozen and dusty depths of the Siberian barrows, are no less indispensable than others to the knowledge of man. The angle of attack from which they are approached in this book, through both text and reproductions, is designed to contribute to this. The publisher and author, who have sometimes perhaps imprudently departed from the beaten tracks, would already be satisfied if—since *errare humanum est*—their more disputable views should prove more interesting than the well-worn themes: should, that is, prove fruitful through the searching criticisms they may provoke.

Besides, even should the result be meager, there would always remain the originals and the reproductions of the fine objects presented. These belong essentially to the museums of Soviet Russia, headed by the Hermitage. For, since the Revolution, archaeology in the USSR has benefited from aid commensurate with its results, and this explains the very considerable number of prehistoric finds in expanses of territories so thinly populated. All the pieces thus recovered are then lovingly restored, protected, and conserved by the community—that is, none of them can be seized upon for the private collections of the rich. So, in the last resort, it is thanks to the civic sense and government of the citizens of that country that we have been able, so we hope, to give the reader a taste for the barbarian arts of their ancestors.

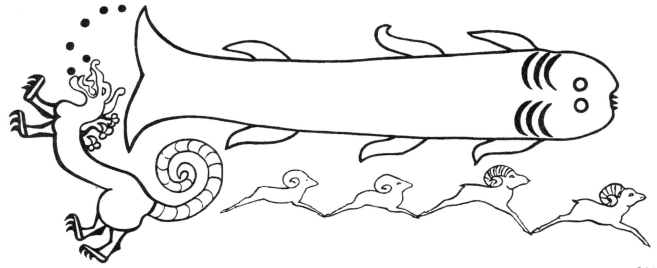

308

309

310

311

312

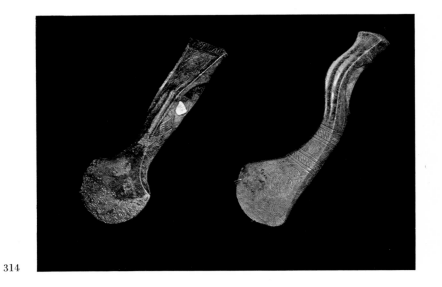

314

313

315

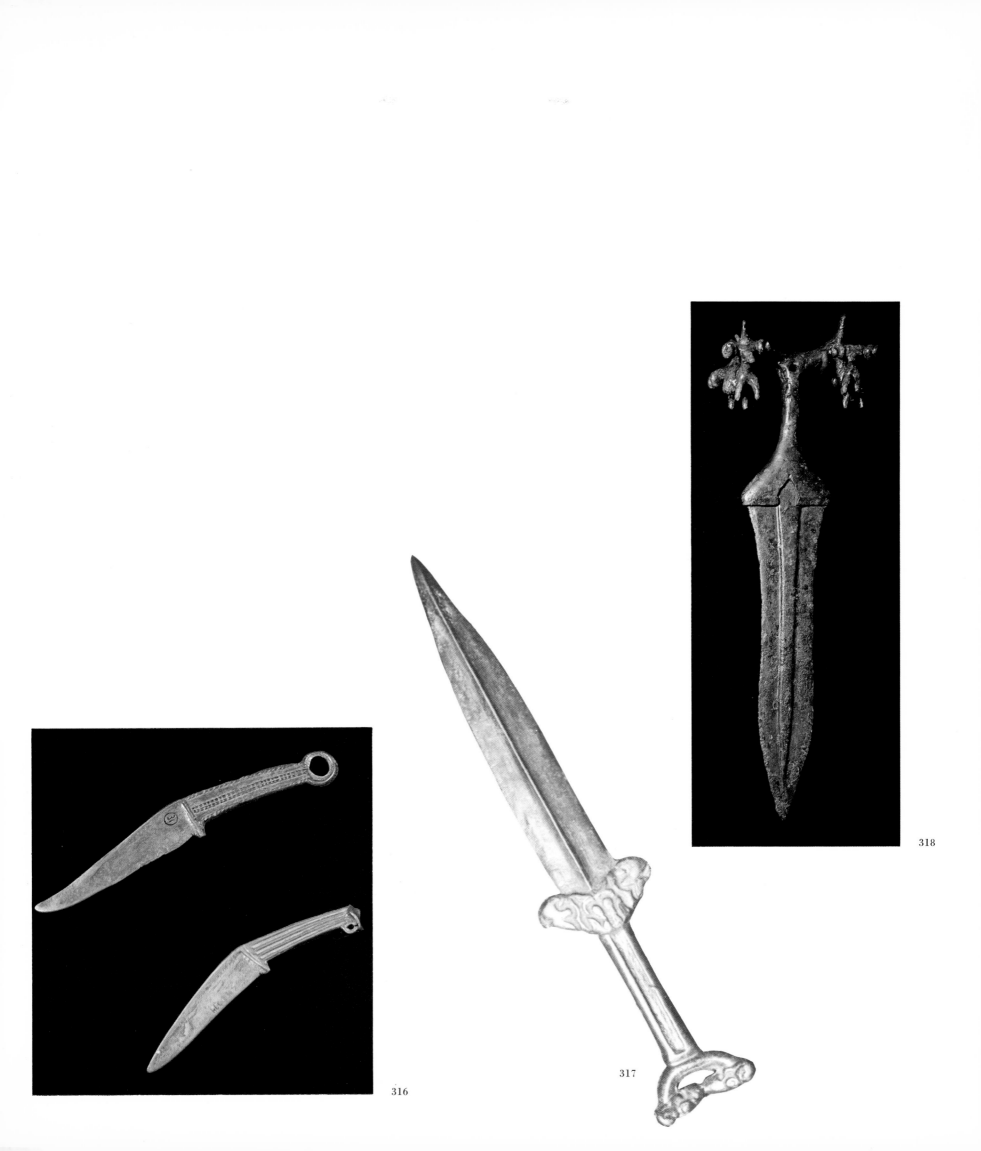

316

317

318

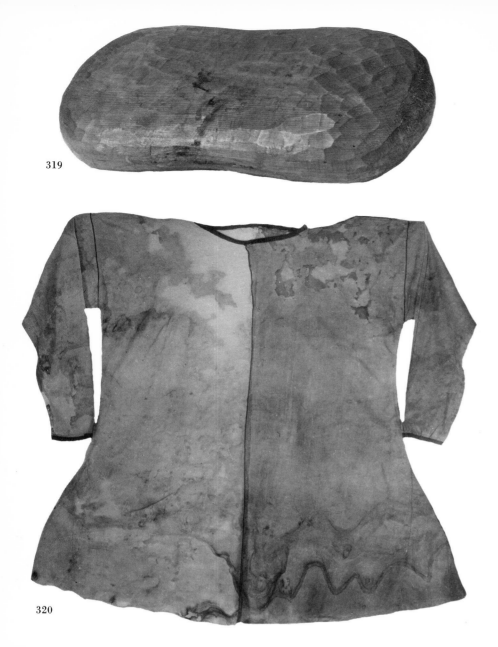

319

320

323

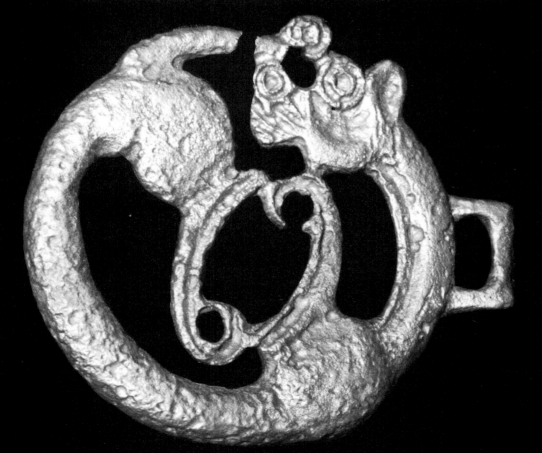

321

322

325

324

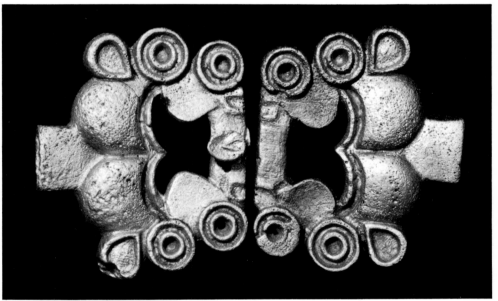

326

327

328

329

330

331

332

333 334 ▶

335

336

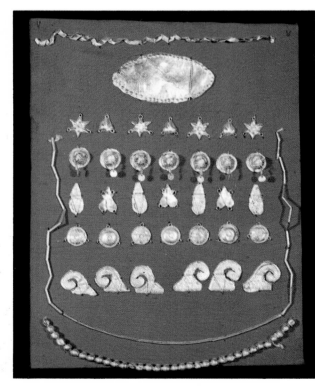

337

338

339

340

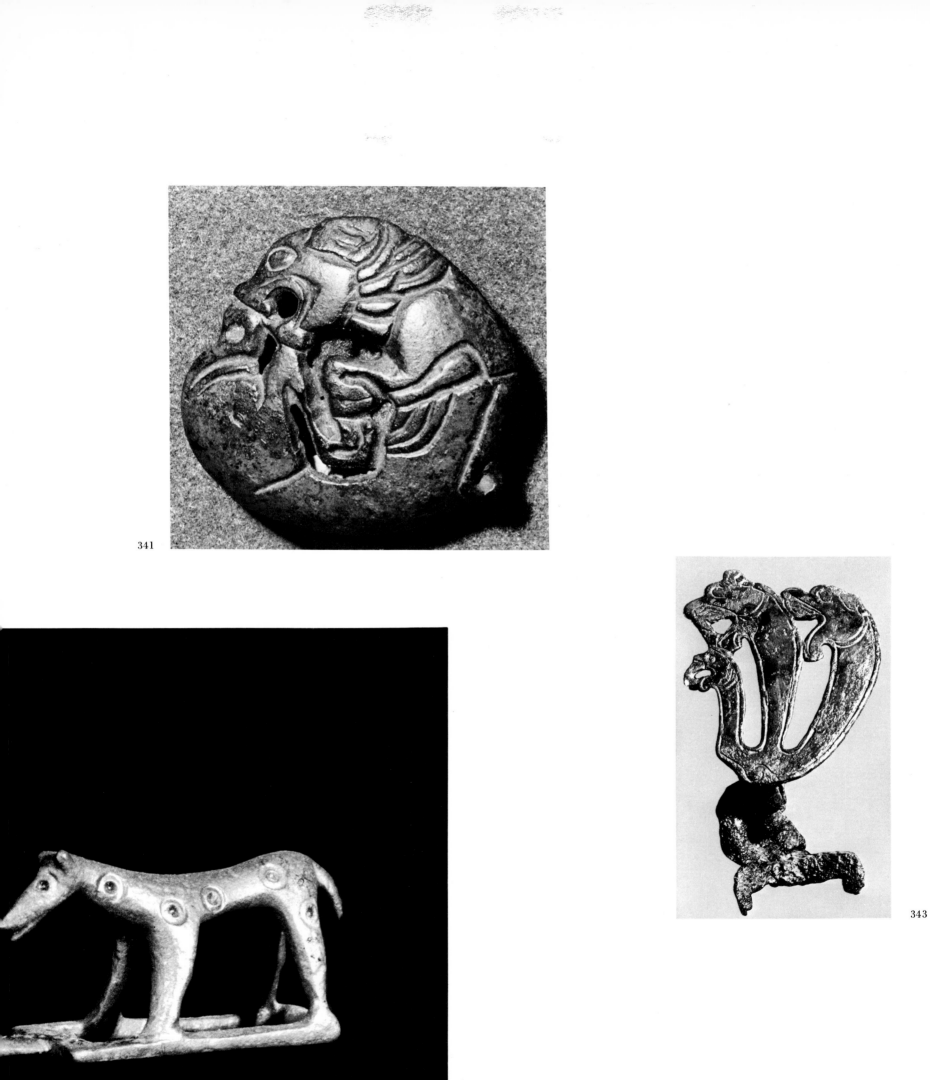

341

342

343

344

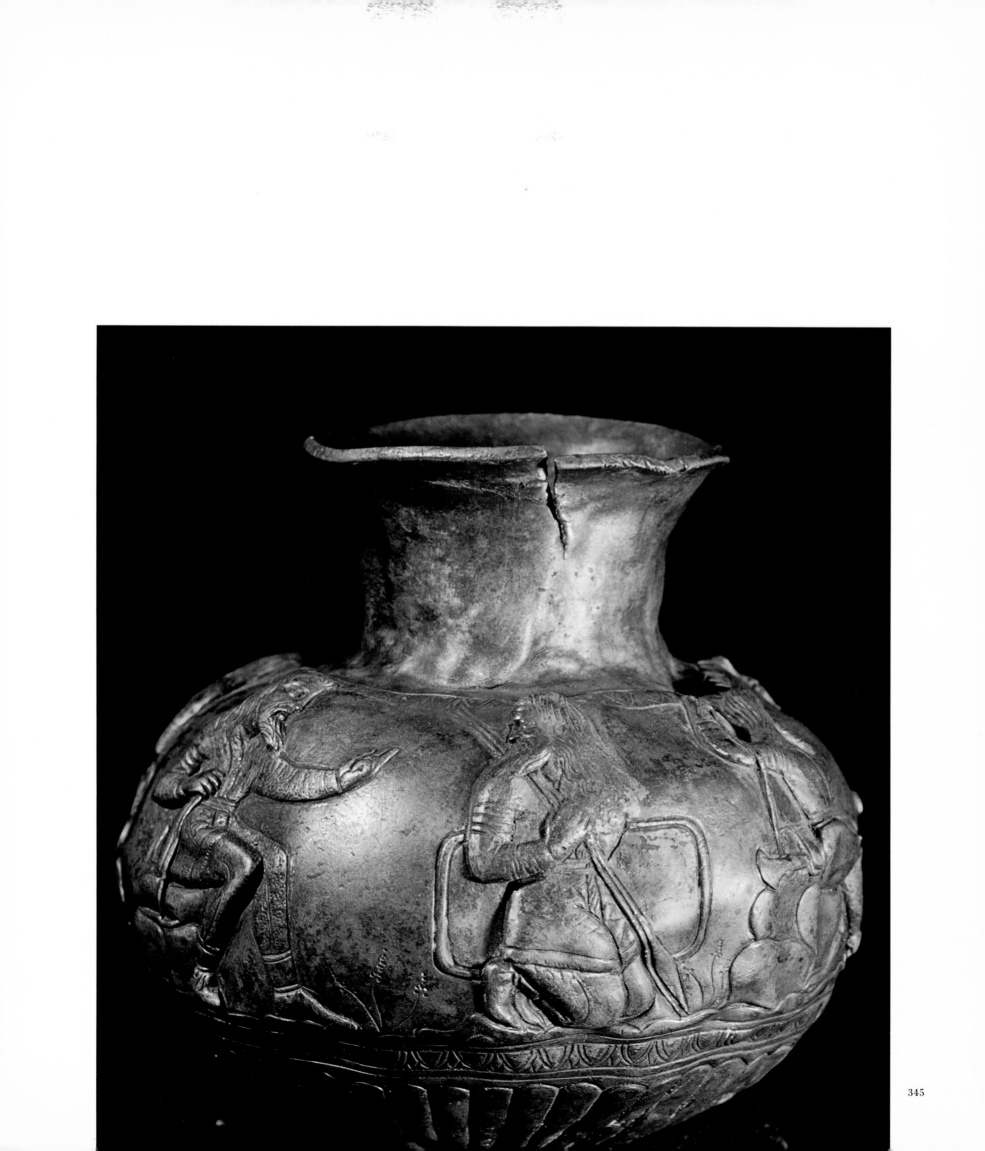

346

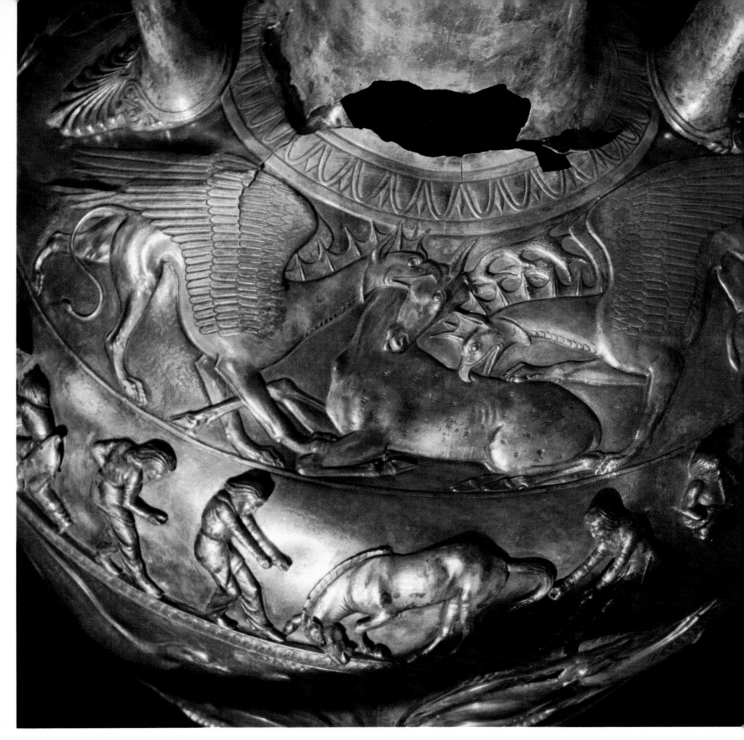

347

348

349

350

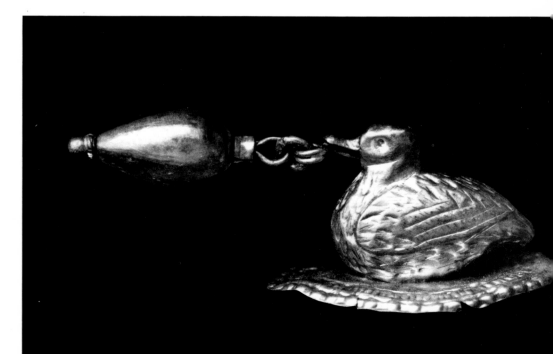

351

352

355

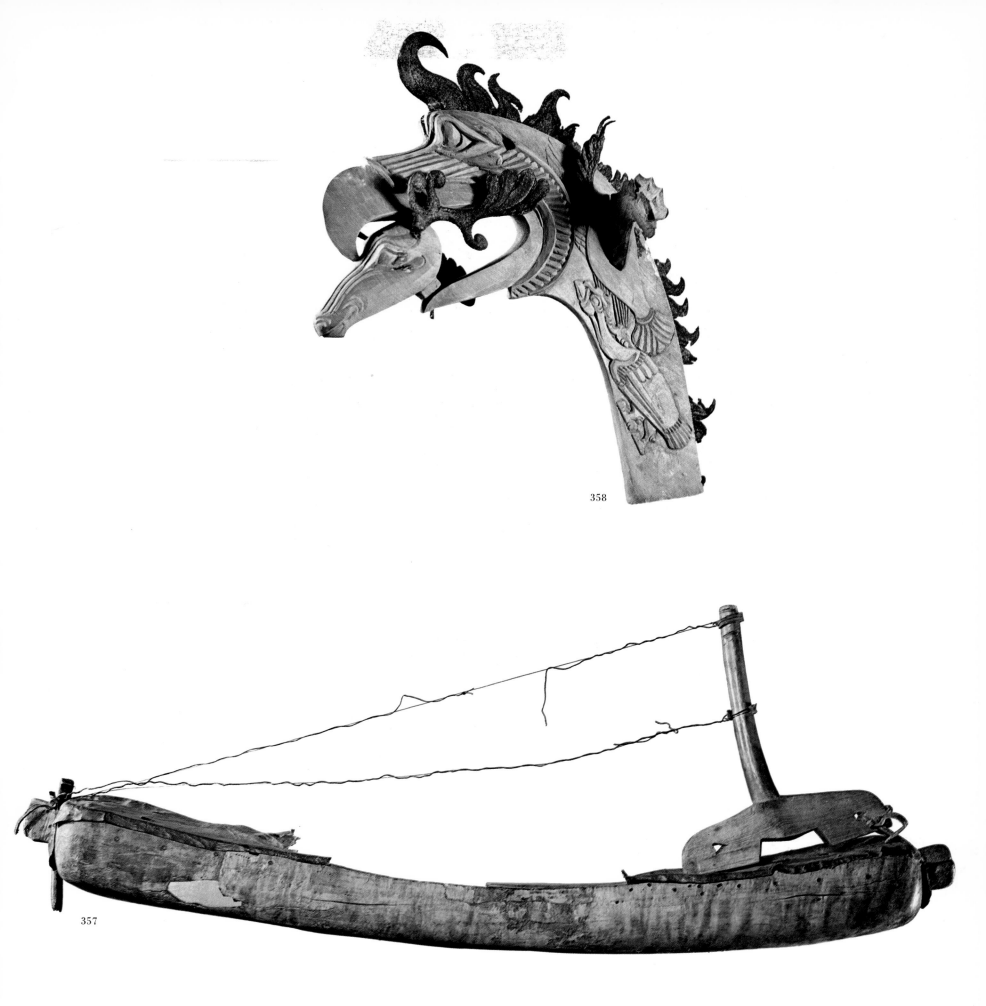

358

357

360

359

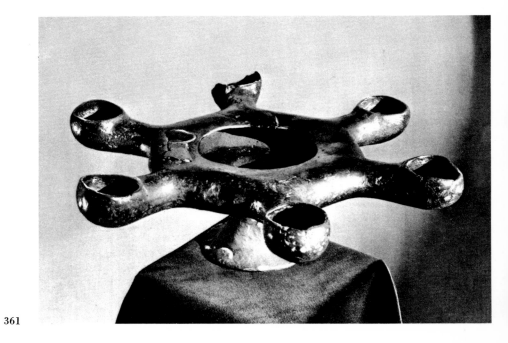

361

364

362   363

365

366

367

369

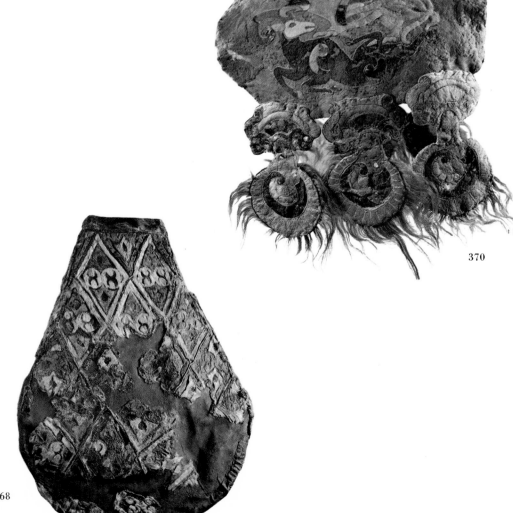

370

368

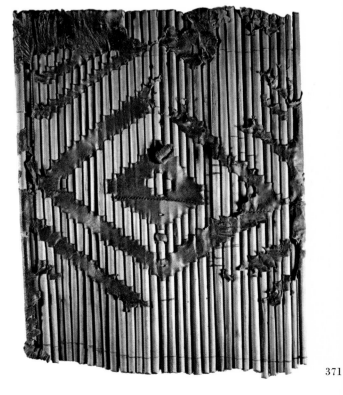

371

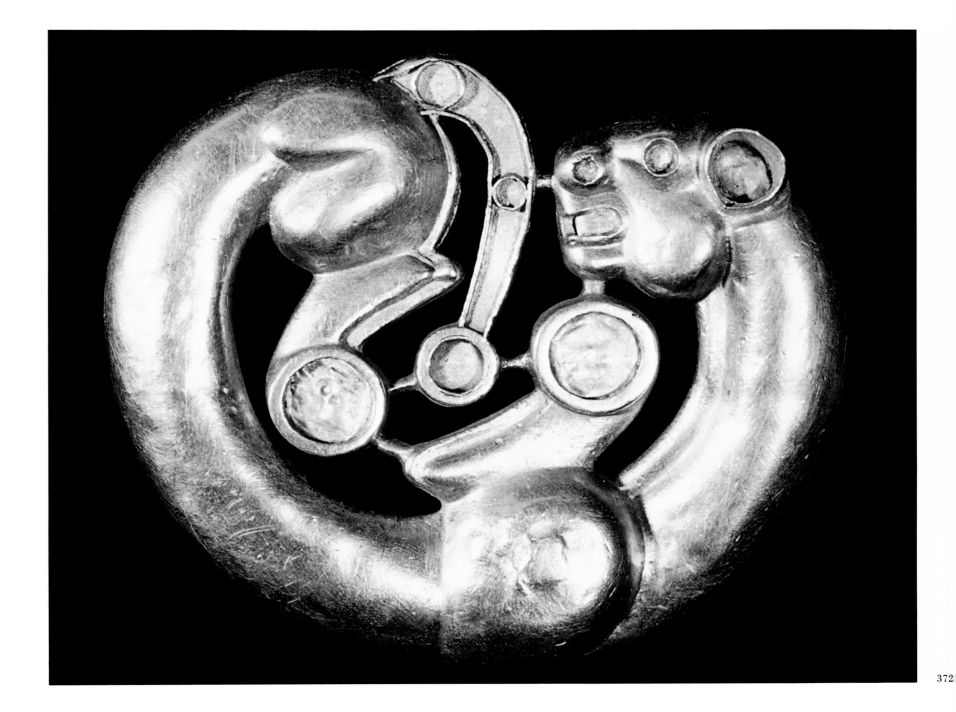

372

374

376

377

378

NOTES ON THE ILLUSTRATIONS

—The Barbarian Modes of Expression —

1 Boar. Bronze. Ninth or eighth century B.C. Private collection, Tehran. After R. Ghirshman.

2 Multipede boar starting from cover. Paleolithic art. Altamira, Spain. After A. Laming.

3 An ideographic aggregate, as is clear from the monstrous constituents: a stag's antlers, a goat's beard, an impressive number of horse's feet, no doubt to convey the idea of speed. Agighiol, detail from vase no. 1. Thraco-Gaetic art, Romania. (See also figs. 222 and 227.)

    These multipede steeds make one think of the Kirghiz stories in which remarkable horses are described as having six, seven, or eight feet.

4 Gold plaque intended to decorate a garment. A winged boar. Fifth or fourth century B.C. Barrow 2, Kerch. Ashmolean Museum, Oxford.

5 An ideographic aggregate. A multipede stag with an ibex beard and horse's hoofs. Agighiol, vase no. 2. Thraco-Gaetic art, Romania. (See also figs. 228 and 240.)

6 Gold plaque 3¾" high, from one of the wooden rhytons from the Seven Brothers Barrows, Kuban. Greco-Scythian style. An ibex being attacked by a winged feline is a characteristic barbarian theme, but it is here treated with a certain realism which betrays a Hellenic influence.

7 Fight, in typical animal style, on a felt hanging: a winged griffin is attacking an elk. Probably of Sarmatian inspiration. Another part of the hanging is decorated with a yak and a lion, and the choice of animals and style suggest Asiatic and Chinese influence. From Noin Ula, on the Selenga River, which flows into Lake Baikal.

    Several tombs have been discovered there. The most remarkable finds come from the sixth. They include a felt hanging or carpet with Chinese motifs, other hangings adorned with tigers embroidered in the same style, or depicting tortoises with grass in their mouths with, in the center, fish and aquatic plants—some even decorated with birds and fishes in air and water.

8 and 9 Bronze Age paintings in ocher, on islands in the Sea of Bratsk, Siberia. Station at Manzi village, near Bratsk.

10 Engraving on the emblematic sword from Medgidia, Romania. On account of its akinakes (dagger) form, this object is considered to be Thraco-Gaetic with Scythian or Persian influence. Ibex are depicted on the sheath (not shown here); the pommel is decorated with an engraving of a bird of prey with, in its beak, a serpent held by the head.

    In its most literal, i.e., warlike, interpretation, this theme seems appropriate to a weapon: such an object, being designed at least to wound, hardly calls for the image of a peaceful, bleating lamb, except insofar as the akinakes may have been used to protect "the widow and the orphan." So the decoration on this dagger may be considered as being in close harmony with its military function.

    But is this the only possible, or the most subtle and adequate, association between the engraving and the object? The beak of the bird of prey is a "gripper," as indeed the hand is in popular language, for the bird seizes with its mandibles and not with hands; and the "pommel"—a word derived from blow, another image!—by which one takes hold of the weapon, is equivalent to the reptile's head which the bird is seizing, i.e., the principle and active extremity, commanding, in the one case, the sword's short blade, and in the other the thick body of the snake. The two elements are strangely similar, with their elongated form and deadly bite. In other words, the engraving might suggest the idea of a firm grasping of the pommel which it decorates.

But are there not other possible interpretations? And more probable ones? Imagination becomes sovereign when it strays into the mire of symbolism—where the very nature of barbarian art and that of the early proto-picto-ideograms do make it necessary to penetrate. (See also fig. 295.)

11 Drawings at the mountain station of Barun-Turen. The image, here reversed, might be entitled: Archer on horseback pursuing two stags. The original might bear the title: Two stags pursued by an archer on horseback.

Siberia, Bronze Age or Iron Age.

12 Copper plaque engraved with griffins. Barrow 2, Pazyryk.

13 Lion's head decorating a saddle-rug from Barrow 1, Pazyryk.

14 Engraved copper plaque. Barrow 2, Pazyryk.

15 Ram's head decorating a saddle-rug from Barrow 1, Pazyryk.

16 Griffins fighting: decoration from a saddle-rug from Barrow 1, Pazyryk.

17 Decoration in the form of roosters' heads on mane hood forming part of a ceremonial caparison. Barrow 1, Pazyryk.

18 Roosters cut out of leather, decorating a terra cotta bottle. Barrow 2, Pazyryk.

19 Carpet from Pazyryk, decorated with a succession of lions. Barrow 5. There are similar felines on Assyrian low reliefs, and they are particularly numerous in Achaemenid Persian art. Hence a dating which cannot be later than the fifth century B.C.

The technique of depicting the muscles with "apples and pears" and with "dots and commas" takes up that of the enameled bricks of Susa—that is, of classic Achaemenid art.

20 Well-known Paleolithic statuette, in the Aurignacian style. Mammoth ivory, height 4⅜". Thirtieth to twenty-fifth millennium B.C. From Kostienki (Voronezh), excavations by P.P. Efimenko, 1936. Museum of Anthropology and Ethnography of the Academy of Sciences, Leningrad.

21 For comparison: Aurignacian Venus from Balzi Rossi, Ventimiglia. Museum of Saint-Germain-en-Laye.

22 Statuette from Sireuil, near Les Eyzies (Dordogne). Closely related to the Venus of Tursac. Museum of Saint-Germain-en-Laye.

23 Aurignacian Venus from Balzi Rossi, Ventimiglia. Museum of Saint-Germain-en-Laye.

24 Aurignacian Venus from Balzi Rossi, Ventimiglia. Museum of Saint-Germain-en-Laye.

25 Venus of Willendorf (Austria). Museum of Saint-Germain-en-Laye.

26 Fragment of a spatula, Middle Magdalenian period. Two breasts or nipples, barely sketched, and a real but unemphatic male organ combine with an elongated body which, in striking contrast to the rounded shapes of the other figurines shown here, asserts a masculine morphology. From Bruniquel, Tarn-et-Garonne. Museum of Saint-Germainen-Laye.

27 Head of an elk. Bone, height 15¾". Neolithic, third millennium B.C. From a tomb at Oleniy Ostrov (Lake Onega). Excavations by V.I. Ravdonikas, 1936-38. Museum of Anthropology and Ethnography of the Academy of Sciences, Leningrad.

28 Female statuette in clay, 5½ × 9½". Chalcolithic, second half of fourth millennium B.C. Excavations by I.N. Khoplin, 1957, at Ialangach-Depe (southern Turkestan.) Hermitage Museum, Leningrad.

29 Detail from a massive gold necklace. This comes from the Scythian tomb at Ordzonikidze, near Nikopol, which is considered the richest funerary treasure of the fifth century B.C., since about 520 gold objects were found there. The enamel ornamentation on the necklace has retained the full freshness of its colors. Figures 33 to 37 show the whole necklace. The find was made by A. Leskov in 1969.

At both extremities it ends in lion heads. In all languages the word "head" has an analogical and technical sense, to describe the upper or end part of certain things and of many objects, this part being generally more or less swollen and spherical, so that its shape reinforces the comparison. We speak, for instance, of the head of a pin, of a screw that has lost its head, of the head of the femur, of an ax head, etc.

30 Ram's head ornament, with a tenon at the back. Bronze, 1⅛ × 2". Tagar culture, fifth or fourth century B.C. From Krivaja (Minusinsk Basin). A chance find, in the I. Lopatin Collection. Hermitage Museum, Leningrad.

31 Ornamental plaque depicting a carnivore; on its reverse side it has two studs to attach it. Bronze, 1¾ × 3½". Tagar culture, fifth or fourth century B.C. From Pavlovshchina (Krasnoyarsk). I. Lopatin Collection, Hermitage Museum, Leningrad.

32 Drinking horn (or rhyton) adorned with a ram's head, found by V. Bidzilya in 1969, in the tomb of Gaimanova Mogila at Balky (banks of the Dnieper, southern Ukraine). Fourth century B.C.
The use of the rhyton was in favor in Media in the eighth to seventh centuries B.C.

33-37 Elements from the Scythian tomb at Ordzonikidze, near Nikopol (southern Ukraine), the richest Scythian funerary treasure of the fifth century B.C.

The small gold plaques covered the dead man's quiver or adorned the covering of his corpse. The animal subjects include: boars depicted as lying down, heavy, seemingly pressed down on their tucked-in feet and with their snouts lowered (a sign of fear), and hounds attacking with menacing fangs; also a leopard, its body shown in profile and its jowl full face, mauling a man's head. Above the lower plaques from the quiver, there is another bearing the effigy of a stag.

The Scythian representations of these various animals could be used as a quasi-ideographic composition to illustrate an epic poem of the Narts (legendary ancestors of the Ossetians), in which men are allegorized by means of typical animals:

He has tracked down great boars . . . .
His fierce hounds with their huge fangs
Attack them from all sides.
To aid the boars . . . .
From the top of the mountain
Has sprung a young leopard,
Agile, with flashing eyes . . . .
Plainly the hounds with the huge fangs
Now will not escape.

It is in fact a symbolic narration concerning the old heroes Uryzmaegt and Haemys, who were saved by the young Batradz.

Even if there be no relation of whole or part with the metaphors of that poem, the symbolism of the animals seems clear from a glance at the plaques: one has the impression that the leopard mauling a human head and another feline attacking a stag are two variants, the one anthropomorphic and the other zoomorphic, for one of the protagonists in the struggle. Another legend of the Narts describes the foolhardy Batradz thus: "the stag has himself come under the ax," to signify the danger that threatens the hero.

38 Female statuette. Coiffure with ringlet and tresses, necklace and (?) dress ornaments, all schematic. Clay, $4\frac{3}{8} \times 6\frac{1}{4}$." Chalcolithic, beginning of third millennium B.C. From Kara-Depe (southern Turkestan). Excavations by V.M. Masson, 1957. Hermitage Museum, Leningrad.

The bosses remind us of those worn on the shoulders of similar Mesopotamian figurines (found at Ur and Eridu) of practically the same dimensions ($5\frac{1}{2}$ and $6\frac{1}{4}$"), dating from the fourth millennium (Obeid period).

39-41 Three busts from female statuettes. Clay, $2\frac{1}{4}$", $2\frac{3}{8}$", and 2" high. Bronze Age, beginning of second millennium B.C. From Khazpuz-Depe (Turkmenia). Excavations by V.I. Sarianid. Institute of Archaeology of the Academy of Sciences, Moscow.

Similar pieces, with a decoration using bosses and in so-called carboniferous pottery have been found in the Elburz region of Persia and are dated at 2400-2200 B.C.

42 Female statuette. Clay, height $9\frac{1}{2}$". Chalcolithic culture of the Ukraine: Tripolye II. Second half of third millennium B.C. From Vykhvatintsy (Moldavia). Excavations by T.S. Passek. Historical Institute of the Academy of Sciences of Moldavia, Kichinev.

Note the dissymmetry of the breasts. Other figurines were found at the same site. The clay often contains grains of wheat. The importance of women and rarity of men are characteristic of the sculpture of a farming society.

43 Harness ornament in the form of a lion's head. Bronze, $2\frac{3}{8} \times 3$". Scythian animal art of the Crimea, fifth century B.C. From Tomb 14 of Barrow 32 at Nymphea (Kerch, Crimea). Excavations by A.E. Lutsenko. Hermitage Museum, Leningrad.

Note the incorrect placing of the canines, which is unusual in purely barbarian art.

44 Paleolithic sling, on which the leaping horse stresses the object's function. In a number of cases the art of the Eurasian nomads seems to convey such correlations between the motif and the object that bears it. Thus Pazyryk yielded a whip-handle, of which one end has on it the image of a hunting feline and the other shows us the head of a horse that is being pursued. There is necessarily a semantic relationship between this object's function and the animal figures decorating it, which illustrates the usefulness of the whip in increasing the speed of the horse: it is as though the horse's desperate flight depended on the bite of the feline predator. There are expressions in modern English and French that can contain a similar meaning, for example "to give a man the cat"—*donner le fouet*—the cat-o'-nine-tails being the most barbarous and medieval type of whip.

Another instance of the same spirit: the airy leap of the vicuña, which was thought to be as swift as the Indian's arrow or as the flight of shooting stars, explains how the Aymaras of Lake Titicaca came to regard meteorites as the mothers of the graceful vicuñas "with their lightning leap like that of the shooting stars." This Pre-Colombian myth of genesis illustrates how abstraction leads to idealist aberrations when a simple verbal image is taken literally.

Extrapolating from this to the art of the Steppes, one may safely admit that the representations of animals on saddlebows and seats, or on shabracks, sometimes have an ideographic relationship with the objects that bear them, and this should make possible a better understanding of the Scythian language.

45 Bison carved on a reindeer's antler and hyena on fragment of an ivory sling. Cave of La Madeleine (Dordogne). The attitudes are typical of a quarry's uneasiness and of the predator's readiness to pounce.

46 Harness ornament in the form of a lion's head. Bronze, $2 \times 3\frac{1}{2}$". Scythian animal art of Taman, fifth century B.C. From the Seven Brothers Barrows, Kuban (northern Caucasus). Excavations by V.G. Tiesenhausen, 1875. Hermitage Museum, Leningrad.

47 Figures of sheep, Greco-Scythian art.

48 Harness ornament in the form of the head of a bird of prey. Bronze, $1\frac{1}{8} \times 1\frac{5}{8}$". Scythian animal art of the Crimea, fifth century B.C. Excavations by A.E. Lutsenko. Hermitage Museum, Leningrad.

   In the Ossetian legends about the Narts the heroes are often compared to birds of prey. "Voice of falcon, cry of eagle, Soslan took charge of the troops of the Narts," says one of them, and another: "Then Soslan, like a kite rising from the high grass, emerged from the cloud," for that prompt rescuer possessed "a horse swift as a cloud, impetuous as the tempest."

49 Woodcarvings, decorating the lidded coffin found in Barrow 2, Bashadar. Total length of coffin, 10' 2".

50 Head of a mountain ram, decorating a bridle. From Pazyryk.

51 Ornament of a saddle pommel. Wood, $4\frac{3}{8} \times 7\frac{7}{8}$", treated and covered as a gilt eagle-griffin on a red felt basis. Fifth to fourth century B.C. From Barrow 2, Bashadar. Excavations by S.I. Rudenko, 1950. Hermitage Museum, Leningrad. There are many analogies with later Sarmatian objects.

52 and 53 Saddle pendants. From Pazyryk 1.

   A ram's head seized by a fish—in this case flesh-eating and with a tapering body, possibly of the eelpout kind. In Altaic art the sheep is, systematically, the victim of predators: doubtless it allegorizes some age class or tribe of mountain people dominated by the powerful barbarians, who are themselves allegorized by griffins, "guardians of the gold"—that is to say, men possessing not only that metal but also cattle and herdsmen or slaves.

54 Head of statuette. Clay, height $2\frac{3}{8}$". Tripolye culture, second half of third millennium B.C. Vykhvatintsy (Moldavia). Excavations by T.S. Passek. Historical Institute of the Academy of Sciences of Moldavia, Kichinev.

55 Horse, from Airum (Noemberian, Armenia). $1\frac{5}{8} \times 2\frac{5}{8} \times \frac{1}{2}$". Seventh to sixth century B.C.

56 Wolf, from Airum (Noemberian, Armenia). $1\frac{1}{4} \times 2\frac{3}{8} \times \frac{1}{2}$". Seventh to sixth century B.C.

57 Statuette of a zebu from Talin (Armenia). Bronze, $2\frac{3}{8} \times 2\frac{3}{4} \times \frac{7}{8}$".

58 Bull, from Airum (Noemberian, Armenia). $2 \times 3 \times \frac{3}{4}$". Seventh to sixth century B.C.

59 Statuette of a stag, from Kamo (Armenia). Bronze, $1\frac{5}{8} \times 2\frac{3}{8} \times \frac{3}{8}$". Tenth century B.C.

60 Handle in the form of the head of a bird of prey or raven, to hold a wooden vase. Gold, diameter of vase, $3\frac{1}{4}$". Greek art of the forest-steppe, fourth to third century B.C. From Barrow 2 (Chastye) at Voronezh. Excavations by P.D. Liberov, 1954. Archaeological Institute of the Academy of Sciences, Moscow.

61 Harness ornament in the form of a ram's head. Bronze, height $1\frac{1}{8}$". Scythian animal art of the Crimea, fifth century B.C. From Ak-Burun barrow (Kerch, Crimea). Found by A.E. Lutsenko. Hermitage Museum, Leningrad.

62 and 64   Two plaques decorated with the griffin motif. Gold, 2¼ × 2¼". Mixed art of Taman, end of fourth century B.C. From one of the Five Brothers barrows (Rostov-on-Don). Excavations by V.P. Shilov, 1959. Regional Museum of Rostov-on-Don.

63   Plaque from a belt. A fantastic winged animal, with a feline head and antelope horns, is attacking a horse. Gold, 5½ ounces, 5 × 3⅛". Scytho-Siberian art, fourth to third century B.C. (Siberian Collection of Peter the Great.) Hermitage Museum, Leningrad.

65 and 66   Two figures of lions decorating the material of a funerary canopy. Gold, 2⅜ × 1¼" and 2 × 1". Third millennium B.C. From the barrow at Maikop (northern Caucasus). Excavations by N.I. Veselovsky, 1897. Hermitage Museum, Leningrad.

67   Wooden cup with a handle made of horn in the shape of a horse's hoof. From Pazyryk 3. Fifth or fourth century B.C.

Hand or foot are animal metaphors to designate the parts of man-made objects by which they are picked up and held. We still talk of a glass as having a foot, and this barbarian receptacle might properly be called a "cup with a hoof." Nomadic art offers several examples of the kind: for instance the bars from horses' bits from Great Blisnitza and from Ak-Burun have a horse's hoof or the clawed foot of a bird of prey.

68   Tiger's head, detail of a bridle. Wood. Fifth to fourth century B.C. From Tuekta 1, Altai.

69   Psalium with ring from horse's bit. Bronze and iron. Height 3½". Scythian animal art, end of fourth to beginning of third century B.C. From the burial at Elisavetinskaya (Krasnodar). Excavations by N.I. Veselovsky, 1917. Hermitage Museum, Leningrad.

70   Tiger's head. Wood. Scytho-Altaic art.

The comparison of a hero to a feline is very widespread, In the Kirghiz epics, the woman in love with that hero of the Steppes, the valiant Töshtük, calls him "my lion, my hero," while his comrades describe him as a "lion among men," the heroes being also, elsewhere, described as "blue tigers."

Thousands of miles away and at the end of the last century, King Glêlê of Dahomey was still represented as a lion-cub, to illustrate one of his parables: "I am the lion-cub who spreads terror on all sides as soon as his teeth have grown." This king was also represented as a man with the head of a lion or tiger. But his successor, Béhanzin, was depicted as a shark-man, an allusion to a phrase in which he compared himself to the shark that disturbs the rudder, the purpose being to express his intention to smash the French expeditionary force then landing at Cotonou (but unfortunately for him this force was not—to use a contemporary Chinese metapor—a "paper tiger").

We are reminded also of the comparisons with animals that were current in Sumerian imagery. The hymn of Shulgi, a king belonging to an ancient dynasty of Ur., provides a significant example:

> *I, the king, from my mother's breast I have been a hero,*
> *I, Shulgi, from birth I have been a man of power.*
> *I am a lion with a fierce gaze, son of the dragon . . . .*
> *The lion of Utu with his great maw wide open . . . .*
> *The proud he-ass clattering along the road,*
> *Swift horse whose tail cracks like a whip,*
> *He-ass of Shakan with the proud gallop—that is I.*

> (After J. Deshayes, *Les Civilisations*
> *de l'Orient ancien.* Paris: Arthaud, 1969)

71   Feline head. Wood covered with gold leaf, height 2". Scytho-Altaic art, second century B.C. From Shibe (Altai). Excavations by M.P. Griaznov, 1927. Hermitage Museum, Leningrad.

72 Stag's head in the mouth of a wolf. A harness ornament. Wood, length 3⅜". From Pazyryk 4.

    (It calls to mind the French expression, *Mettre quelqu'un à la gueule du loup,* more vivid than the English "throw to the wolves.")

73 and 77 Pottery jars from Pazyryk.

74-76 Three round ornamental plaques (phalerae). Gold, with animal decoration and incrusted stones; diameter 2". Sarmatian art from the Volga, first century B.C. From Barrow 1 at Novocherkassk. Excavations by S.I. Kaposhina. Regional Museum of Rostovon-Don.

78 Top of a sword hilt in the shape of a griffin's head. Iron, silver, and gold; 2⅜" long. Seven Brothers, Barrow 3 (northern Caucasus).

79 Horse's head ornamenting a pole. Bronze, 5⅞ × 4 × 1⅞". Teshebani period. Seventh century B.C. From Karmir-Blur (Armenia).

80 Funerary mask considered to belong to a Mongoloid type. Gold, height 6". Mixed art of Taman, fourth century A.D. From Olbia. Found by A.S. Uvarov, 1842. Hermitage Museum, Leningrad.

81 and 82 Above: Vase with pointed bottom and a handle in the shape of a horse's head. Clay, height 11⅜". Beginning of first millennium B.C. From a burial at Mingechaur (Azerbaijan). Excavations of 1933. Azerbaijan Historical Museum, Baku.
Below: Vase with three compartments, with inscription of white paste done by pricking. Clay, height 2½". End of second to beginning of first millennium B.C. From burial at Mingechaur (Azerbaijan). Excavations of 1947. Azerbaijan Historical Museum, Baku.

83 Vase with handles and lid, supported on a horse. Pricked decoration. Clay, 6 × 7¾". From burial at Mingechaur (Azerbaijan). Excavations of 1946-48. Azerbaijan Historical Museum, Baku.

84 and 85 Simple and evocative forms of "testa": two gold pots, undecorated. Height 5⅛" and 4¾". Art of southern Siberia, eighth century A.D. From a chaatas or tomb at Kopeny on the Yenisey. Excavations by L.A. Evtyukhova and S.V. Kiselev, 1939-40. Historical Museum, Moscow.

86 Wooden griffins' heads, the one on the left still having its leather ears. From Pazyryk 2. Fifth to fourth century B.C.

87 Heads of wild sheep (detail from a saddle). Wood, partly covered with gold and felt. Fifth to fourth century B.C. From Bashadar 2. After M.P. Griaznov.

88 Cylindrical mount for a rhyton; decorated with four griffins. Gold, height 3⅛". Sarmatian art from the Kuban, second century A.D. From burial at Severskaya (Krasnodar). Historical Museum, Moscow.

89 and 94 Vases with animal-head spouts. Seventh century B.C. From Ardebil. The Louvre, Paris.

90 So-called head-shaped urn, the concentric motifs representing eyes and the vertical handles noses. Painted pottery: height 11⅜". Tripolye culture, first half of third millennium B.C. From Varvarovka (Moldavia). Excavations by V.I. Markevitch, 1958-61. Historical Institute of the Academy of Sciences, Moldavia, Kichinev.

91 and 93 Mask and fragment of vase with geometrical decoration. Clay, height 5". Neolithic, third millennium B.C. From Voznessenovka (eastern Siberia). Excavations by A.P. Okladnikov, 1964. Academy of Sciences, Siberian Section, Novosibirsk.

92 Urn with motifs of stags, hounds, and horses. Painted pottery, height 13¾". Tripolye culture, first half of third millennium B.C. From Varvarovka (Moldavia). Excavations by

V.I. Markevitch, 1958-61. Historical Institute of the Academy of Sciences of Moldavia, Kichinev.

95 Urn with geometrical decoration; pair of breasts near the neck. Painted pottery, height 23¼", diameter 19⅝". Tripolye culture, first half of third millennium B.C. From Varvarovka (Moldavia). Excavations by V.I. Markevitch, 1958-61. Historical Institute of the Academy of Sciences of Moldavia, Kichinev.

96 Back of a mirror, with a handle whose form is more Western than Asiatic. The mirror consists of two plates of silver, clamped to each other, and the front one is inserted into a handle made of ox-horn. Between the small central boss and the pronounced flanged rim of the back plate, an extremely fine network of decorations in concentric rings is engraved. From Pazyryk 2. Fifth or fourth century B.C.

97 Bracelet, a spiral making three turns, with, at each end, the stylized motif of a feline with a stag in its clutches. Gold, diameter 3⅛". Sarmatian art of the Volga, first century B.C. From Tomb 2 of Barrow 1, Verkhnee Pogromnoe (Volgograd). Excavations by V.P. Shilov, 1954. Historical Museum, Moscow.

98 Ornament for a garment: a plaque decorated with the Greek motif of Pegasus, the horse whose wings made him the swiftest of his kind. Gold 2 × 2". Greek art of the Crimea, fourth century B.C. From the burial at Kul Oba (Kerch, Crimea). Hermitage Museum, Leningrad. Former Tolstoy Collection.

"The mare with wings" is current among the Kirghiz as an image for a swift mount. Similarly, in their legends, the horse of the hero Töshtük is called the "wing of its master."

99 Finely worked underside of a gold cup, with a hemispherical bulge at the center. Diameter 8½". From Solokha (left bank of the lower Dneiper).

The surface is broken up into three rings, each having engraved within it a composition of images which is repeated: in the outer one, an ungulate being devoured by two lions; in the middle one, a deer being attacked by a lioness and a lion: in the one nearest the center, a stag in the clutches of a lion. On the outer rim of the cup there is a stamped inscription in Greek (the letters are reversed), which seems to be: ΕΛΕVΘΡΕΙΑ ΗΕΡΜΟΝ ΑΝΤΙΣΘΕΝ ΕΙ. And on the same rim, but in smaller characters, the word ΛΟΧΟ is written, meaning "ambush" or "detachment."

What is the meaning of such a decoration on this vessel, whose workmanship and inscription are Greek, though the animal themes and ideology are more nearly barbarian? The word "ambush" or "detachment" surely refers to what the lions are engaged in: lions are the most gregarious of the felines, and this precisely when hunting and attacking.

The lion, in fact, often goes in for collective life, in a group of as many as ten to twenty animals. The greater part of the troop forms a semicircle to round up the game, terrorizing it by roaring and driving it back toward the claws of a few members of the troop who lie silently in wait. The lionesses are generally detailed for this work of execution: they pounce on the throat or shoulders of the victim, and sever its arteries with a single bite. This is what the lioness is doing on the middle ring of the Scythian cup.

But when the quarry is being shared out, precedence dictates that the males begin the meal alone—and so it is that we see them, apparently, in the outer ring.

It is thus a good allegory for a warlike and patriarchal society, in which brotherhood in arms is the main source of strength against enemies who are also well armed. For, as indeed the Greek inscription says, "freedom and solitude weaken," and the maxim receives concrete illustration from all the compositions on the cup: isolated and therefore free, undisciplined and without the restraints of gregariousness, the herbivores are falling into the ambush laid by a detachment of hunters and predators, which the lions symbolize. So the message of the cup is simply a dialectical variant of "united we stand" which recurs, in its modern context of the class struggle, in the hopeful slogan "workers of the world unite."

Thus the Solokha phalera is the best Rosetta stone of Greco-Scythian art: a Greek text and a barbarian ideography illustrate a theme which recurs in many forms in nomad symbolism. Often, even when a single predator would be perfectly capable of mastering his prey, the Scythian artist sets two of them against the isolated victim, who is attacked from two sides and will succumb in what is no longer single combat. And on the famous comb from the same kurgan, the struggle between a horseman, aided by a man on foot, and an attacker who has been dismounted illustrates, with a classical and Hellenizing realism, what is expressed by numerous more archaic and purely native depictions of animal fights.

100   Earrings. Gold, length 1¼". From Pazyryk 2.

101   Triangular appliqué, which no doubt adorned a rhyton. The common motif of an eagle carrying off a hare. Gold, height 3⅞". Seven of the twenty-one holes along the edges have retained traces of silver inlays. Mixed art of Taman, fifth century B.C. From the Seven Brothers Barrows (Taman). Excavations by V.G. Tiesenhausen, 1876. Hermitage Museum, Leningrad.

102   Plaque belonging to a belt: detail of the head and neck of a stag at rest. Gold, 12½" long, 7½" high. From Kostromskaya, Barrow 1.

103   Figurine of a Scythian standing. Gold, height 2⅜". Fifth or fourth century B.C. From burial at Kul Oba (Kerch, Crimea). Hermitage Museum, Leningrad.

The man, in a caftan and breeches with slanting folds, is holding in his left hand a quiver and in his right a spherical vase.

104   Detail from a plaque, the centerpiece of a shield. Gold, length 12¼". From Kul Oba. (See fig. 250.)

Note the anatomical exactitude, stylization notwithstanding: the tear duct of the old stag's eye is clearly shown.

105 and 108   Pair of pendants. Gold and enamel, diameter of disk 2¾". From Kul Oba.

The head of Athena is represented, wearing a richly worked helmet. Below the disk rosettes and amphorae ornamented with granulations are suspended from small crossed chains. After M.I. Artamonov.

106   Women's ornaments, art of the Steppes. The geometrical play of balls and rings shows clearly, by its abstraction, that in this case there is no message and that, apart from a display of wealth, the pleasure of the eyes was the artist's only aim and the test of his mastery.

107   Bracelet with lion's head. Diameter 3½". From Ziwiye. Eighth or ninth century B.C. Private Collection of A.B. Martin, New York.

109   Plaque belonging to a bridle. Bronze, length 7¾". From Seven Brothers, Barrow 4.

110 and 111   Pair of swans in white felt stuffed with hay, with appliqués of black, red, and yellow felt. Length of body 17¾". Fifth century B.C. From Pazyryk. Excavations by S.I. Rudenko, 1949. Hermitage Museum, Leningrad.

These birds decorated the canopy of the ceremonial wagon found in the tumulus. They seem, in this case, particularly appropriate as domestic symbols.

Swans, like barbarian nomads, migrate together, seasonally, to more favorable territories. This indeed is why the swan finds a place in so many mythologies as an attendant or transporter of the gods; it is also the entirely nonreligious reason why, in the time of sailing-ships, many of them had a swan figurehead.

But the swan symbolism has other references, in connection with marriage conventions: the pairing of the wild swan is permanent, with the two birds migrating together and producing a family every spring at their habitual nesting grounds until one of them dies. This is rather the impression given by the attitude of the two depicted here—by no means a warlike one, but rather one of display, with the neck bent back in an S and the wings extended.

Such an allegory, in the context of barbarian polygamy, may seem strange. But there is nothing to prove that the Scythian chieftain was not obliged to remain faithful to his various wives, who were subjected to a reciprocal loyalty. Marco Polo, after reporting, without blinking an eyelid, that among the Tatar nomads each man could take as many as one hundred wives if he was rich enough to keep them, goes on to praise his hosts as follows: "They drink mare's milk, and for nothing in the world would a Tatar touch the wife of another, for they hold that to be an evil and disgraceful thing. The wives are virtuous and loyal to their husbands."

In addition, Rudenko thinks that the wagon in question may have been part of a marriage gift, made when the old chieftain married a young princess (no doubt not his first wife), who was buried with her protector in the tumulus. The Soviet archaeologist has looked to ancient China for analogies: similarly decorated wagons have been found in that country, dating to the period of the Warring Kingdoms. There is also written evidence of such vehicles having been presented by the Chinese court to the great Hun chieftains. (N.Y. Bichurin, *Collected References to Peoples Inhabiting Central Asia in Antiquity*. Moscow-Leningrad)

Chinese emperors contemporary with the Pazyryk burials often tried to ensure peace on their western frontier by giving their daughters in marriage to nomad chieftains. Although the anthropological data concerning the woman found in Pazyryk 5 are not sufficient to assign her to any particular ethnic group, and even if she was of European descent, one cannot help thinking of cases in which the woman was at the man's mercy: a relevant story is the one in which a migrant bird provided allegorical support for the nostalgic dreaming of Princess Hsi-Chün, the unlucky wife of a king of Central Asia who, being old and ill, visited her only once or twice a year to drink a cup of wine in her company. The girl sang of her misery in a melancholy poem:

My people have married me to the far end of the world.
They have sent me into a strange land,
To the house of the King of the Wu-Sun.
My dwelling is a tent,
My walls are of felt.
Raw meat and mare's milk are my food.
I think of my country without ceasing and my heart is sad.
Oh, why am I not like the yellow stork?
I would fly with all wings' strength to my old home!

112 Bit-bar (psalium): bird of prey stylized as clawed feet. Bronze, length 6½". Scythian animal art of the Crimea, fifth century B.C. From Ak-Burun (Kerch, Crimea). Hermitage Museum, Leningrad.

113 Boot-shaped vase, as still used in the Caucasus region. Clay with inscription in white paste by pricking, height 8½". End of second or beginning of first millennium B.C. From a burial at Mingechaur (Azerbaijan). Excavations of 1946. Azerbaijan Historical Museum, Baku.

Another well-known example of a boot-shaped vase—more narrowed near the bottom, bell-mouthed at the top, and very finely ornamented—comes from Karmir-Blur; it is dated as from the seventh century B.C., and is preserved in the Armenian Historical Museum, Erevan.

114 Part of a Chinese silk shabrack. From Pazyryk 5. This dreamlike decoration, with its marvelous, more or less real, birds (phoenix or pheasant), has been interpreted by

Alekseev as the translation of an ancient story to illustrate a wedding present: the bird is thought to be singing in honor of some young lady or princess for whom he is yearning.

Rudenko also suggests that the poem to which it refers is the Eighth Shih Ching ode:

The phoenix sings
On the high branch;
The wu t'ung trees grow thick, luxuriant,
On the slope that looks toward the rising sun.
A tuneful, gentle song.

(The wu t'ung tree is *Dryandra cardifolia*.)

But the birds with outstanding plumage are seldom songsters. Whether those here are birds of paradise, peacocks, or (more likely) pheasants, all of these being large birds that dwell in forests and in forest trees, their cries are by no means tuneful or gentle.

However that may be, the essential motif of the embroidery is male birds perched on magnificent flowering trees, while female birds flutter about among them. It is the theme of the mating season, in springtime, the time of blossom, when the parents will soon be able to nourish their young with sprouting seeds and delicious ants' eggs. As with many species of birds, the male is displaying on the branch where he is perched: he is the owner of a territory whose limits he determines. A female is about to join him, for she accepts his decisions. An excellent allegory for a patriarchal society where the woman must follow her master! The theme confirms what we already knew: such textiles were manufactured in China for very rich people, especially for princesses who, for reasons of state, were going to be married in a distant land. (See also figs. 141-50.)

116   Roosters cut out of leather. From Pazyryk 1.

115 and 117   Elk cut out of leather. From Pazyryk 2.

118   Shabrack. Felt with appliqué, scale design; $85\,^{7}/_{8} \times 26\,^{3}/_{4}$". From Pazyryk 5.

119 and 121   Tiger attacking an elk. Ornaments cut out of leather and applied on saddle cushions; length 13". From Pazyryk 1.

120   Shabrack. Felt. From Pazyryk 5.

122   Roosters cut out of leather. From Pazyryk 1.

— Art Demystified —

123   Detail of the engraved and gilded silver mirror from Kelermes (Kuban). Seventh or sixth century B.C. Mistress of daunted felines, often considered to be the Great Goddess of the Scythians.

124   Shabrack: praying women. From Pazyryk 5. Reconstruction. Each picture is 2" to $2\,^{3}/_{8}$" high. Not only are elements of the embroidery on the women's clothes different, but so are also their toenails and fingernails.

The altar-cum-censer at the center of each scene—flanked by women wearing crowns and in a ceremonial attitude, with their right arms raised and their left hands holding a flower—also occurs on Assyrian low reliefs; and at a later date the motif still figures on Persian cylinder seals, the best known of which is the one in the Clerk Collection: here a queen or goddess, or at any rate a woman who is important, is stressed ideographically by her greater stature; a (? female) bearer is giving her at least a bird, if not the flower which the mistress is already holding in her hand; and, behind, there is an altar-cum-censer, like the one illustrated here, with a similar small chain joining the lid to the pedestal. Next comes another crowned figure, very much like the ones on the textile we are examining—having in particular the long veil attached to the royal headdress.

One of the gold dishes from the Oxus treasure also shows a woman in a similar ceremonial attitude: she has her right arm raised to the height of her forehead, while her left hand holds a flower. It looks as if all these female officiants are using accessories that denote their function, at least on the plane of the ancient division of labor—that is to say, attributes that are rustic, floral, or connected with fire and thus derived from sedentary activities (belonging to the farm or home): activities complementary to those of the men, which are more nomadic and itinerant, having to do with hunting or warfare. Both in the case of the cylinder from the Clerk Collection and that of the Pazyryk textile it should be noted that the secondary people are drawn smaller than the principal ones. This is particularly marked as regards the officiants in the Altaic example, who are holding looped stoles like the ones held by exactly similar servants in an Assyrian low relief from Kuyunjik, depicting a ceremony under Assurbanipal.

The ritual character of the scenes on this shabrack is obvious. It is more difficult to determine whether their essence is profane or sacred, but the signs of a social classification are clearly marked.

125 Master of animals (? Gilgamesh). Bronze from Luristan. After A. Godard.

126 A person mastering felines which may represent allegorically prisoners dedicated to agricultural work: the cereal grains dotted about the scene would be relevant to this. Pin from Luristan. After A. Godard.

127-29 Figurine of stylized woman, from three different angles. Paleolithic art (Aurignacian). From Mezin (Ukraine). After H. Golomshtok.

130 A person, apparently female, with animals as prisoners. Bronze pin from Luristan. After A. Godard.

131 Scene of a strong man (? Gilgamesh) mastering powerful monsters. Bronze. From Luristan. After A. Godard.

132 Half-human, half-animal creature, with animal muzzle and wearing horns and a domed crown; depicted in the attitude of the hero, with animal prisoners. Bronze pin from Luristan. After A. Godard.

133 Hero mastering animals (? Gilgamesh). Bronze. From Luristan. After A. Godard.

134-39 Tattoo marks on the body of a man buried in Barrow 2, Pazyryk: fantastic animals on the left arm (134-39); tattoo marks on the right arm and right leg (136 and 137); front view and back view, showing the position of the tattoo marks on the man's body (138 and 139). The decorated parts may be those not habitually covered by clothes. (See also figs. 151-60, 194, and 308.)

140 Fight between two fantastic creatures. Felt hanging. Fifth century B.C. From Pazyryk 5. (Fig. 274 shows a detail in color.)

The fight between two well-matched predators makes one think of the later themes of the "seeker of strength" or "seeker of one stronger than himself"—a theme common to several Circassian and Ossetian legends.

141-50 Details from a shabrack: pheasants and blossoming trees. Chinese silk, embroidered. From Pazyryk 5. (Fig. 114 shows a detail in color.)

151-60 Tattoo marks, and details from them, on a mummified male body from Pazyryk 2. Right arm and details (151-57); left arm and detail (158-60).

The state of the skin shows that the man was of Tungusic-Manchurian type, aged about sixty, and that the tattooing was done when he was young.

More or less monstrous felines and ungulates are depicted. The details of the former tend to be spiral, of the latter sinuous; they, and the antlers also, often end in a bird's head. But endings in a serpent's or a bird's head occur in upper Asia from at least 2000 B.C. onward: Mesopotamia and the Hittite cities have supplied several examples. Sometimes indeed, with the griffins of Persia or Assyria, a scorpion's tail is substituted for the kind that would be natural to the body to which they are attached.

Such excrescences, at first sight merely fabulous, may have their origin in the semantic requirements of Indo-Iranian languages. And indeed, in hunting terminology, antlers are given names according to their form or attachment—brow, bay royal, and crown are expressive radicals describing four types. In the same way the nomads may possibly have referred to some stags as "birdhead," since the shape of a beak makes it enter into technical terminology of all kinds.

But why is the movement of the bodies of these ungulates pushed to the point of unreality? The spiral movements stressing their articulations or motor muscles, and the helical torsion of their foreparts as against their hindquarters—a twist of as much as 180 degrees, their front hooves pointing downward and their hind ones upward—produce a total impression of extreme agitation.

These exaggerations contrast with the stillness of the big cats, planted firmly on their claws. One thinks of the common expression "to fall on one's feet like a cat." And, as if to stress this idea, the leader buried in Pazyryk 2 has one of these carnivores tattooed on his ankle, thus asserting that he is no colossus "with feet of clay" but that he has "both feet firmly on the ground," or is "on a war footing," or "has his best foot forward."

The reason why only the ungulates are depicted in hallucinatory contortions is no doubt because the ecstasy-producing drugs come from plants. Herbivores begin by eating these plants accidentally; then, like men, they become intoxicated and dependent. Individual animals have been seen to leave some herds of ungulates in order to search for the plants which they can no longer do without. And the weakness of the roebuck is well known: he eats such quantities of fresh leaves and sugary buds that the nectar in them goes to his head and makes him so drunk that he staggers about, knocking into trees.

In such a condition the herbivore would find it hard to escape from the sober predator, as one sees him tattooed on the skin of the chieftain from Pazyryk 2. So the themes of the tattoo marks describe their bearer by what seems to be a clear allegory: strength of character as opposed to aimlessness.

Among the Kirghiz, even quite recently, only the bravest of the brave laid claim to these skin decorations. It seems natural that the Soviet archaeologist Rudenko, quoting in his support the statements of Herodotus, Hippocrates, Xenophon, and Pomponius Mela to the effect that among certain Asiatic peoples tattooing was a mark of rank, should see in the examples discussed here evidence merely of a social distinction. (See also figs. 134-39, 194, and 308.)

161 An animal archer: detail of the sword-sheath from the Melgunov barrow (Ukraine).

162 Horse-headed archer: rock wall engraving in the Tassili (Sahara).

163 Detail, the strange archer from the kudurru (boundary stone) of Nebuchadnezzar. Twelfth century B.C. British Museum.

164 Classical Greek representation of a centaur.

165 Griffins: detail of the knotted carpet from Pazyryk 5.

166 and 167 Details from the Pazyryk carpet: flower and star motifs.

168-74 Details from the Pazyryk carpet: horsemen on foot or on horseback. The horses are parade ones, with plumes on their heads and with their tails braided. One of the horsemen (171) seems to mark the beginning of the decline of his troop, in view of the presence of rosettes above and below his horse's tail.

175 Details of saddle rugs.

176 Detail: a buck. In addition to the dapples on the animal's coat and along its back—all of which are characteristic details—the large spots on the flanks are typical of the way in which muscles were rendered in Achaemenid art.

177 Sole of a woman's boot. From Pazyryk 2.

178 Mummified woman's corpse from Pazyryk 5. The head and back display the sutures made after embalming.

179 Small table with carved, removable legs. Height 14⅛". From Pazyryk 2. The table top and feet are joined by tenons and mortices. The feet end in lion paws at the bottom and heads of the same species at the top.

180, 181, and 183 Human heads carved in hard stone. Height, from 1⅛" to 1¾". Afanasievo culture of Okunev, beginning of second millennium B.C. From Barrows 8, 9, and 10 at Chernovaya (Krasnoyarsk). Hermitage Museum, Leningrad.

182 Male statuette, with rounded headdress which has a ribbon hanging down the back. Clay, 5¾ × 3". Chalcolithic, second half of third millennium B.C. Kara-depe (Turkmenia).

184 "Baba" placed on the tumulus of a Petcheneg lord. Stone, height 74¾", breadth 19⅝". Twelfth century. Northern Black Sea coastal region. Hermitage Museum, Leningrad.

185 Neolithic statue-menhir from Saint-Sernin (Aveyron, France). Woman with tattooed face, mouth not depicted.

186 Statue of a woman bearing a vessel in her hands; her clothes have spiral decoration. "Baba" stone, height 54⅜". Tenth century A.D. From the Volga steppe.

187 Bridle ornament in the form of a human head. Wood. From Pazyryk 1.

188 Saddle ornament: human head. Leather cutout. From Pazyryk 1.

189 Ancient terra cotta: characteristic Gorgon (Medusa) head. Sixth century B.C. Syracuse Museum.

190 Fragment from a paving stone showing a person brandishing two tridents. Detail of the head. Afanasievo culture of Okunev, beginning of second century B.C. From Barrow 4, Chernovaya (Krasnoyarsk). Excavations by G.S. Maksimenko, 1963. Hermitage Museum, Leningrad.

191 and 192 Felt wall hanging from Pazyryk 5: detail showing a woman seated on a throne and holding a flowering branch; a horseman is facing her.

One is reminded of another representation of an authoritative woman, likewise seated on a throne, and who has a vessel in her hand, a tree to her right, and a horseman (offering a rhyton) also on her right: this scene decorates a silver rhyton from the tumulus at Merdjana; it is a little less ceremonious than the one on the hanging, in view of the libation about to take place.

In both cases the seated woman is greater in stature than the horseman, apparently to mark a difference of rank. On the cylinder (of Persian origin) from the Clerk Collection, a very tall woman wearing a crown and holding a flower is receiving offerings from people who are shown smaller to mark their subordination—or at least their attitude of respect. An exactly similar difference in stature is found in the people in one of the Persepolis reliefs, where Artaxerxes I, seated on his throne, dominates all the others with his exaggerated height.

By analogy, therefore, there is no proof that in the case of the felt hanging the seated woman is a goddess. While one of her hands holds a spray of flowers and buds, the other is raised close to her mouth, as if to send a kiss. Possibly she is already married, if we relate her shaven head to Herodotus's observation that the Argippeans, both men and women, were bald—and, especially, to the report in an ancient Chinese chronicle that, among the northern Wu-huan, young girls wore hair and tresses only until their marriage. Some of the dead women in Pazyryk burials did, in fact, have shaven heads.

The horseman is elaborately elegant, with his short floating cloak and his well-smoothed mustache. He is riding a thoroughbred suitable to his rank and to the ceremony depicted, a well-caparisoned animal with its tail braided; with his bow in his bow-case, he might be a knightly bridegroom, paying his respects to the high-ranking fiancée waiting for him on the throne. Not only is she holding a flowering branch, but there is a rhythmic arrangement of floral motifs round the two decorative bands bordering the composition. The atmosphere is one of springtime, of the mating season of the birds and (why not?) of human beings. The hanging might therefore be designed to recall the union between the man and the woman buried in the kurgan.

Nonetheless, the writing is not so legible as to exclude our seeing in it a scene of a nomad chieftain paying allegiance either to a barbarian queen (for it was possible, in rare cases, for a woman to be at the head of the state) or to a goddess, if the divine nature of the theme were proved.

This hanging is often compared with a rhyton from Karagodeuashkh, on which two horsemen are advancing toward one another, wearing Scythian costume and bareheaded. While one of them is raising his hand in sign of adoration, the second is holding a lance or scepter in one hand and a rhyton in the other. Their horses are trampling slain enemies. The whole scene reminds one of the well-known relief at Naqsh-i-Rustam in which one sees the god Ahuramazda bestowing royal power on Ardashir I while, similarly, their mounts are trampling their respective enemies, in particular the god of the lower regions and of darkness.

The luminous springtime atmosphere of the Pazyryk hanging may, therefore, also suggest some kind of investiture, in which the divinity is on the throne and has the appropriate stature. But there is nothing about the gesture of her free hand to incline one toward a mythic rather than a profane hypothesis, or vice versa. No choice can be made a priori between interpreting it as a gesture of summons, a hand transmitting a kiss, or a hand placed before the mouth in sign of respect for the person addressed (as, for instance that of a chiliarch addressing Darius in one of the Persepolis reliefs). Certainly one may also think of the very ancient and strange Sumerian stele of Urnammu, on which—twenty-two centuries B.C.—the king is shown pouring a libation at the altar of the sacred plant by the side of the goddess, while she sits on her throne with her hand raised, as though in a gesture of intercession.

But the chief conclusion from these comparisons, with their wide difference in time and in possible meaning, is how clearly the language of art shows its weakness as soon as it has to convey abstract notions.

And indeed the artist of the Pazyryk hanging has betrayed his difficulties in the actual pictorial expression, for the clumsiness with which the figures are depicted shows clearly that the artists of that time had less ease, skill, and training in conveying human beings than in conveying animals, to which the symbolic bestiary used by the Eurasian nomads had accustomed them.

193 and 195 Pieces of a woman's necklace from Pazyryk 2: wooden griffins covered with metal leaf.

194 Fantastic theme from the tattooing of the man in the Pazyryk burial. It suggests some hallucination caused by drugs. A book by Cocteau on the drawings of the insane shows clearly how pictures by, for instance, schizophrenics may come quite close to those by famous artists: the latter often spend a lifetime freeing themselves from the stylistic conventions of their period or class, while the mentally sick man shakes free from himself much more quickly and has no hesitation in distorting or caricaturing—partly because a certain kind of graphic expressionism liberates his language, and partly because his crazy visions are conveyed with all their anomalies. His "rendering" comes still closer to that of the sane man when both of them are speaking in graphic symbols, with motifs devoid of lights and shades and belonging to the realm of thought.

Among the barbarians, tattoo marks were a sign of distinction. Herodotus reports of the Thracians: "They consider bearing tattoo marks as a sign of nobility, bearing none as a sign of the contrary." (See also figs. 134-39, 141-50, and 308.)

196 Six-footed support, with a small bronze pot. Height of the hexapod 48⅜"; height of the pot 5⅜". From Pazyryk 2.

In the vessel, which was filled to the brim with large stones, partly burned grains of hemp were found. From one of the rods there hung a leather gourd decorated with appliqués in animal style: it was full of grains of hemp.

Ancient texts such as the Avesta provide evidence that hemp was used in the Iranian world (to which the nomads of the Altai belonged) to produce ecstatic states of mind. Zarathustra himself used this technique to nourish his mystique. In this he was imitating his protector, King Vishtasp, who received from the gods the cup with the narcotic ingredients, "haoma and hemp." Thanks to this "illuminant beverage" the possessed could "open the eye of the soul to obtain knowledge"—in other words, he experienced hallucinations and an intoxication that was certainly real, though considered as magico-religious. The king thought he was in this way escaping from his body and sending his soul to travel in paradise. But descriptions of the place or state of mind in question as being full of "illumination" are typical of the visions experienced by the consumer of hashish, along with a sleeplike trance which obliges him to lie down.

At the same time, since haoma was reputed to "hold death at a distance" and was associated with prescriptions governing blood sacrifices (which Zarathustra denounced), it may also be considered that the sacred and hallucinogenic drinks were used in sinister rites for their insensibilizing or exhilarating powers.

The nomads of the Altai seem to have made use of still more effective ecstasy-producing techniques. Smoking allows these drugs to enter the bloodstream (through the bronchial tubes) more quickly than does ingestion.

Grains of coriander have also been found at Pazyryk 5: they must have been imported, since the plant does not grow in that region. Apart from its aromatic qualities, coriander also produces a euphoric intoxication and, like hemp, has powers which can hardly be limited to the purely medicinal.

197 Bronze mirror. Diameter 3 ⅜ ". From Pazyryk 2.

198 Half of a mirror from Pazyryk 6. Diameter 4½". Chinese, period of the Warring Kingdoms. The illustration shows its back.

199 The famous carpet from Pazyryk 5. Fifth century B.C.

This work of art is about forty square feet in area; it contains about 240 knots to the square inch, giving a total of about 1,250,000 and a thickness of eight hundredths of an inch. It may therefore be estimated to have taken about a year and one-half to make. Another carpet, found in the Bashadar burial, is of even finer workmanship, having nearly 470 knots to the square inch.

In the Pazyryk example, the warp count gives 56 to 66 threads per inch, the weft count as many as 100 to 250 threads per inch.

This textile has two faces and is of many colors; none of the figures exactly repeats any of its fellows in detail or in coloring. The motifs are stressed by colors that harmonize with one another: pale green, lime green, and soft yellow predominate. And against this background of pastoral tone, floral, animal, and human subjects stand out; sometimes, indeed, a vigorous red tone, though with paler variants, brings out these motifs on the bands in which they are placed.

The way in which the various subjects are arranged invites enumeration: certain markings in the outer series of griffins, in the procession of horsemen, and, lastly, in the band of starry flowers seem to indicate the origin of each specific number.

Is the carpet therefore a kind of gaming board? In support of this interpretation it may be pointed out that in ancient eastern burials it was customary to place gaming boards by the dead man's side, and this custom is to be found also in Hittite and proto-Greek traditions, and generally in Asia Minor. A mural fresco from the first century B.C., found in a funerary chamber at the Scythian Neapolis, the present Simferopol, even depicts a checkerboard with yellow, black, and red squares; close by it, a nomad is playing an Ionic lyre; then comes a scene in which the horseman, preceded by his hounds, is hunting a boar. One's impression is that all these themes are there to evoke the life of the dead man in paradise, with his favorite amusements—playing checkers, hunting, and music.

By their coloring and their spirit, the motifs of the Pazyryk carpet seem to be illustrating this happy life. Moving in the opposite direction from the neighboring horse-men and chargers, but in an equally peaceful manner, twenty-four deer seem on the point of browsing, if they are not doing so already. Their male sex is clearly stressed, and the dappling of their coats marks them as Anatolian fallow deer. To anyone who knows the habitually aggressive mood of these animals, the choice of them for depiction in such an attitude reinforces the serene atmosphere of the carpet as a whole. It is uncertain whether they are there in their capacity as highly valued game, but certainly the twenty-eight horsemen of the neighboring band seem by no means equipped for hunting them: some, indeed, are on foot, keeping pace with their mounts, as if there were no hurry about anything—including the pursuit of the fine game nearby.

Some authors have supposed that the strangely large patches decorating the deer are representations of internal organs, coveted delicacies—that the bodies are imagined as transparent, conceived with the stomach rather than by a scrupulous eye. Exactly similar forms are traced on the flanks of many animals in the Persian reliefs: in the present case, therefore, they are simply the sign of a foreign—Persian—stylization, and proof that the textile was imported.

On the other hand, the punctuations of the coats and along the backs of the deer are realistic markings, showing that they have their summer coats. This may well be done on purpose, because—at least according to the pre- and post-Zoroastrian scriptures—the light of paradise, where an eternal summer is enjoyed, seems to be one of the fundamental elements of the divine environment which awaits the elect of the Indo-Iranian world (to which the nomads of the Steppes were related).

For, the eastern version of the Elysian Fields, where the souls of the departed are ethereal bodies, differs little from the Greek one, in which the happy place, likewise exempt from intemperate weather, is covered with flowers as beautiful as those of the carpet in question. These starry corollas, which speak both of the fields and of the heavens, doubtless explain the no less important part assigned to the lotus in the impor-ted plant motifs used by the Altaic and Scythian artists. Does not the flower of the water lily also open at sunrise and close at sunset?

In this connection, the name of the king of the Sogdians, which signified "light of the land," and the title "son of god" given to the Kushan sovereigns, help to explain why those princes are represented either with haloes, or holding a lotus flower—a symbol whose choice is then more easily understood in the context of a paradisal and divine royalty.

For men to find their way to the luminous country of the dead, the Eurasian le-gends, in many of their variants, bring into play the hunting of a stag, an animal which, as is well known, purposely leads the hunters after it in order to protect its young at-tendant. Led away from his initial purpose in this fashion, the hunter, according to the legend, gradually penetrates into the lower regions or into paradise. It is apparent, then, that this animal is the sovereign of the realm of the dead, or is related to the celestial and solar god enthroned there. The stag, as guide or *psychopompos* (guide of souls), leads

245

the living into the other world, to a radical change of situation and existence.

The most characteristic legend is that of the Narts, fabled ancestors of the Ossetians (who are elsewhere said to be the descendants of the Scythians). In it the hero Sosryko, when he sees a companion of his returning weaponless from the pursuit of a mysterious deer against which he has spent all his arrows, himself sets out in search of so extraordinary a beast. And the same thing happens to him. Then the deer leads him into the Beyond, to a celestial fortress where, in due course, the valiant man marries the daughter of the Sun.

On the Pazyryk carpet horsemen, as weaponless as Sosryko, are leading or riding fine horses adorned from head to foot, like the parade horses led by similar masters—the poses and dress are the same—on the Persepolis reliefs.

By their number the twenty-eight horsemen of the Altaic carpet remind us also of the twenty-eight Izeds, celestial officers of the cohort of the god Ahuramazda.

For all the uncertainties, and there are many, it does seem possible that we are near an archaic mythology common to various Indo-Iranian peoples. For—to turn to other bands of the carpet—the griffins, winged felines with hooked beaks, fit into the same idea. Through Herodotus, as well as in our present-day metaphors where the bird of prey is treated as a hoarder of treasure, the griffins—"guardians of the gold" and, in this case, turning their heads in all directions, uneasily, keeping a lookout—illustrate the idea of a fierce watch kept over the holy of holies. The country of the dead, whether they be elect or damned, always has some celestial, and often winged, gatekeeper: angel, Cerberus, or some other demon. May not the fortress to which the deer in the Ossetian legend leads the hero be also symbolized by that toothed rectangle, like the ground plan of a turreted enclosure, where the vigilant griffin reigns? Entering or leaving such realms is not easy!

It is easy to draw a parallel also with that fabled fortress, the Kangdiz, or with its pendant castle of Afrâsyâp, both of which are described in ancient Iranian texts or by the medieval poet Firdausi—a paradise-citadel, full of gardens and springs, recalling the Vara which the peaceful Yima, first king of the Beyond according to the pre-Zoroastrian traditions, had made, on orders from Ahuramazda, for the best of men after their deaths. The exact meaning of the Pahlavi word *var* must be "fortification," "walled enclosure." And the Soviet archaeologists excavating in eastern Iran (in the region formerly called Xuvârizm) have found a walled colony with a square ground plan, which sheltered a whole clan. An earthly dwelling seems to have served as model for the imagined celestial one.

The representation of Scythia itself in the form of a square ties up with this: its correspondence with the evidence from ancient Iran reveals a mythic geography, which is to be found not only in ancient Europe and the ancient East, but also in Scythian ritual square forms, at least if Herodotus is to be believed.

But, if the Pazyryk carpet has some relationship with the mythology of the ancient Indo-Iranians, so imperfectly known to us, the other hypotheses that have been formulated (gaming board in carpet form, cosmogonic map) are not necessarily contradictory: since, in the old religions of Persia and neighboring lands, the special numbers (those of the revolutions of the stars in particular) were those of the gods, the genii, the demons, and other supernatural components of the mythology of the time, the same syncretism may have marked the beliefs of the nomads of Eurasia.

There are, however, so many uncertainties and contradictions in all the interpretations of this carpet here put forward, that it must remain a key subject for the sagacity of future seekers. (For details see figs. 165-74.)

200 and 207 Bridle ornaments in carved wood: cheekpieces with a monster's head at the upper end. From Pazyryk 4.

201-6 Bridle ornaments, carved wood: cats' heads. From Pazyryk 4.

208 Stag. Wood and leather partly covered with gold plates. Fifth to fourth century B.C. From Pazyryk 2.

209 Small seated figure with an aureole of flames. Bronze, height 5½". Bronze Age, second half of second millennium B.C. From Galich, central Russia.

210 Women before an altar. Shabrack. Iranian woolen textile. From Pazyryk 5. (See fig. 124.)

211 and 212 Dress ornaments. Gold plaques, 1⁷/₈" × 1⁷/₈". Decorated with the Greek motif of the crowned head of Perşephone-Kore, flanked by a torch. Mixed art of Taman, fourth century B.C. From the burial at Great Blisnitza (Taman). Excavations by I.E. Zabelin, 1864. Hermitage Museum, Leningrad.

213 Gold plaque, probably a dress ornament, found at Kul Oba. Two agitated women: the one on the left seems particularly excited, perhaps because she has absorbed the contents of the receptacle still being offered to her by her companion opposite. An allusion to drug-taking? Or to the alcoholism of the Bacchantes?

214 Wall hanging with finely colored felt appliqué; bordered with lion heads. From Pazyryk 1.

215 Horned carnivore mastering two geese. Chamfron of a horse's harness. Carved and painted horn. From Pazyryk 2.

— The Symbolic Animal Species —

216 Large half-moon pectoral from Ziwiye, Iranian Kurdistan. Breadth 14¹/₈". Archaeological Museum, Tehran.

A similar ornament is worn by a human-faced bull of Urartian manufacture, which was found at Toprak Kale, near Lake Van.

The composition of the Ziwiye pectoral is basically in two concentric rows: these are bordered by a frieze of fir cones and are separated by a twisted fringe or rope molding. At the center, within each row, there is a tree: in one row the tree is flanked by two bulls, in the other by two ibexes; these animals are Urartian in style.

The tree is doubtless the tree of immortality, and the theme is taken up and completed by the fir cones: the conifer, being an evergreen, is well fitted to fill in with concrete symbolism the abstraction of such a concept, which is the more real for being bound up with its intrinsic idealism.

The two ruminants—the ibex and the bull—seem to have led the other participants to the miraculous tree: they have their heads over their shoulders to see that they are indeed being followed. The choice of these two indicates clearly their function as *psychopompoi*: it is common in both species for an experienced male to serve as mentor to a younger companion, and even to draw the predator away from him. Instances are to be found in various Eurasian myths, as Mircea Eliade has clearly shown, basing his demonstration particularly on legends in which the stag, ibex, or bull lead their follower to the country of the dead, whether paradisal or infernal.

Each of the pectoral's two rows presents also two processions, whose participants vary slightly from row to row, although they seem to answer and complement one another, like classes or age categories within a given society.

On either side of the center in the lower row there is a winged, man-headed, bearded bull standing on its hind hooves and raising its human hands as though in an exclamation of happiness at the approach of his desired aim. The corresponding figures in the upper row are female sphinxes, each with the full-fleshed face of a respectable matron.

Behind each man-headed bull comes a griffin (an appointed "guardian" according to Herodotus); behind each female sphinx there is a "lamassu" (a winged, human-headed bull), another domestic guardian who did duty at the gates of the Achaemenid palaces—though in this case the ears are human, not animal.

In the lower row, the male section of this part of the procession is closed by a kind of ram-headed sphinx. This is followed by a female sphinx, sitting down and apparently followed by her young—a feline cub and a rabbit, depicted in the same spirit in which mothers of the present day may affectionately call their children "puss" or "bunny."

The childhood allegory is even clearer in the upper row: here the skittish rabbit is turning its back on the rest of the troop, like a disobedient child; and a winged lion, sitting even more idly than the female sphinx below it, seems to be her graphic pendant.

Thus the Ziwiye pectoral seems to be telling a complete story, but its translation is made difficult by the fundamental imperfection of the language used.

217-21 Handles of mixing-bowls, featuring the Gorgon. From the British Museum, London (217), Trebenishte (218), southern Russia (219), Munich (220), and the Louvre, Paris (221). After R. Joffroy, *Le Trésor de Vix* (Paris: Fayard, 1962).

222 Detail from vase no. 1 from Agighiol.

Almost exactly like the two examples from Agighiol (see figs. 3, 5, 227, 228, and 240) and in a characteristic Thracian animal style, there is a silver vase from the Iron Gates which presents a scene and an ornamental motif that are to be found also on the Gaetic helmet preserved in Detroit. A bird of prey—a kind of griffin equipped with a fully developed male ibex horn—is holding in its beak a fish and in its claws a quadruped that seems to be a hare. But in addition, on the vessel, a smaller bird of prey is coming toward the monster, and the difference of scale suggests that it is a dependent or subordinate. The Herculean creature seems to be there in the capacity of master not only of the air, but also of land and water, to judge from the herbivore and the fish it is holding prisoner. But whether this kingship is divine or civil, sacred or profane, is unknown.

223 Engraving on stone, from Chernovaya (the Minusinsk Steppe): bird-footed wolf. Beginning of second millennium B.C.

The Kirghiz heroes are often called blue wolves; and the legends say, of a woman who has brave sons, that "she had seven sons like wolves."

224 Fight between wild animals and monsters. Siberian Collection of Peter the Great. After Rudenko.

225 Tiger killing an elk: detail of carving on wooden coffin from Barrow 2 at Bashadar (central Altai). The style prefigures that of Sarmatian goldsmiths' work.

226 Leather covering from Pazyryk 2.

227 and 228 Griffins attacking boars: decorations on the bottoms of the Agighiol vases, nos. 1 and 2. (See figs. 3, 5, and 222.) Thraco-Gaetic art.

One of the monsters is holding in its beak the substantial leg of a fully grown animal. It may have been the father or mother of the young boar which the predator is either threatening or already gripping in its claws.

229 Horned lion-griffins attacking elk: detail of the leather covering from Pazyryk 2 (fig. 226).

230 Lion-griffin attacking an elk: from the Seven Brothers Barrows.

231 Lion attacking a stag. From Kul Oba.

232 and 233 Zooanthropomorphic paintings. Verknaya-Burriet.

234 Lion attacking a bull. Persepolis.

235 Decoration of saddle cover from Pazyryk 1: a tiger pouncing on a wild sheep.

236 Lion attacking a wild goat. From Kelermes, Kuban.

237 Horse mask. Felt and leather. From Pazyryk 2.

Has this funerary head some relation with the belief in an afterlife? In the legends about the Narts as told by the Ossetians, the idealist and abstract notion of the immortal soul belonging to each individual is conveyed by concrete images; and the motif of the soul as an exterior threefold appearance is also found in northern Caucasian stories apart from the Narts cycle. But its commonest form occurs in the story in which Soslan fights the sons of the czar: one of these—Bibyts—loses his soul in the form of three doves that are killed, one after the other, by Soslan; the first of them represents his strength, the second his assurance, and the third his thought.

238 Human head crowned with a stag's antlers. Wood carving. Fourth to third century B.C. From Changsha, Hunan province, China. British Museum, London.

The thirsty stag—as he is after an exhausting exertion—has often served as a symbol in historic periods. In China it occurs in connection with prophecies of drought. In our own time the way in which the tongue is treated in this carving survives in the description of a man with "his tongue hanging out" with desire or need.

239 Ibex in repose. Ninth or eighth century B.C. Private Collection, Tehran. After R. Girshman.

240 Decoration from vase no. 2, Agighiol. (See also figs. 5 and 228.)

Below a frieze consisting of a chain of heads of birds of prey, there is a stag and an ibex. These two species, one a forest dweller, the other a mountain dweller have (as we have seen) some similarities in their way of living—in particular the association of a mature male with an attendant, which explains how these animals have come to symbolize guides or *psychopompoi*.

241 Stag-shaped bronze brackets, from the Amlash region. Height $3^3/_8$" and 4", respectively; lengths $2^3/_4$" and $2^7/_8$". The Metropolitan Museum of Art, New York City.

242 Cernunnos, the antlered god of Gaul, as he appears on the stele in Reims Museum.

243 Two opposed stags—but if in combat, so lacking in violence that they appear to be ideographic rather than anecdotic. Late Paleolithic art. Lascaux (France).

244 Stag-shaped rhyton: terra cotta. Ninth or eighth century B.C. From Amlash. Private Collection, Tehran. After R. Ghirshman.

245 Anthropomorphic figure with antlers. Trois Frères cave (Ariège, France).

246 Old man, bald and bearded, with antlers and horse's tail. Engraving on slate. Magdalenian style, France. After H. Breuil.

247 Part of a bronze breastplate, depicting a Gorgon. $16^1/_8$" × $17^3/_8$". From Elisavetinskaya.

Besides the ophidian affinities that have been given to the face, this Medusa has the characteristics that are caused by strangling or beheading—the protruding tongue and staring eyeballs. The terrifying aspect attributed by legend to this monster(and are not the faces of the asphyxiated also purplish?) may have its origin in some decapitation, the reason for which was then forgotten, its physiological and morphological consequences alone being remembered. This theory would make it possible to harmonize all the legends, those that describe the Gorgons as a terror to look at and those stating that they were very beautiful women. Their name suggests the Indo-European root which has given us "gorge," the French *égorger* (to cut the throat), and the Spanish *gorgo* (a gulf). This root has entered into everything concerning the *gorge* (throat); for instance into the old French word *gargon* and the up-to-date Italian *gergo,* both of which mean "jargon."

248 Small gold figure of a griffin: possibly a cap ornament—it has two ties at the back; it also has hollows to take incrustation. The tail ends in a leaf. $2^3/_8$". From the Oxus treasure. British Museum, London.

249 Bridle plaque in the form of a stag lying down. Bronze, length 1³/₈". From Seven Brothers, Barrow 4.

   This is not the only example from this tumulus of an old stag shown laying back a highly developed set of antlers denoting his great age. The animal gives the impression of repose, rather than active presence: it is not clear which is the primary purpose here—to symbolize withdrawal, or to pull together a more or less rectangular composition so as to avoid letting thin and weak parts stick out.

250 Centerpiece of a shield. Gold, length 12¼". From Kul Oba (See fig. 104.)

   The plaque takes the form of a stag lying down and having, imposed on its sides, small figures of a hare hemmed in by a lion and a griffin. A dog is lying under the stag's neck, apparently sheltered but nonetheless still nervous and on the alert, with its head turned back in the direction of the conflict about to break out between the small figures. This dog also has its tail lowered, reminding us of the one on the vase from Solokha with its tail between its legs as it cowers behind the feet of a horse whose rider is attacking an angry lion. On the same vessel another rider is approaching the lion from behind, and the dog close to the feet of his mount, being in less danger, is moving bravely to the attack and has its tail held high. Thus the plaque from the Kul Oba belt, with the royal stag protecting the dog and the hare tracked down by the two carnivores, is a double illustration of the idea of brotherhood in arms, the usefulness of companionship, the way in which "unity is strength."

   The stag's neck is also adorned with a Greek inscription, ΠΑΙ. This word comes from the Indo-European root PU and means "child" or "young" (of an animal). In Greek the root has yielded *pais* (child), *paizo* (I play), and *polos* (colt). Latin owes to it *puer* (child) and *pullus* (young of an animal). And English has inherited from the two dead languages such words as pupil, pullet, pony, and foal. Clearly the Greek inscription confirms the ideographic sense of the dog sheltering beneath the adult stag, and thus, to some slight extent, this work of art from Kul Oba is a Rosetta stone.

251 Detail from a belt: a tiger mauling a goat. Length 2³/₈". Fifth to fourth century B.C. From Pazyryk 2. Excavations by Griaznov, 1929. Hermitage Museum, Leningrad.

   The belt is a leather one, decorated with catgut circled with tin wire, with gold-leaf appliqué. The buckle is of silver.

252 Chamfron ornament; a creature with a stag's antlers and an elk's mouth. Bronze, height 3¾". Scythian animal art of the Crimea. Fifth century B.C. From Ak-Burun (Kerch, Crimea). Hermitage Museum, Leningrad.

253 and 254 Two ornaments in stag's-head form, with, at the base of each, four holes for fixing. The wide spread of the antlers at their ends shows that it was intended to depict old animals. Note also, at the springing of the antlers from the head, the emphasis on the burrs and their bedding. Mixed art of Taman, fourth century B.C. From burial at Sennaja (Taman). Excavations by C.I. Verebrjusov, 1880. Hermitage Museum, Leningrad.

255 Mouthpiece of a rhyton, carved in the form of the forepart of a winged he-goat. From Seven Brothers, Barrow 3.

256 Ornament in the form of a small bell surmounted by an ibex. Bronze, height 3⁷/₈". Tagar culture, fifth to fourth century B.C. Minusinsk Basin. Hermitage Museum, Leningrad. Kuznetsov Collection.

257 Ensign from a Hittite royal tomb (Alaca-Hüyük). An old stag is leading bulls or bull-calves.

258 Chamfron ornament depicting a stag's head. Bronze, height 2½". Mixed art of Taman, fifth century B.C. Seven Brothers Barrows. Hermitage Museum, Leningrad.

259 A griffin's head with, on its neck, filigree cloisonné to receive enamel incrustations.

Detail from the crown found at Kelermes, Barrow 3.

260 Crown in the form of a band adorned with eight-petaled rosettes, with a griffin's head, and with numerous drop-shaped pendants. Two rams' heads also hang from it by longish chains.

Gold, with traces of enamel. Diameter 8¼", height ⅝". From Kelermes, Barrow 3.

261-64, 267, 268 Bridles and harness of horses buried in the Altai kurgans; some are displayed on casts.

265 and 266 Masks for horses. Leather, fur, gold, and hair, forming respectively a lion-griffin's head and a stag's antlers. From Pazyryk 1.

269 Two heads of fantastic birds, made of wood still partly covered with gold; they may have been ornaments for the heads of horses. Fifth or fourth century B.C. Pazyryk 3. Between them is shown a more natural bird's head, from the same tumulus.

270 Bronze from ancient Iran representing half-human, half-animal creatures.

The mountain dwellers of ancient Iran, as early as the fourth millennium B.C., worked out a repertory dominated by the strange figure of a "master of animals"; sometimes he was booted, and his deliberately simplified head might be replaced by that of a wild sheep or an ibex. In such cases he is associated with various animals, but more specially with serpents.

The Susians represented this monster in a way obviously intended to be impressive: his horns seem to be the forerunners of those which, in historic times, adorned the tiara of gods. Their hero is also shown grasping a pair of lions or huge snakes. He looks like a kind of ancestor of the animal tamers that were so dear to the ancient East, and in whom were mingled the characteristics of heroism, royalty, and divinity, in accordance with the economic and historical development of their social context: the links between these three types of personages reflect the fundamental problem of the transition from a communal organization to a class society, with its consequent ideology and with correlative religious aberrations.

From Luristan, eighth century B.C. The Louvre, Paris.

271 Back of a round mirror (6¾" in diameter) found at Kelermes, Barrow 4. The images, which are engraved and coated with gold leaf, are arranged in eight sectors. In one of these a goddess is grasping two felines. In the next sector to the right, a lion and an ox are locked in a titanic fight, and below them is depicted a courageous boar. In the first sector to the left of the goddess, two lions are confronting each other above a goat and a ram's head, for which the two lions seem to be acting either as defenders or as the allegory of their male rivalry and combativeness. In general, most of the sectors are divided into two layers, the lower seeming to have a symbolic link with the upper one: for instance, a lion is passing calmly in front of a tree, while below him a ram is resting; two female sphinxes sit face to face above an equally fantastic and aggressive griffin; two other female sphinxes have turned their heads as if to avoid each other, while below them there is a panther with lowered head; and a bear and a bird of prey are arranged above a wild specimen of the dog tribe, like them a predator.

272 Repoussé gold plate, height 6¼". Stags and ibexes in the fields: they have obvious Scythian features, while the execution of the knotwork, on the contrary, corresponds to the Urartian style. From the Ziwiye treasure. Archaeological Museum, Tehran.

273 Master of the animals on a bronze disk from primitive Iran. Luristan, eighth century B.C. The Louvre, Paris.

274 Detail showing the right-hand protagonist in a fight between two fantastic beings. Felt hanging from Pazyryk 5. Fifth century B.C. (See also fig. 140.)

275 Strange bird's head. Leather, length 5⁷/₈". From Pazyryk 4.

276 and 278 From the bull frieze at Lascaux. Two facing groups; in the lower one, classical representations of stags.

277 Engraving on stone. Lake Onega (USSR).

279 Water jar imported from Clazomenae; decorated with a siren with outspread wings and a band of lotus buds. Clay. Ancient Greek art of the Aegean region, sixth century B.C. From Parutino (Olbia). Hermitage Museum, Leningrad.

280 Stags carved in wood, with leather antlers. From Pazyryk 2.

281 Twisted bracelet terminating in busts of female sphinxes with wings outspread. The core of the bracelet is of bronze. The rings from which the sphinxes spring are bands of palmettos and filigree, with traces of blue enamel. Gold, diameter 4". Greek art of the Crimea, fifth or fourth century B.C. From burial at Kul Oba (Kerch, Crimea). Hermitage Museum, Leningrad.

282 Hittite statuette of a stag, in copper and electrum. Before 2000 B.C. From Alaca-Hüyük (northern Anatolia). It is shown against a background of Hittite ideograms.

283 Ornamental plaque in the form of a stag with its legs gathered under it. Bronze, 2¼ × 3¹/₈". Tagar culture, fifth to fourth century B.C. From the Minusinsk Basin. Hermitage Museum, Leningrad.

284 Head of a stag in the jaws of a griffin. Horn and hide. The stag's antlers end in birds' heads. Length 9". From Pazyryk 2. (See commentary to fig. 358, same subject.)

285 Harness ornament in the form of a stag lying down. Bronze, 3 × 2¾". Mixed art of Taman, fifth century B.C. From the Seven Brothers Barrows, Kuban (northern Caucasus). Hermitage Museum, Leningrad.

286 Buckle in the form of a stag. Bronze, diameter 3½". Scytho-Sacian art, seventh to fifth century B.C. From Tomb 41 at Uigarak, near the Syr-Darya (Central Asia). Excavations by S.P. Tolstov. Institute of Ethnography of the Academy of Sciences, Moscow.

287 Wolf with ram's horns. Sino-Siberian culture. British Museum, London.
     The ram's function as a leader is well brought out in one of the Ossetian legends, where Uryzmaegt tricks the one-eyed giant as Ulysses tricked Polyphemus: the giant has no need of a shepherd for his flock because a single ram leads it, and so the hero gets hold of the ram's skin and uses it to escape from the cave where he has been imprisoned; he takes with him all the rest of the flock, to the great dismay of the stupid giant, who has been blinded by a stroke from a cooking spit and therefore could not see the subterfuge.

288 Bridle ornament; lotus and palmetto. Bone, diameter 2¾". From Pazyryk.

289 Bridle ornament representing a highly stylized wild beast's head. Bronze, 1¼ × 2¾". Scythian animal art, from Tuzla (Taman, northern Caucasus). Found by Begitchev in 1852. Hermitage Museum, Leningrad.

290 Ornamental plaque in the form of a feline curled in a circle and bearing an ibex on its back. On the reverse side, an eyelet for attachment. Bronze, diameter 4". Scythian animal art, fifth century B.C. From the Kulakovsky burials, Simferopol (Crimea). Excavations by J.A. Kulakovsky, 1895. Hermitage Museum, Leningrad.

291 Pole top, pear-shaped and pierced, with two iron bells inside; the upper end treated as a griffin's head. Bronze, height 12¼". Scythian animal art, sixth century B.C. From Kelermes (Krasnodar). Hermitage Museum, Leningrad.

292 and 293 Small ornamental plaques from Pazyryk 2. (Also reproduced as line drawings, figs. 14 and 12.)

294 Gold bracelet with horned eagle-griffins. From the Amu-Darya (Oxus) treasure. The same kind of monster is to be found on a silver rhyton from Armenia and on a gold necklace in the Siberian Collection of Peter the Great.

— The Artist in Barbarian Society —

295 Ornamentation of sword hilt. From Lito (Melgunov) kurgan (Ukraine).

The guard is decorated with two ibexes. They suggest those experienced males who keep watch, lying down, for the sake of their group. This characteristic attitude of the ibex is reinforced by the depiction of them with their heads turned back—keeping a lookout in all directions.

In the case of many species of gregarious herbivores, the males, since their means of protection are weak, defend their troop by circling around it, with their backs toward those in the center or even toward one another (when the circumference is not exactly circular) so as to present, as nearly as possible, a complete and even front of determined defenders.

One is reminded also of the male bisons at the end of the composition that covers the walls of the main nave at Lascaux: they suggest the same defensive theme. Here, though the attitude of the two bisons back to back and ready to face any threat from outside lends them realism, the scene seems to be already some way toward ideography, for the vigilance suggested by them is definitely symbolic, seeing that there are only two of them.

The allegory is still more naturally expressed on a piece of gold appliqué from Kul Oba: there, two Scythians are represented back to back with their bows drawn to shoot any enemy who might appear, from whatever part of the horizon.

These plastic variations on the word "guard" (whose synonyms are "look-out," "defence," "vigilance," "protection") are so many examples illustrating the relation there is between the ornamentation on the guard, or hilt, of this sword and its function.

The same was observed in the case of the pommel of the Medgidia sword, where again decoration seemed to be in harmony with function (see fig. 10). This Thraco-Gaetic weapon has a guard adorned with two ibexes, their heads turned back, as on the Lito example.

Such correlations between engraving and function are so real that they are often to be found. Thus, in the sarcophagus of a warrior at Kul Oba, an iron sword was found complete with the gold coating on its sheath: on this there is a scene of bloodshed, with a lion and a griffin dividing up a stag, while a leopard is attacking another herbivore—a scene that fits in well enough with the weapon's function. But at the end of the sheath there is also a lion mask surmounted by an inscription in Greek characters: ΠΟΡΝΑΧΟ. This may be the name of the owner or of the craftsman, but it may, like the aggressiveness of the lion, have to do with the function of the object and so be similar to Roland's name "Duranda." The Indo-European roots *per* (= *por* = *pro*) and *nek* (= *nekus* = *nocere*) are the ones that recur in the adjective "pernicious."

296 Saddle from Pazyryk 5. After S.I. Rudenko.

297 Bridle from Pazyryk 5. After S.I. Rudenko.

298 Saddle from Pazyryk 5. After S.I. Rudenko.

299 Bridle from Pazyryk 5. After S.I. Rudenko.

300 and 301 Chariot found at Lshashen, on the shores of Lake Sevan (Armenia). Triangular form. There are still similar vehicles on the Anatolian plateau. Second millennium B.C.

302 Covered wagon with large disk wheels, about 3,500 years old. It was found in Armenia, on the shores of Lake Sevan.

The wheel seems to have made its first appearance in about 3650 B.C. in Lower Mesopotamia, about 3700 B.C. in Transcaucasia, and to have been known in central Europe before 2500. Its appearance is bound up with the age of metals in its early stages—when the use of copper made it possible to have cutting tools.

At Lshashen the wheels were usually made of elm wood, the axles, shafts, and yoke of oak, and the arches for the covering of yew. The diameter of the wheels—over a yard—shows that considerable supplies of good timber were needed, which accounts for the relatively early appearance of the invention in Transcaucasia.

Apart from the classic depictions of archaic wagons on pottery from Susa and Khafaje, on the famous Ur standard, and in pictograms from Uruk (IVa), a representation of a wagon dating back to the Bronze Age has also come to light in the Altai.

303 Clay copy of a wagon, possibly religious in function, from Dupljaja (Banat), dating from the end of the Bronze Age. It has three wheels and is ostensibly drawn by aquatic birds, reminding one of the swans of the chariot of Hyperborean Apollo, whom the Thracians and the Greeks worshiped. See also the swans adorning the covering of a wagon at Pazyryk (figs. 110 and 111).

304-6 Earthenware models of covered wagons as used on the Steppes: the lower one with two wheels, 2000 B.C.; the upper one with four wheels, 600 B.C. After E.D. Phillips.

307 Gold helmet from Cotofenesti (Prahova District, Romania). Weight 27 ounces, height $9^7/_8$". Gaetic art, beginning of fourth century B.C., like the helmet from nearby Agighiol.

The two cheek pieces are decorated with a scene of a ram being sacrificed in the ancient manner, by having its throat cut. This is being done with a short blade of the akinakes type, which is considered as being of Scythian origin. One thinks of the Ossetian tale, possibly stemming from nomad tradition, in which the hero Uryzmaegt has the privilege of himself cutting the throat of a wild ram; also of the expression *doe foequa foeuon*—"let me be your sacrifice, your victim!"—a formula for devotion and willing subordination. And indeed, in many of the legends about the Narts, the cutting of the sheep's throat is the privilege of any self-respecting hero, host, and master of the house.

The helmet from Agighiol (Tulcea District) is in the same spirit: its cheek-piece is adorned with a brave horseman armed with a lance.

On both the helmets, at forehead level, there are two large eyes with arching eyebrows: they evidently express domination, like those of Soslan, the brave Nart, who had two pupils per eye. These eyes plastically reinforce the authority of the *couvre-chef* (head-cover). One may wonder whether the curves of the eyebrows are not a stylization of those of the ibex, that leitmotiv of the Thraco-Gaetic bestiary.

The surface of the neck-piece is decorated with two friezes. The upper one represents a succession of half-animal, half-human creatures; the lower one depicts aggregates that are more animal, being made up of extremely dynamic carnivores and winged creatures.

All this belongs to a princely art: it bears witness to the existence of an autochthonous Thraco-Gaetic animal style, to some extent independent of the Scythian, though one finds in it traces of Persian and Phrygian influence. The themes are those of sovereignty, their purpose being the exaltation of a warlike aristocracy.

Another helmet, a silver one, at the Institute of Arts, Detroit, also illustrates this Gaetic type. Its left cheek-piece depicts a rampant wild animal with powerful horns, very probably an ibex. The right cheek-piece shows a bird of prey holding a fish in its beak and in its claws a herbivore that seems to be a hare (cf. fig. 222).

308 Detail of tattoo marks on the right leg of the man from Pazyryk 2. (See also figs. 134-39, 141-50, and 194.)

309 Decorated leather gourd: fight between two winged creatures. Fifth to fourth century

B.C. Pazyryk 2.

310 Gourd with appliqué. Pazyryk 2.

311 Detail of a felt hanging: lotus and palmetto. Pazyryk 2.

312 Pickax with its heel decorated with a feline. Bronze, $3\frac{1}{4} \times 7\frac{1}{4}$". Tagar culture, sixth to fifth century B.C. From River Pit (Yenisey region). Hermitage Museum, Leningrad. Collection of I. Lopatin.

313 Dagger with button-shaped pommel, stripe decoration on the front of the handle, and two eyelets on its reverse side: it was no doubt a weapon that was kept hung up as a decoration. Bronze, length 11". Karasuk culture, thirteenth to eleventh century B.C. From Amurskoe (Achinsk). Hermitage Museum, Leningrad. Collection I. Lopatin.

314 From left to right:

a) Ax with engraved geometric decoration. Bronze, $6\frac{3}{4} \times 2\frac{3}{8}$". Beginning of first millennium B.C. From Koban burial in northern Ossetia (central Caucasia). Historical Museum, Moscow.

b) Ax with engraved geometric decoration, with a wild-beast motif on the blade. Bronze, height $7\frac{1}{8}$", breadth $2\frac{1}{4}$". Beginning of first millennium B.C. From Koban burial in northern Ossetia. Historical Museum, Moscow.

315 and 317 Daggers with their pommels surmounted by two facing griffin heads, their guards having a stylized zoomorphic decoration. Bronze, length $10\frac{1}{2}$" and $11\frac{3}{4}$". Tagar culture, sixth to third century B.C. Znamenka and Bateni. Chance finds. Hermitage Museum, Leningrad. Collection I. Lopatin.

316 Above: Knife with ring pommel. Bronze, length $9\frac{3}{4}$". Karasuk culture, thirteenth to eleventh century B.C. From Baikalovo (Minusinsk Basin). Hermitage Museum, Leningrad. Collection I. Lopatin. Below: Knife with button-shaped pommel with an eyelet; fluted decoration on the handle. Bronze, length $7\frac{3}{4}$". Karasuk culture, thirteenth to eleventh century B.C. From Kazantsevo (Minusinsk Basin). Hermitage Museum, Leningrad. Collection I. Lopatin.

318 Dagger with pommel decorated with heads of horses seizing ibex. Bronze, length $14\frac{5}{8}$". From Koban burial. Collection A.S. Uvarov.

The theme of an animal being caught by another may, as we have seen, be not unrelated to the function of the weapon it adorns, and this is not incompatible with a decorative purpose.

319 Wooden headrest from Pazyryk.

320 Shirt made of plant fiber. Length $42\frac{1}{2}$". Pazyryk 2.

321 Buckle in the form of a curled-up feline. Bronze, diameter $2\frac{3}{4}$". Scytho-Sacian art, seventh to fifth century B.C. From Tomb 33 at Uigarak, on the Syr-Darya (Central Asia). Excavations by S.P. Tolstov. Institute of Ethnography of the Academy of Sciences, Moscow.

322 Buckle in two parts; decoration of horses' heads. Bronze, each part $2\frac{1}{2} \times 2\frac{1}{4}$". Scytho-Sacian art, seventh to fifth century B.C. From kurgan at Tagisken (Central Asia). Excavations by S.P. Tolstov.

323 Phalera (decorative plaque from harness) originating from the Black Sea coastal region. Silver coated with gold leaf. About second century B.C. Cabinet des Médailles, Paris.

324 Man's felt stocking. Pazyryk 2.

325 Frontal plaque from a bridle. Diameter 5". Tuekta 1.

326 Buckle in two parts; decoration of stylized feline heads. Bronze, each part $2\frac{1}{2} \times 2\frac{1}{4}$".

Scytho-Sacian art, seventh to fifth century B.C. From Tomb 27 at Uigarak, on the Syr-Darya (Central Asia). Excavations by S.P. Tolstov. Institute of Ethnography of the Academy of Sciences, Moscow.

327   Pierced ornamental plaque: two oxen. Bronze, $2\frac{3}{8} \times 5\frac{1}{2}$". Tagar culture, fourth to third century B.C. Kopterevo (Minusinsk Basin). Found by A.V.Adrianov, 1894. Hermitage Museum, Leningrad.

328 and 329   Earrings in the form of round shields with large hooks ending in rams' heads. Gold, $1\frac{1}{4} \times 1\frac{1}{4}$". Ancient Greek art of the Black Sea, sixth century B.C. From Parutino (Olbia). Excavations by V.V. Farmakovsky, 1913. Hermitage Museum, Leningrad.

330   Four-wheeled wagon from Pazyryk 5. The wheels are $55\frac{1}{8}$" in diameter and have thirty-four spokes each. The body is adorned with balusters and covered with a hanging. It was drawn by four horses, and these were buried with it. The vehicle is an elegant and refined one, but the wheels do not have the outer rim of iron with which wheels of Scythian manufacture were always provided.

     This wagon could be taken to pieces and transported on an animal's back over very rough ground. Moreover, the shaft was firmly fixed to the body, so that turning was not easy. All this suggests that its function was ceremonial rather than practical. For this reason Rudenko thinks that it was a wedding present and that it originated in China, in view of its sophisticated appearance: there is, as we have seen, documentary evidence that such presents were customarily given by the lords of China to their daughters when these were married to the great nomadic chieftains for reasons of state.

331   Body of a horse. Pazyryk 1.

332   Chariot drawn by four horses. The driver and his companion are wearing Iranian clothes and jewels. The style is related to that of the one from Pazyryk 5 (fig. 330). Ghirshman cites the annals of Sargon II to the effect that the king of Assyria found in the temple at Musasir (a city of Urartu), besides thirty-three silver chariots, a "statue of Ursa [Rusa I] with his two chargers and his charioteer, with their seat, the [whole] in melted bronze, [a statue] on which his pride could be seen expressed as follows: With my two horses and my charioteer, my hands have conquered the realm of Urartu."

     Length $7\frac{1}{8}$". Sixth to fourth century B.C. Oxus treasure. British Museum, London.

333 and 334   Two pottery models representing wagons of the type used by the nomads. End of second or beginning of first millennium B.C. From burial at Mingechaur (Azerbaijan). Excavations of 1946. Azerbaijan Historical Museum, Baku.

335   Necklace with slender chain and nine medallions containing seven garnets and two pieces of green glass; hanging from it by a slender chain, a butterfly-shaped pendant; on either side of this, arrow-shaped pendants. Gold, length $10\frac{5}{8}$". Mixed art of Taman, first to second century A.D. From the Chersonese (Seastopol). Excavations by K.K. Kost-siushko-Valiuzhinich, 1898. Hermitage Museum, Leningrad.

336   Gold diadem in the form of a broad ribbon. In the center the Greek motif Hercules' Knot and on either side of this, two tripods, two bacchantes, and dolphins. The feeling of this piece suggests that of Delphi. Mixed art of Taman, fourth to third century B.C. From kurgan near Karantin (Panticapaeum). Excavations by A.D. Ashik, 1838.

337   Art of the Royal Scyths of Neapolis; objects belonging to a collection of jewelry decorating clothes of a Scythian king:
     a) Three plaquettes in the form of flies. Gold, $\frac{3}{4} \times \frac{3}{8}$".
     b) Oval plaque. Gold, height $1\frac{1}{4}$".
     c) Three bud-shaped plaquettes. Gold.
     d) Four plaquettes in the form of six-pointed stars. Gold, $\frac{5}{8} \times \frac{5}{8}$".
     e) Seven buttons in the form of lion heads, with a pendentive at the end of a slender

chain. Gold, ¾ × ½".

f) Four drop-shaped plaquettes. Gold.

g) Three disk-shaped plaquettes. Gold, ½ × ⅝".

h) Six wave-shaped plaquettes. Gold, ¾ × ¾".

i) Forty-two tubular ornaments. Gold, ⅜".

j) Thirty-four biconical grains of old gold.

k) Twisted ribbon. Gold, ⅛ × 3⅞".

This is work of the settled Scythians of the Crimea. End of second, beginning of first century B.C. Mausoleum at Scythian Neapolis (Simferopol). Pushkin Museum, Moscow.

338 Art of the Royal Scyths of Neapolis: collection of jewelry decorating the clothes of a Scythian queen:

a) Three segment-shaped plaquettes. Gold, 2 × ¾".

b) Needle with eye. Gold, length 3⅛".

c) Hollow drop in the form of two cones.

d) Spiral ring (eight turns): Gold, diameter ⅝".

e) Rosette; Gold, diameter ¾".

f) Pendant with slender chains. Gold, length 1⅜".

g) Pendant with moon crescent.

h) Two bicylindrical keepers. Gold, 1 × ½", and 1¼ × ½".

i) Necklace with eighteen drops. Carnelian, from ⅜ × ¼" to ¼ × ⅛".

j) Necklace with thirty-seven drops. Amber, glass, and various pastes, ranging from ½ × ⅜" to ⅛ × ⅛".

k) Two parts of a buckle in the form of animals. Bronze, 1⅝".

Art of the settled Acythians of the Crimea, second half of first century B.C. Pushkin Museum, Moscow.

339 Ornament from a breast-piece. Bronze. Nomadic design based on herbivores (?ibex) from Tuekta 1.

340 Wood carving, a winged tiger. Siberian nomad art.

341 Harness ornament in the form of a wild beast rolled in a ball. Bronze, diameter 2⅜". Scythian animal art of the Crimea, fifth century B.C. From Ak-Burun (Crimea). Found by A.E. Lutsenko. Hermitage Museum, Leningrad.

342 Two parts of a buckle, in the form of animals. Bronze, 1⅝". Art of the settled Scythians of the Crimea, second half of the first century B.C. From mausoleum at Neapolis (Simferopol). Excavations by P.N. Schultz, 1947-48. Pushkin Museum, Moscow.

343 Bit-bar (psalium), with decoration of griffins. Bronze, 2¼ × 4½". Scythian animal art, fifth century B.C. From Tuzla (Taman). Found by Begitchev, 1852, Hermitage Museum, Leningrad.

344 Shield with very prominent boss and a raised rim bearing inscriptions. Three concentric bands carry ornamental friezes of bulls and lions passant. Bronze; diameters 22⅞" and 32⅝". Culture of the kingdom of Urartu; Iron Age, seventh or sixth century B.C. From Karmir-Blur (southern Armenia). Excavations by B.B. Piotrovsky, 1949. Hermitage Museum, Leningrad.

345 Vessel with spherical belly; the chased decoration represents Scythian warriors. Work of a Greek master on the northern coast of the Black Sea. Silver, height 4". From Barrow 3 (Chastye) at Voronezh. Excavations by the Archives Commission, 1911. Hermitage Museum, Leningrad.

346 and 347 Details of the ovoid amphora from Chertomlyk; it has a cylindrical neck with a widely flared brim, and two large curved handles descending from the top of the neck to the belly of the amphora. The lower part of the vessel has three spouts, one shaped like a hor-

se's head, the others like lion heads. The whole body is covered with figures: on the upper part griffins in pairs—unity doubling their strength—are attacking an isolated stag; immediately below, and like a leitmotiv or a translation of the above, Scythians can be seen helping one another tame a wild horse which, like the stag above, has sunk to its knees. The rest of the band depicts the antithesis: horses at liberty, one of which is grazing, while others are escaping from isolated men, whose failure to catch them is no doubt explained by their isolation.

On the walls of the vessel there are also stylized palmettos and brambles, from which birds with their wings spread stand out.

Silver gilt, with relief carving and engraving; height 27⅝", diameter 15¾". The vessel must have been used for koumiss, a fermented juice based on mares' milk, prized by the Scythians. The spouts and the neck are provided with filters. The paradisal part of the decoration—the luxuriant vegetation with the fluttering birds—may perhaps be connected with the intoxication produced by that drink.

348 View of the inside of the Gaimanova Mogila kurgan, showing the state in which it was found. A Scythian bronze caldron is clearly visible.

349 The objects found in this kurgan, after cleaning. The Gaimanova treasure. (See fig. 32.)

350 Cup from Gaimanova. Gold, but the face and hands of the two Scythian warriors are modeled in silver. Scythian art of the fourth century B.C.

The two men have beards and long hair; wearing caftans decorated with a design of branches, long trousers and pointed boots drawn close at the ankles by thongs, they have a calm, serene expression. One of them is holding a sword, with his hand on the hilt, and the other a quiver containing arrows; close by him there are a bow and bow-case. Each of them has a whip in his free hand.

On the opposite side from this scene there are two beardless people, seated and holding out their arms to each other. On the knees of one of them there is a goblet. To the right of them, a kneeling man is hiding his face with one hand and offering or holding out something to them. On their left someone is drinking from a gourd.

The two principal persons on each side, bearded in the one case, beardless in the other, seem to indicate two different age groups.

In Ossetian literature the *histaertae* and the *kaestaertae* (seniors and juniors), as in all Caucasian society, illustrate two age groups—the elders, and the younger men who are subordinate to them.

351 Pendant from an eardrop with a duck at the end.

352 Painted pottery urn, caterpillar motifs. Height 7¾". Tripolye culture, first half of third millennium B.C. From Varvarovka (Moldavia). Excavations by V.I. Markevitch, 1958-61. Historical Institute of the Academy of Sciences of Moldavia, Kichinev.

353 Painted pottery urn, dog motifs. Height 22⅞", diameter 22⅞". Tripolye culture, first half of third millennium B.C. From Varvarovka (Moldavia). Excavations by V.I. Markevitch, 1958-61. Historical Institute, Academy of Sciences of Moldavia, Kichinev.

354 Bronze dish on a stand; round the rim lions passant, molded in the round; there are thirteen of them, matching the thirteen lunations of the year, and they are moving in the direction of the daily movement of the moon. Height 7⅞", diameter 8¼". Scytho-Sacian art, middle of first millennium B.C. From Lake Issyk-Kul (Central Asia). Acquired from the Frunze Educational Institute, 1939. Hermitage Museum, Leningrad.

355 Caldron with two handles and a narrow foot; with relief ornamentation of stylized oxen, concentric circles, palmettos, and triangles. Bronze. From kurgan at Mikhailovo-Apostolovo (Kherson). Excavations by D.I. Evarnitsky, 1897. Hermitage Museum, Leningrad.

356 Silver statue of an ox; ornament belonging to a funerary canopy. Height 3¹/₈". Third millennium B.C. From kurgan at Maikop (northern Caucasus). Excavations by N.I. Veselovsky, 1897. Hermitage Museum, Leningrad.

357 Stringed instrument made of wood. Hypothetical reconstruction on the basis of two models found in Pazyryk 2.

In a country of bowmen, the stringed instrument is almost the logical conclusion, in musical terms, of a weapon whose string vibrates at the slightest touch. Harps and lyres were already in use in the first half of the third millennium B.C., as is shown by the royal tombs of Ur. The technique of musical notation also was practiced by the Kassites as early as 1500 B.C., and was done on clay tablets.

358 Pole-top, made of wood and leather; fifth or fourth century B.C. From Pazyryk 2. Hermitage Museum, Leningrad.

A stag's head in a griffin's beak. Since the two heads (the two "chiefs") are facing in the same direction, the allegory can hardly be connected with hunting, since such a position would not be natural. The old stag and the "gold-guarding" griffin—the one held, guided, or thrust forward by the other—may together symbolize some inspiring theme connected with the pole whose top they adorn.

A carved griffin's head sticks out from one side: it is inserted in the middle of an engraving of the beast's body, which is also holding a goose in its claws. (See also fig. 284.)

359 Woman's headdress, made of wood, leather, and felt. Fifth or fourth century B.C. From Pazyryk 5. It is of the type called in English "pigtail," and in French *queue-de-cheval* (horse's tail).

360 Bronze mirror with a handle in the form of a figure of Aphrodite. Height 9", breadth 4³/₄". Annovka (Ukraine).

361 Bronze lamp with six wicks. Height 4 ", diameter 14". From Chertomlyk. The number may possibly be seven, corresponding to the seven days of the week, one of them being ceremonial. There is a somewhat similar lamp, but of terra cotta, in the Armenian Historical Museum, where it is assigned to the Teshebani period (seventh century B.C.).

362 and 363 Fragments of ornamentation of an ivory sarcophagus from Kul Oba; Aphrodite with Eros, and woman holding part of her dress.

364 Gold comb from Solokha, the work of Greek goldsmiths, described by M.I. Artamonov as follows:

The back of the comb is decorated with a frieze of five lions lying down, below a group of Scythians fighting. There are three warriors, one of whom, on horseback, is aiming a lance at a second, who is sheltering behind his shield while his wounded horse lies at his feet. A third warrior, on foot, brandishing a sword, is running to the assistance of the unhorsed man. The first two are probably leaders, and are clothed and armed in half-Scythian, half-Greek fashion. Their breeches and their soft boots done up with thongs are Scythian, but one of them has Greek leggings, and both of them are wearing Greek helmets. The one on horseback is wearing armor with a scale pattern, and the unhorsed one has smooth armor bordered with semicircular strips of metal. The third man is bareheaded; he is wearing the usual Scythian caftan, decorated with sewn-on appliqués, as are the breeches of the second warrior. The man on horseback has in his hand a short lance with a leaf-shaped point. The other two are armed with akinakes. All three have small shields, of different shapes. The men on foot are holding their shields in their left hands, by means of a handhold fixed to the center; the man on horseback, whose left hand is holding the reins of his mount, wears his shield on his left shoulder. Two of the men have a bow-case attached to their belt, on the left side; the third wears a dagger sheath. Many details of the clothing and weapons in this scene correspond completely with the objects found in the Scythian burials. The horses are small and have long tails and short manes, a thoroughly characteristic type of horse. The rider has reined his horse in violently, and it is rearing. The other horse, wounded in the neck, is lying on its back with its feet in the air. Blood is flowing from the wound; the harness, including decorated bits and bit-bars, very closely resembles the usual Scythian type.

So these warriors are fighting like lions, to use a still current expression. The comparison is the more appropriate since lions, being particularly gregarious, help each other to lay an ambush for their prey, and it does look as if one of the three barbarian protagonists on the back of the Solokha comb has fallen into an ambush. The frieze of lions below them may therefore be connected with the symbolism of the nomads, in spite of the anecdotic Greek style in which the fight above them is depicted.

365 Saddle, saddle cover, and breast strap. Felt, leather, wood, hair, gold. On the cover, a leather appliqué in the form of a silhouetted tiger. On the breast strap, carved wooden plaques: heads of wild sheep in a wolf's mouth, and other wild sheep heads. From Pazyryk 1.

366 Saddle cover, of felt and leather. Felt appliqué in lively colors—a griffin with a tiger's body. $15 \times 29^{7}/_{8}$". Scytho-Altaic art, fifth or fourth century B.C. From Pazyryk 2. Excavations by S.I. Rudenko, 1947-48. Hermitage Museum, Leningrad.

367 Saddle cover. From Pazyryk 1.
An elk is being attacked by a griffin. Leather cut-outs of disheveled heads hang down from the sides of the saddle cover. These are perhaps vestiges of an ancient custom of the Scythians reported by Herodotus: according to him the nomad warriors, after scalping the heads of those whom they had killed, using a circular incision close to the ears, made from these skins "hand-towels which they hang from the bridle of their horse and in which they take great pride, for the more of these hand-towels a Scythian has, the greater his reputation for valor. There are also some who make themselves cloaks with these human skins, sewing them together like shepherds' cloaks."
The practice of scalping is attested not only by the decoration of a few of the objects surviving from the barbarian period, but also by the tattooed man from Pazyryk 2, whose head had had its skin removed by an incision from one ear to the other—a technical detail which confirms the report of the Father of History.
Moreover, in one of the Ossetian stories (Sosryko or Batradz cycle), the hero tells the women to make him a cloak with the skins of the heads he is bringing them—and they are the heads of those women's own relatives.

368 Leather bag decorated with cheetah and colt fur. Fifth to fourth century B.C. From Pazyryk 1.

369 Scene of animals fighting, on a saddle cover: a lion-griffin attacking an ibex. From Pazyryk 1.

370 Saddle and its pendants. Felt, leather, and hair. Fifth to fourth century B.C. From Pazyryk 1.
The motif on the cover: a griffin killing an ibex.
From the saddle hang motifs formed of a ram's head caught between two griffins' heads—or, more precisely, between two heads of horned felines, a kind of monster common in Altaic art. These rams' heads remind us of the human ones hung from another saddle from the same kurgan (fig. 367), and there may be a symbolic correlation between the ram and the man in these similar uncomfortable situations.

371 Shield from Pazyryk 1.

372 Gold plaque: a feline. The eye, nostril, ear and claws were at one time inlaid. Weight 7¾ ounces. Diameters 4³/₈". Sacian art. Hermitage Museum, Leningrad. Collection of Peter the Great.

373 Glass cup with gold handles and a broad trimming of gold work in filigree, with garnets inlaid; this trimming has drops of carnelian and gold hanging from it by slender chains. It is a fine example of ancient polychrome work. Height 3³/₈". Sarmatian art of the Kuban, second century A.D. From kurgan at Severskaya (Krasnodar). Chance find, 1881. Historical Museum, Moscow.

374 Ornament in the form of a two-headed stag, with ten pendants and a small bell suspended by chains. Bronze, 12⁵/₈×5½". End of second to beginning of first millennium B.C. From Dolanlar (Azerbaijan). Excavations of 1933. Azerbaijan Historical Museum, Baku.

375 Finial in the form of a stylized bird's head, with the beak of a bird of prey and a human eye; it has three eyelets (one of them broken) for hanging small conical balls. Above the eye, the crest is formed by three similarly schematic birds' heads. The eye proper of the principal head leads to another, inside it, reversed and defined by relief lines. At the base of the plaque, an ibex with its head turned backward is depicted. Bronze, 10¹/₄ × 7¹/₈". Scythian art, fifth century B.C. From kurgan at Ulskii (Krasnodar), Tomb 2.

376 Gold pot with handle; it is covered with a decoration—a tracery of branches and medallions with flowers. Height 5½". South Siberian and Kirghiz art, eighth century A.D. From chaatas tomb at Kopeny on the Yenisey. Excavations by L.A. Evtjukhova and S.V. Kiselev, 1939-40. Historical Museum, Moscow.

377 Gold pot with handle, decorated with branches and animals face to face, arranged in medallions. Height 4½". South Siberian and Kirghiz art, eighth century A.D. Chaatas tomb at Kopeny on the Yenisey. Excavations by L.A. Evtjukhova and S.V. Kiselev, 1939-40. Historical Museum, Moscow.

378 Dish with decoration consisting of birds face to face and branches. Gold, diameter 7⁷/₈". South Siberian and Kirghiz art, eighth century A.D. Chaatas tomb at Kopeny on the Yenisey. Excavations by L.A. Evtjukhova and S.V. Kiselev, 1939-40. Historical Museum, Moscow.

379 Cup adorned with feather motifs and with a medallion depicting a vintage. Silver, diameters 7⁷/₈ and 8". Sarmatian art of the Volga, first century B.C. From Barrow 1 at Novocherkassk. Excavations by S.I. Kapochina. Regional Museum of Rostov-on-Don.

Silver was no less prized than gold by the nomads and ancient peoples of Russia. In one chamber of the Solokha tumulus a silver kylix (two-handled cup) with the inscription ΛΥΚΟ was found. The laudative Indo-European root *leuk* implies the idea of whiteness, of brilliance proper to a metal whose Greek name "argos" came from a root that expressed the same idea and gave its name also to ἄργιλλος (English, argil), the white clay used in the ancient potteries.

GLOSSARY

A

ABORIGINES:
The first inhabitants of a country. The term is often used to describe indigenous Australians.

ACHAEMENID:
The name of the dynasty that reigned over the Persian Empire during the fourth to sixth centuries B.C.

AHURA MAZDA, AHRIMAN:
The first was the supreme god of the Iranians during the Achaemenid epoch. He symbolized light, as opposed to Ahriman, god of darkness.

AKINAKES:
The handle of a saber, sword, or dagger which characterizes oriental arms, particularly those of the Scythians.

ALACA HÜYÜK:
An Anatolian site known for the graves of its princes.

ALTAI:
The range of high mountains (summit at 4,520 meters) at the western border of Siberia and Mongolia, notable for its gold and silver mines. The Altai are populated in part by Europeans. They form the large ethnographic family (Turks, Turkomans, Hungarians, and Khirghiz) which comprise the group formerly known as Tartars.

The Uralo-Altaic languages are nearly all agglutinate, characterized by multiple word structures and a rigidly organized construction of the proposition by juxtaposition of word endings. There seems to be a repercussion of artistic language which precedes the writing.

ALTAMIRA:
The paintings in this grotto were discovered in 1879 by an archeologist's daughter who had wandered into the cavern. It took many years to make certain the authenticity of the painted bison at Altamira. It is located near Santander (Spain).

AMLASH:
Site of the Guilan mountains, Iran, near the southwest coast of the Caspian Sea. Its name is given to a civilization dated from the eleventh to the tenth century B.C. There are numerous tombs adorned with animals, human figures, and deer beautifully executed in wood.

ANATIDAE:
A family of web-footed birds which includes geese, swans and ducks.

ARSLAN TASH:
A site in northern Syria where some sphinxes were created during the eighth century B.C. These ivories seem to have been a part of the tribute paid to the Assyrian king.

ASIANIC:
The language of the non-Indo-European people of Asia.

ASSYRIA:
Part of the Tigris River Basin, between the section of the river flowing through Iraqi territory and the adjoining Little Zab River. It was during the 19th century B.C. that the first dynasty was founded. After the collapses of Nineveh in 612 and Haran in 610, Assyria, a hitherto important state, became nothing but a province in the Persian Empire.

AZERBAIJAN:
A region stretching from Persia through the U.S.S.R. which comprises the Soviet Republic whose capital is Bakou. South of the Caucasus, it adjoins the Caspian Sea.

B

BACTRIA:
The Greek name for the northern part of Afghanistan divided by the Oxus River. It was populated by the Iranians, who were perhaps originally the Medes. After its capture by Cyrus, it constituted a part of the Achaemenid Empire.

BASHLYK:
A hood worn by the Scythians.

BATRADZ:
Hero of a Nartian epic (see Narts).

BIOTOPE:
A biological system which includes climate, flora, and fauna.

BUCRANE:
A bull's head reproduced in simplified graphic style on prehistoric ceramics and water urns.

C

CALATHOS:
An ancient Greek image or statue of a crow, particularly one used by the agrarian cult of Eleusis in honor of Demeter.

CANIDAE:
The family of carnivorous mammals which includes dogs, wolves, foxes, and jackals.

CANNABIS:
The resin from the flowers of Indian hashish, whose active ingredient is cannabinol.

CAPRIDAE:
The family of ruminants which includes goats.

CATALHUYK:
A site in Turkey to the southwest of Konya. There is a large layer of deposits from the Neolithic Age beneath the surface there.

CHALCOLITHIC:
A cultural phase characterized by the simultaneous use of metal (copper) and stone.

CHERSONESE:
The Greek etymology signifies a peninsula. A name study designates, thus, the peninsula of Galipoli (Chersonese of Thrace), the Crimean (Tauric Chersonese), Jutland (Cimbric Chersonese).

CHTHONIAN:
A title given to gods that reside beneath the earth's surface; Hades, for example.

CIMMERIANS:
People of Indo-European origin. Forced to leave their sedentary occupations in the central plains of Russia by Scythian invasions of the eighth century, the Cimmerians crossed the passes of the central and western Caucasus to spread out over the Urartian, Manaean, and Phrygian states, and to menace the Syrians, who pushed them in the direction of the Assarhaddon.

COMPUTIST:
He who works to arrange the religious calendar (*comput*).

CRIOCEPHALIC:
Any imaginary being having a head in the form of a ram. The Greek symbol of a ram's head is *criocephore*, which is the surname of Hermes, the god who saved the village of Tanagara from an epidemic while traveling with a ram on his back. There was a discovery in the Seven Brothers Barrow of a portion of a mirror in the form of a nude youth, with two rams on his outstretched hands, recalling the heroic action of Hermes.

CYLINDER SEALS:
Small stone cylinders engraved with cultural scenes or depicting hunting and animal combat, which were rolled over soft clay tablets. They have been found in Mesopotamia, Elam, Syria, Assyria and Palestine and are among the fundamental references used in the study of ancient oriental art.

CYNEGETIC:
Relating to the hunt.

D

DACIAN-GETO-DACIAN:
Referring to an early group of people who inhabited the west bank of the Danube River (Bessarabia). The Getae were absorbed by the Dacians who were in turn conquered by the Roman, Trajan. The Dacian people still have direct descendants in a group called the Motses who live in Rumanian Transylvania. The major communication problems between the Dacians and the Scythians seemed to be related to the fact that they were civilizations of the same type.

DARIUS THE FIRST:
The greatest Achaemenid king (522-486 B.C.). He founded the capital of the Persian Empire. Various conquests in India and Europe, and the annexation of Thrace hardly affected the Scythians who lived north of the Black Sea, failing to drive their armies to disaster. He failed at Marathon as well in his attempt to conquer Greece.

E

ELAM:
The ancient name of the Iranian region east of the Mesopotamian basin; the inhabitants of the Iranian plateau during the first half of the third millennium B.C. were called Elamites.

EREBUNI:
An Urartian site near Armenia. It was a powerful and important place until the construction of Karmir Blur.

EXPRESSIONISM:
The artistic procedure which consists of giving the maximum expression and style to the work being produced. Thus, the inhabitants of central New Guinea have a highly developed expressionist art, consisting of masks, figurines and graphic representations which are symbolic of the culture. For example, if an individual who dies had good eyesight, all artwork created in his image will have large eyes; if he was a good speaker, his mask would be enhanced by an enormous tongue.

One could almost say that expressionism is an essential characteristic of all barbarian art.

G

GILGAMESH:
A celebrated hero of Mesopotamian mythology, dated during the 27th century before our era.

GNOSEOLOGY:
The theory of knowledge, from the Greek *gnosis*, knowledge.

GORYTUS:
A quiver fixed to the belt of a Scythian nomad which also contained a short bow.

H

HELIAC:
One who has communication with the sun.

HIEROGLYPHICS:
An incorrect name given to the pictorial characters of certain writing.

HITTITES:
A people whose principal home was Anatolia. They arrived there in the beginning of the second millennium B.C. The Hittite presents important associations with the Tokarians of oriental Turkestan, implying that the two groups spoke the same language—a tongue which came from the Caspian steppes, seemingly by way of the Derbent Pass.

HOMOMORPHIC:
Having the same form.

HOMOTAXY:
A concept borrowed from biology which

encompasses and designates those groups which are in the same evolutionary stages. It was used especially by the English Marxist prehistorian, Gordon Childe.

HOPLOLATRY:
The worship of weapons.

HURRITES:
Their constant presence in the mountains of Armenia two thousand years ago leads us to believe that their original home was Azerbaijan. Their language, of an agglutinate type, has Asiatic affinities which are present in Urartian languages.

I

IBEX:
A wild goat found in the Alps.

IDEOGRAM:
A figure representing a word or an idea of a language. An ideogram is a sign-image which can be read in any language as an aid. In various Chinese dialects, for example, the design of a word remains the linguistic connection between the individual provinces.

K

KARMIR BLUR:
The ancient Teshebani, a very important Urartian site, near Erivan in Soviet-Armenia. It was founded by King Russa II (685-645 B.C.).

KASSITES:
Emigrants from the northeast who came through the mountain chains that separated Iran from the Mesopotamian plain around 2000 B.C. Their language was not Indo-European.

KIRGHIZ:
Nomadic people between the Urals and the Irtysh.

KUDURRU:
A stone which served to mark the divisions of property in Mesopotamia and which is decorated with symbolic reliefs.

KURDISTAN:
Mountainous region divided between Iran, Iraq, and the U.S.S.R., located between Mesopotamia, Anatolia and northern Armenia. In this northern portion of the Zagros Mountains the oldest remains of Neolithic sedentary life have been discovered. The Kurds are of Iranian

origin. Their literature of popular stories and epic recitals is typical.

KURGAN:
From the Tatar, *Kurgan*. Old nomadic sepulchre in the form of a mound.

KUSHAN:
The history of the Kushan Empire covers the five centuries between the fall of the Greek kingdom of Bactria from the second to the first century B.C. and the appearance of the Empire of the White Huns at the end of the fourth or at the beginning of the fifth century A.D.

The Empire extended from the Aral Sea, to where Balkhach Lake empties into the Ganges, and to Afghanistan into the Sikkim.

KYLIX:
A wide-mouthed Greek cup with two handles, with or without feet.

L

LAMASSU:
A bull with a human head who guarded the palace doors of Assyria and the Achaemenid Empire.

LASCAUX:
One of the most important grottos decorated by prehistoric man. It was discovered December 6, 1940. Some paintings are as large as 5 meters in length. Dated from the Magdalenian period, the cave is near Montignac (Dordogne region).

LURISTAN (LUR):
The ancient country of Lur was in the part of the Zagros Mountains which is south of Iran. This region is known for its bronze artifacts, of which the oldest appear to be those of Suse, dated between the third and second millennia B.C.

M

METAPHOR:
A figure of speech in which one object is likened to another by speaking of it as if it were that other.

MINUSINSK:
The basin of the central Yenisey River.

MOUFLON:
A type of wild sheep with horns that curve in a spiral.

MOUSASIR:
A major city located between lakes Van and Urmiah, fought over for many years by the Assyrians and the Urartians.

N

NARTS:
The indigenous legendary figures of the northern Caucasus who became popular during the Iron Age as "life ideals" among the various peoples of the region. The Narts divided their time between three activities: joyous reunions, warring, and hunting expeditions. The stories describe the adventures of Satana, respected female leader of housewives and Caucasian amazons; or Uryzmaegt, head of a whole group of powerful heros, often represented as an older person. The courtly individuals Sosryko and Batradz must also be mentioned.

NEOLITHIC:
The age of polished stone.

NINGIRSU:
A divinity of fertility, adored primarily in Lagash. Symbol: a lion-headed eagle.

O

OKUNOV:
The culture of Okunov (dated at the beginning of the second millennium B.C.), appeared in the Minusinsk Basin after the Afanasievo culture, which began at the end of the third millennium. The most recent belongs to the Bronze Age, the earliest Neolithic period.

OMBON:
The central ridge of a buckle.

ONAGER:
Horses of the desert tamed and harnessed to chariots, represented on artifacts from Ur, Mari, and Khafadje.

OPHIDIANS:
Another term for serpents.

ORDOS:
The desert region of China in the large curl of Hwang Ho. One finds excellent examples of art from the Steppes in this region; not only knives, daggers, and hatchets, but also bronzes of fantastic flesh-eating animals, and even extremely erotic scenes.

OSSETIANS:
The people of Iranian origin who occupy the Caucasus Mountains and form two autonomous republics of the U.S.S.R.

OVA:
An ornament in the form of an egg.

OXUS:
The ancient name for the Amu-Darya, a river in Soviet Turkestan. The river irrigates the rich land of Uzbekistan and Turkmenia.

P

PALEOLITHIC:
The period of shaped stone tools.

PARTHIA:
The Iranian dynasty formed by the nomad Aparnians. Arriving from the steppe which divides the Aral and Caspian seas, they progressively dominated the Seleucids, successors of Alexander. They came to Iran in 250 B.C. and were conquered in 224 B.C. by the founders of the Sassanid Dynasty, in a country where they had always been considered foreigners.

PERSIA:
The group of agricultural and nomadic tribes of which the Achaemenids were a part. The Persians came from the Satem group of Indo-Europeans.

PHALERA:
A round plaque which served as honorable decoration to courageous Roman soldiers. The flagstaff of Roman eagles was also adorned with phaleras.

PHIAL:
A Greek vase for holding wine or water that was often used as a gift or offering.

PHRATRIE:
A subdivision of the tribe among the Athenians, the phratrie comprised thirty families or clans.

PICTOGRAMS:
Painted or engraved figures depicted in such a way that language is not necessary to understand them, but which nevertheless are perceived similarly by all those within a given culture. (Definition of M. Cohen.)

There is a difference between pictogram signals and pictogram words. The signals are abstract, serving as memory aids, catalyzers for recitation. The pictogram words carry their own signification, imparting a vision. They are talking drawings.

PICTO-IDEOGRAM:
An ideogram is a character or a group of characters that represents an idea which is expressed in a word, enabling it to be read in any language; the picture expresses the fact that the character consists of a recognizable drawing. This is what is called a direct rebus. (M. Cohen.)

PROTOME:
The forequarters of an animal.

PSALIUM:
A bit bar.

S

SELENIAN:
Of or pertaining to the moon.

SEMANTICS:
The science of the meaning of language.

SEMIOTICS:
A science that is directed to the study of signs, particularly those of language.

SOGDIANA:
An ancient country in high Asia, corresponding today to the Soviet republic of Uzbek. Capital: Samarkand.

SUIDAE:
The family of ungulates to which pigs and wild boars belong.

T

TANTRISM:
A late form of Hinduism, tantrism has engendered a crowd of emblems and symbols whose forms and colors permitted their artists an imagery as individual as that of the nomads of the northern Steppe region.

THERIOMORPHIC:
Having an animal form.

THRACIANS:
The people of an ancient country situated to the north of Macedonia between the Danube, the Black Sea, the Sea of Marmara, the Greek Archipelago and the Struma. The Thracian people were ancestors of the Geto-Dacians, who in turn were direct ancestors of the Rumanians.

THREE BROTHERS; TUC OF AUDOUBERT:
These two caverns together are part of six great grottos defined as the peak sites of prehistoric art by the Abby Breuil, who worked on this group along with Begouen and his three sons. The grotto gets its name from the Begouen brothers.

TURKESTAN:
A region in Asia which is divided in two by Pamir. The Soviet part of Turkestan is divided into several republics. The Syr Darya and the Amu Darya flow through the area to the Aral Sea.

Z

ZAGROS:
The Greek name of the central part of a mountain chain separating the Iranian plateau and the Mesopotamian plain. This is actually the central region of Kurdistan.

ZIWIYE:
An Iranian site in oriental Kurdistan; earlier site of the Manaean Kingdom. In 1947, there was an important discovery of a treasure which dates from the eighth to the sixth century B.C. A variety of art forms have been found in this location.

ZOROASTER, ZARATHUSTRA:
The reformer of the old Iranian religion who favored a monotheistic worship of Ahura-Mazda. He lived about 600 B.C.

PHOTOGRAPHIC CREDITS

Nos 21, 22, 23, 24, 25, 45 : ÉDITIONS ARTHAUD. Nos 26, 44 : YAN. Nos 105, 108 109, 247, 255, 259, 260, 271, 360, 361, 362, 363, 364 : ARTIA, PRAGUE. No 185 : L. BALSAN. Nos 217, 218, 219, 220, 221 : ÉDITIONS FAYARD. Nos 257, 282 : ARA GULER. Nos 29, 32, 33, 37, 348, 349, 350, 351 : CHOUPRININE. Nos 89, 94, 270, 273 : REVUE DU LOUVRE. Nos 107, 248, 272, 287, 291, 323, 332 : HOLLE VERLAG. No 189 : MARGRET EGGER.

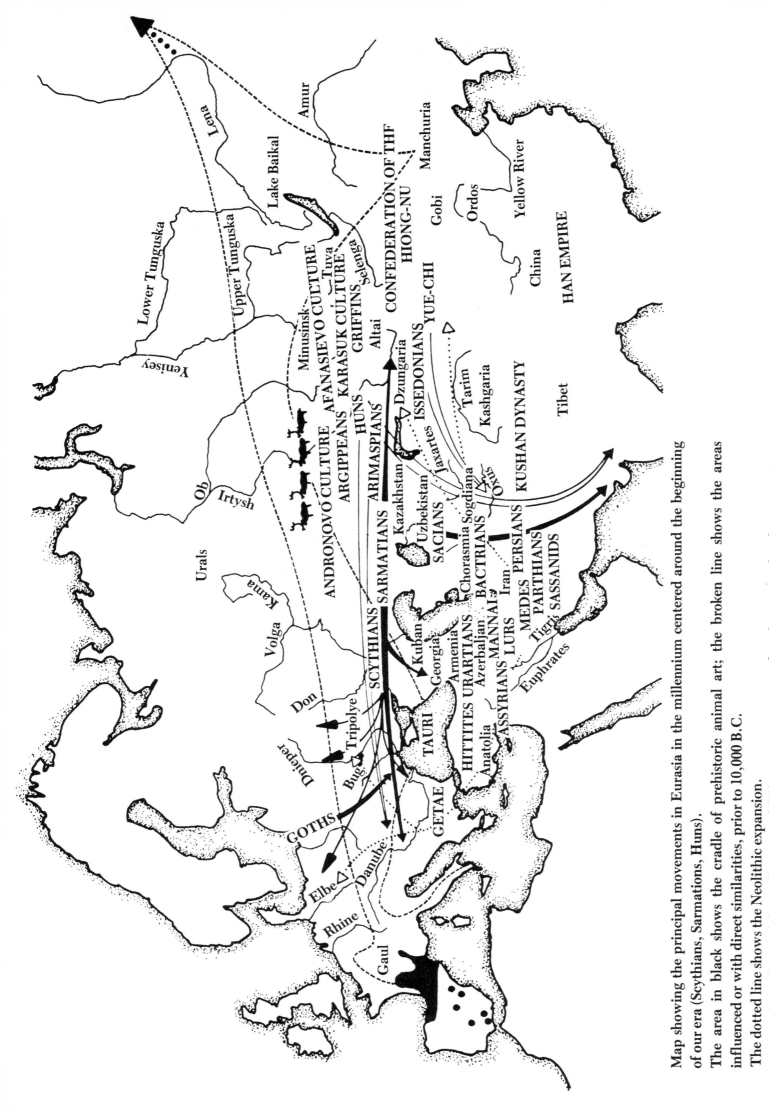

Map showing the principal movements in Eurasia in the millennium centered around the beginning of our era (Scythians, Sarmations, Huns).

The area in black shows the cradle of prehistoric animal art; the broken line shows the areas influenced or with direct similarities, prior to 10,000 B.C.

The dotted line shows the Neolithic expansion.

Names of peoples or of the civilizations of different ages mentioned in the text with reference to their artistic aspects are shown at the point from which they started out.

They are not all contemporary.

The line of reindeer marks the present southern limit of their biotope.

For the incursions of the Scythians into southern Caucasia, see monographs on the countries concerned.

266

CHRONOLOGICAL TABLE

Top axis label: **Area in the historic period: army, social classes, first writing**

Time scale (top, A.D. → B.C.): 200, 100, 0, 100, 200, 300, 400, 500, 600, 700, 800, 900, **1000**, 1100, 1200, 1300, 1400, **1500**, 1600, 1700, 1800, 1900, **2000**, 2100, 2200, 2300, 2400

Time scale (left, A.D. → B.C.): 100, **0**, 100, 200, 300, 400, **500**, 600, 700, 800, 900, **1000**, 1100, 1200, 1300, 1400, **1500**, 1600, 1700, 1800, 1900, **2000**, 2100, 2200, 2300

Region	Events / periods (recent → ancient)
Armenia, Iran, Asia, Middle East (Asia)	Decline of the Parthians; Kushan kingdom; Sacian invasions; Parthian kingdom; Barbarians in Bactria; Bactria and Parthia independent; Decline of the Persians; Persian expansion toward Central Asia; Scythians appear in great number; Cimmerians threaten Urartu; Medes and Persians in the Zagros mountains; Constitution of Mitanni kingdom; Hittites and Kassites; First Assyrian Empire; Royal tombs of Alaca-Hüyük; Sargon of Akkad
Central Europe (Europe)	Sarmatian influences; Contacts with the Scythians; Thracian princely tombs; Scythian incursions
Pontic Scythia	Scythian state in the Crimea; Royal kurgans; Scythian dominance; Cimmerians
Caucasia	Sarmatians occupy northern Caucasia; Settlements of the Pontic Scyths; Nomadism in the western steppes; Kuban civilization; Dolmens; Bronze Age; Nachik, Maikop
Central oriental Russia	Passing to the Piany Bor civilization; Beginning of the animal style; Ananino civilization. Caucasian influence; Nomadism in the western steppes; Beginning of equestrian nomadism
Tuva	First nomads; Beginning of the animal style; Beginning of equestrian nomadism; Spread of pastoral societies; Origin and birth of pastoral societies
Minusinsk basin (Eurasia)	Tess' period; Saragash period; Podgornov period; Tagar culture; Bainov period; Kamenny Log period; Karasuk culture; Andronovo culture; Okunev culture; Afanasievo culture
Kuznetsk basin	Karasuk culture; Andronovo culture
Altai plain	Period of Berezov culture; Period of Bija; Bolshaya Rechka culture
Altai mountains	Predominance of the Altaic nomads; Shibe period; Nomads of the Asiatic steppes; Pazyryk period; Time of the first nomads; Mayemirskaya period; Afanasievo culture

Left vertical age bands: **Period of the first Nomads** — **Bronze Age (Middle and Recent)** — **Aeneolithic or Chalcolithic Age**

Right vertical region bands: **Asia** — **Europe** — **Eurasia**

267

BIBLIOGRAPHY

The bibliography has been very much shortened: a longer one would only have meant repeating those of the main works listed here, to which the reader can refer. The aim has been to direct the reader to basic works on the principal themes considered or touched on in this book; in other words, they are not works exclusively on the subject of the archaeology of the Steppes.

THE SCYTHIANS AND THEIR NEIGHBORS:

Artamonov, M.I. *The Splendor of Scythian Art. Treasures from Scythian Tombs.* New York: Praeger, and London: Thames and Hudson, 1969. (Title of English edition: *Treasures from Scythian Tombs in the Hermitage Museum Leningrad.*)

Griaznov, Mickhail. *The Ancient Civilization of Southern Siberia.* New York: Cowles Book Co., and London: Cresset, and Barrie and Rockliff, 1969. (Title of English edition: *Southern Siberia.*)

Herodotus. *The Histories.* Book IV. Various editions.

Mongait, Aleksandr L'vovich. *Archaeology in the USSR.* New York: Heinman, and London: Central Books, 1960.

Phillips, E.D. *The Royal Hordes: Nomad Peoples of the Steppes.* London: Thames and Hudson, 1965; New York: McGraw-Hill, 1966.

Talbot-Rice, Tamara. *The Scythians.* London: Thames and Hudson, 1957 (third edition, 1961); New York: Praeger, 1957.

BARBARIAN ECONOMY:

Childe, Gordon. *What Happened in History.* Revised edition with foreword and footnotes. Baltimore: Penguin Books, and Harmondsworth: Penguin Books, 1964.

Clark, Grahame. *Prehistoric Europe: the Economic Basis.* New York: Philosophical Library, and London: Methuen, 1952.

Engels, Friedrich. *Origin of the Family, Private Property and the State.* Various editions.

HASHISH:

Baudelaire, Charles. *Œuvres complètes: Les Paradis artificiels.* Various editions.

Dardanne, A. *Contribution à l'étude du chanvre indien.* Paris: Vigot Frères, 1955.

Gautier, Théophile. "Le Club des haschischins." In *La Presse.* Paris, July 10, 1943.

ART AND RELIGION:

Hainchelin, Charles. *Les Origines de la religion.* Paris: Éditions Sociales, 1955.

Marx, Karl and Engels, Friedrich. *Sur la Littérature et l'art.* Selected texts. Paris: Éditions Sociales, 1954.

LANGUAGE AND WRITING:

Cohen, Marcel. *La Grande Invention de l'écriture et son évolution.* Paris: Imprimerie Nationale, 1958.

Guiraud, P. *Structures étymologiques du lexique francais.* Paris: Larousse, 1967.

Kondratov, A. *Sounds and Signs.* Moscow: Mir, 1969.

UNESCO. *Collection UNESCO d'œuvres représentatives, série des langues non russes de l'Union Soviétique.* Collection Caucase. Paris: NRF.

BY THE PRESENT AUTHOR:

Charrière, Georges. *La Signification des représentations érotiques dans les arts sauvages et préhistoriques.* Paris: G.P. Maisonneuve et Larose, 1970.